Sir Watkin's Tours

Excursions to France, Italy and North Wales, 1768–71

Paul Hernon

bridge
books

Sir Watkin's Tours Excursions to France, Italy and North Wales, 1768–71
was first published in Wales in 2013
by
BRIDGE BOOKS
61 Park Avenue
WREXHAM
LL12 7AW

www. bridgebooks.co.uk

CIP data for this book is available
from the British Library

ISBN: 978-1-84494-088-2

Cover illustration:
Sir Watkin Williams Wynn, Mr Apperley and Captain Hamilton
by Pompeo Batoni, Rome 1768. © National Museum of Wales.

Printed and bound
by
Gutenberg Press Ltd
Malta

CONTENTS

To

James Manley and John Peacock

PREFACE

Sir Watkin Williams Wynn, fourth baronet of Wynnstay and the second 'Sir Watkin' is one of those shadowy figures who crop up in history in various guises, none of them of extreme importance, but in the sum of their parts, of much significance. As a patron of artists, actors, architects, musicians, landscape gardeners and purveyors of luxury goods he has often merited a footnote but only occasionally a monograph. The sheer diversity of his interests has perhaps been a factor in his confinement within specialised articles, each concentrating upon a specific aspect of his patronage. Only T. W. Pritchard, in a series of articles in the *Transactions of the Denbighshire Historical Society* has attempted to draw a comprehensive picture of the young baronet and, in *Country Life*, of the architectural and social history of Wynnstay.

The present publication is not a comprehensive study but is concerned mainly with four formative years in the life of Wales' most distinguished connoisseur and looks at his grand tour to France and Italy and his tour of his own land-holdings in north Wales and at the social and artistic milieu in which the young man developed.

The National Library of Wales houses the Wynnstay Papers, which were deposited there from 1934 until 1940 and purchased by them in 2001. The scope of the deposit is immense but importantly, for our purposes, includes the account book for the 1768 tour through France and Italy and the bills and receipts from the 1771 north Wales tour. The transcriptions of the documents printed here were made by me and I accept responsibility for any errors contained within them. I am grateful to the National Library of Wales for permission to publish the relevant papers and to the staff of the South Reading Room for their unfailing courtesy and helpfulness.

There were many practical things about the tours which I did not quite understand whilst reading the papers and therefore I decided that the best option was to undertake those two journeys myself and discover exactly how the tours were made and what their influence could have been. I am happy to record my thanks to John Peacock and James Manley for separately accompanying me through north Wales and Italy, following in Sir Watkin's footsteps and learning a lot about both countries in the process.

I am also grateful for the enlightened and liberal attitude of the British Museum and the Yale Centre for British Art regarding the supply and reproduction of images in their collections and must, in addition, thank the National Museum of Wales, the National Library of Wales, the Tate Gallery, the Trustees of Ruabon Parochial Church Council and the National Gallery of Ireland for permission to reproduce images of works contained within their collections.

I must thank Alister Williams of Bridge Books for his detached appraisal of my sometimes over-loaded prose and his help as both editor and publisher.

Both of Sir Watkin's tours have been the subject of exhibitions in the Wrexham County Borough Museum. The first, in 2006, concerned Paul Sandby and his publication of the *XII Views in North Wales* and the second, in 2013, concerned Sir Watkin's Grand Tour. The research contained within this volume is a direct result of the preparation for those exhibitions. Jonathon Gammond, the Exhibitions Officer of the County Borough Museum of Wrexham, has been responsible for facilitating both of those exhibitions and I thank him most sincerely for his extraordinary devotion to his task.

Paul Hernon
Llangollen, 2013

Author's Note

In transcribing the various papers and manuscripts, which I have quoted from throughout this book, I have made no attempt to modernise the original spelling. Williams Wynn was not hyphenated in the eighteenth century and I have followed the original practice. Mr Sidebotham's spelling can be highly original at times and I have preserved the English, Welsh, French and Italian as he wrote it.

Welsh place names can have several forms. The eighteenth-century English and Welsh form, the modern English form and the current Welsh form. Historical usage I have preserved, but in writing from my own perspective I have used the modern Welsh version. Therefore the English 'Conway' will always appear as 'Conwy' and 'Carnarvon' will appear as 'Caernarfon'. Mr Sidebotham's accounts used both eighteenth-century forms and Paul Sandby uses some names which are no longer in normal usage. Llyn Tegid can therefore also appear as Bala Lake or as Pimble Meer.

Some of the accounts for the north Wales journey may have entries made by somebody other than Mr Sidebotham. Here the rendition of English words appears to have been made by a person whose first language was Welsh and those spellings are likewise preserved.

ILLUSTRATIONS

Endpapers: *Elevation of the proposed new mansion at Wynnstay. c.*1770, James Byers. © National Library of Wales.

Byers' elevation shows us the sheer scale and ambition of the proposed new house at Wynnstay. The block to the left hand side was the, still existing, stable court built in 1738 by Francis Smith of Warwick. Byers proposed replicating it on the other side of a vast forecourt before the palatial central block. The drawings were widely exhibited in Rome before their despatch to London and Byres may have been exploiting them as an advert for his own genius. One thing is absolutely certain, the whole project was completely unaffordable and would have ruined men much richer than Sir Watkin.

Between pages 64 and 65

Plate 1. *Sir Watkin Williams Wynn and Lady Frances Williams Wynn. c.*1769. Sir Joshua Reynolds. © Tate Britain.

Sir Joshua Reynolds seems to have almost become the official family painter. He was undoubtedly very friendly with Sir Watkin and, unusually, allowed him to extract works from his studio before payment had been made but there must have been an intense bond between the bumbling baronet and the highly-strung artist. This painting was probably begun before Sir Watkin embarked upon his Grand Tour and was finished upon his return. We may question Sir Watkin's apparent dependence upon his mother's support in the very year in which he was to be married himself. Lady Frances cost the Wynnstay inheritance rather a lot of money in later years. Alas, she outlived her son and with that 'alas' she recorded her grief upon the commemorative column she had erected in the grounds of Wynnstay.

Plate 2. *Sir Watkin Williams Wynn, Mr Apperley and Captain Hamilton.* Rome 1768. Pompeo Batoni. © National Museum of Wales.

Batoni was famed for his ability to capture a likeness but in this, probably the greatest of his Grand Tour portraits, he excelled himself. The shy Sir Watkin, the eager Mr Apperley and the sophisticated and slightly arrogant Captain Hamilton are delineated with a psychological precision, which demonstrates how Batoni could rise well above his normal efficiency when presented with sitters in whom he could be interested. The British seemed to have bored Batoni a lot of the time but here he created a work of unusual intensity when faced with an intriguing set of personal interactions. The painting took the notoriously dilatory artist four years to complete and was finally delivered in 1772.

Plate 3. *Terracotta bust of Sir Watkin Williams Wynn*, Rome 1769, Christopher Hewetson. © National Gallery of Ireland, Dublin.

Christopher Hewetson was an Irish artist who built up an impressive list of clients in Rome. Sir Watkin collected the finished bust in January 1769 as well as six copies, which had been cast from it. The whereabouts of the copies is unknown. It must be admitted that Hewetson has given the nineteen-year-old youth the gravitas of a Roman senator but perhaps that was what was required. He was generally known for his ability to capture a good likeness and the bust is not dissimilar to Sir Joshua Reynolds' portrait of the young man with his mother (Plate 1) or with his intended bride (Plate 9)

Plate 4. Sir Watkin's Coat. *c.*1769 © Museum of Welsh Life, St Fagans.

This is one of two embroidered coats which belonged to Sir Watkin and have survived. It is richly embroidered and could be thought of as a 'court suit'. It is cut for a relatively slim figure and unfortunately Sir Watkin did not retain his youthful shape for very long, which may account for the fine state of preservation of the coat. When he was in Lyon in August 1768, 552 *livres* were spent upon an embroidered velvet suit and some waistcoat pieces. Upon the return journey, in Paris, Mr Pernon of Lyon was paid a further £84 for the delivery of the suit, described in the account book as 'Sir Watkin's best'. Pernon was one of the best and most important manufacturers of silk velvet in the late-eighteenth century and, although unproven, the present suit may be that mentioned in the accounts. Sir Watkin seems to have been a generally neat man and was described as such by Thomas Apperley's son. The account books for the early 1770s record many payments to tailors and in 1769 as his first marriage approached, he paid Hinchcliffe & Co £18 for velvet for a suit. His tailor, a Mr Morse, presumably made the velvet up and would be another candidate for the manufacture of the present coat. By 1771, when good eating was beginning to take its inevitable toll, this coat would not have fitted the young baronet.

Plate 5. Extract from the elevation of the proposed new mansion at Wynnstay. *c.*1770. James Byers. © National Library of Wales.

This is the central section of the large design shown on the endpapers. The main block is an italianate version of Palladian classicism and contrasts strongly with the side pavilions containing the offices. The design is slightly weak in that the height of the staterooms and of the Egyptian Hall (Plate 6) has created a large area of masonry between the windows of the main floor and those of the bedroom floor. Byres has occupied the space with recessed panels and sculpture in the portico, but the slightly awkward design betrays his inexperience at handling such a large project.

Plate 6. Section of the Egyptian Hall at Wynnstay. *c.* 1770. James Byers. © National Library of Wales.

This admirable section of the central hall is one of the most beautiful architectural drawings to survive from the eighteenth century. The hall itself took up most of the main floor of the central block and more resembles a concert hall or an assembly room than the salon of a domestic dwelling. Sir Watkin's musical ambitions were perhaps the motivation behind this spectacular room, known as the Egyptian Hall because of its conformation to a type described by the Roman writer Vitruvius. The room must have been central to Sir Watkin's ambitions for Wynnstay and the rich musical life he envisaged. The balconies were intended as places for musicians or additional spectators and the importance of the space to the baronet is adequately demonstrated by the fact that he intended his bedroom to connect directly with the hall. It is likely that the hall would have only been used in summer, as the provision for heating is quite inadequate. It might also be noted that he neglected to provide any toilet facilities on the reception floor where an audience of over one hundred could have been expected at Sir Watkin's musical 'Jubilees'.

Plate 7. Samuel Sidebotham's Account Book. © National Library of Wales.

This is the account book kept by Samuel Sidebotham. It is not concerned with a narrative of the journey but merely records expenditure incurred upon it. On page 7 he heads it 'Expenses & Disbursements in Sr Watkins Expedition into foreign Parts by Saml Sidebotham'. Glued inside the front cover is a trade leaflet for an artist's suppliers in Paris and it may be that Sidebotham bought the notebook whilst on the tour. Altogether, ten such account books survive and cover expenses until 1781 when Sidebotham was appointed as steward to Wynnstay. Throughout the pages of this dry financial account, Sidebotham emerges as a most engaging figure. His mastery of French and Italian improves, his appreciation of theatre, and especially opera, becomes a regular expenditure, his slight irritation with cheating postillions and his intense irritation when he could not reconcile the accounts is evident, but most of all, his devotion to Sir Watkin are endearing features of the notebook. Read carefully, this slight book gives us a fascinating insight into what must have been a great adventure for them all. Here it is open at pages 62 and 63, which record the payments to Piranesi for his complete works, to Pompeo Batoni for the triple portrait, and a history painting (*Bacchus and Ariadne*) cameos and antiquities from Jenkins and Byres and the terracotta bust from Christopher Hewetson.

Plate 8. Engraving of a classical urn. G.B. Piranesi. © Trustees of the British Museum.

Piranesi was quite adroit in dedicating his engraving to eminent connoisseurs, mainly in the hope of increased sales. Whilst in Rome Sir Watkin had bought complete volumes of engravings from the artist and this may have been belated thanks. The plate, from his *'Vasi, candelabri, cippi, sarcofagi, tripodi, lucerne, ed ornamenti antichi'* was dedicated to Sir Watkin, described as an English knight and a lover of fine arts. It was published in 1778, and may have been a response to rumours that Sir Watkin was planing a second visit to Rome.

Plate 9. *Sir Watkin Williams Wynn and Lady Henrietta Somerset. c.*1769. Sir Joshua Reynolds. © National Museum of Wales.

On the surface, this appears to be a conventional pre-nuptial portrait. Sir Watkin and his bride to be are dressed in the fashionable 'Van Dyke' style but the rendition of their clothes in funereal black may indicate that the painting was finished after Lady Henrietta's untimely death and adjusted from a celebratory portrait into a memorial one. It is unfortunate, but one must admit that Sir Watkin, at nineteen or twenty, does seem a little bit prematurely aged.

Plate 10. *Sir Watkin Williams Wynn.* Pastel *c.*1772. Hugh Douglas Hamilton. © National Museum of Wales.

This portrait, one of a pair, was based upon earlier versions Hamilton had made (British Museum) and is paired with that of Lady Charlotte Grenville, Sir Watkin's second wife. The frame, which is original, is one of a standard type which Hamilton frequently used to present his work. Of all the paintings and sculptures made at about this time, it is the one which most clearly captures the image of a nineteen-year-old man.

Plate 11. *Portrait of Richard Wilson*. Raphael Mengs. © National Museum of Wales.

Mengs and Wilson were part of the artist's colony in Rome and seem to have admired each other. Mengs is reputed to have painted this portrait in exchange for one of Wilson's landscapes. Wilson's florid complexion hints at the demons which were to pursue him in later life. On his return from Rome he brought the portrait with him and at some time, in the 1770s may have sold it to Sir Watkin when he was in financial straits. Sir Watkin owned at least six large landscapes by Wilson and when the artist was falling from fashion continued to patronise him.

Plate 12A. *View of Tivoli*. Richard Wilson. © National Museum of Wales.

The heat of Rome can sometimes become unbearable and two favourite excursions away from the city were to Frascati and Tivoli. Sir Watkin, in the company of the Duke of Devonshire, visited them both. Tivoli, a town of great antiquity, lies some twenty miles away in the Tiburtine Hills. Mostly celebrated now for the gardens of the Villa d'Este; it was, in the eighteenth century, perhaps more famous for the two temples which cling to the cliff edge over the enormous ravine at the edge of the town. Known, not entirely accurately, as the temples of Vesta and the Sibyl they provided points of interest in a most satisfyingly romantic landscape. Richard Wilson produced innumerable versions of the view and upon his return to London continued producing Italian scenes assisted by Thomas Jones, Joseph Farringdon and other assistants. He reportedly called his views of Tivoli 'good breeders' and would produce copies for clients who perhaps had not been to Rome or had demurred at the high cost of souvenir paintings whilst in the city. The present view exists in several versions and was probably one of the 'good breeders'.

Plate 12B. *View of Castell Dinas Bran*. Richard Wilson. © National Museum of Wales.

Curiously, this seems to be one of the canvases which Wilson brought back from Rome. It is in fact a re-working of an earlier painting and its somewhat strained resemblance to Castell Dinas Bran is explained by the fact that it was originally a view of Tivoli which Wilson has modified; presumably with the hope of selling it to a British client who was more attracted to ancient Wales than ancient Rome. X-ray photography has revealed that the over painting has covered the original view. In fact the river in the foreground would be flowing uphill were this an original view of Dinas Bran. The sketches, upon which the modification was based, were probably done around the time of his visit to Wynnstay in 1770.

Plate 13A. *View from Wynnstay*. Richard Wilson. © Yale Centre for British Art.

Castell Dinas Bran, often known as Crow Castle, was the subject of several of Wilson's paintings. In 1770, during Sir Watkin's summer Jubilee, he was ensconced in a tent at the southern edge of the park at Wynnstay and painted views of the Vale of Llangollen, of which this is one. It was exhibited in 1771 at the Royal Academy and for it and a companion piece he was paid £480 by Sir Watkin. The viewpoint he painted from was later chosen by Sir Watkin's son, when 5th baronet, as the site of a recon-struction of the tomb of Cæcilia Metella which is on the ancient via Appia outside Rome.

Plate 13B. *View of Castell Dinas Bran from Llangollen.* Richard Wilson. © Yale Centre for British Art.

This and the previous painting, appear to be the companion pieces which Sir Watkin acquired directly from Wilson. The painting shows a very faithful rendition of the view of the bridge over the river Dee in Llangollen with Castell Dinas Bran dominating the scene from its perch, an almost conical hill on the north bank. Contrary to his normal practice, in this canvas Wilson has rendered the scene with topographical accuracy. The castle is a little bit more battered today but the bridge, the church tower and the corn mill by the river's edge still exist as he has shown them. The castle is rich in legend and here Wilson shows it in a haze of light, which presumably proclaims its antiquity and its status as an icon in Welsh mythology. Sandby's aquatint (Plate 23 B), although from a different viewpoint and slightly more capriciously composed, gives us a similarly 'romantic' view of the vale and its light effects. Sandby would have seen this painting when it was exhibited at the Royal Academy and his aquatint, if reversed, bears a remarkable similarity to Wilson's view.

Plate 14A. Tickets for the Wynnstay Theatre. Henry Bunbury. © Trustees of the British Museum.

Henry Bunbury was an old school friend of Sir Watkin and developed quite a reputation as a caricaturist. The theatre at Wynnstay rapidly became oversubscribed and a strict system of ticketing had to be introduced. Bunbury designed a series of witty, sometimes bawdy, and often quite elegant tickets for the theatre, which, amongst those who treasure theatre ephemera, are very collectable. The theatre was run with a curious mixture of rustic incompetence and deadly professional seriousness and was another of the ways in which its proprietor managed to reduce his fortune

Plate 14B. Tickets for the Wynnstay Theatre. Henry Bunbury. © Trustees of the British Museum.

Another of Bunbury's tickets shows a group of devotees circled around a bust of Shakespeare on a pedestal. Shakespeare was a staple of the Wynnstay repertoire and the history plays and the comedies were regularly performed with varying degrees of success. Both Garrick and Sheridan witnessed performances, although both wisely declined to participate. On one occasion, Sir Watkin and his friends seem to have ransacked the Wynnstay wardrobe and went to a masked ball in Chester dressed as characters from the *Merry Wives of Windsor*. The costume catalogue survives in the National Library of Wales.

Plate 15A. Silver gilt dessert service. John Carter. © National Museum of Wales.

It was most unusual to employ an architect to design a dinner service but Sir Watkin did precisely that when he commissioned designs for his great service from Robert Adam. The realisation of his designs was entrusted to several silversmiths, the most notable being Thomas Hemming, the royal silversmith. Some difficulty in paying Hemming's bills caused Sir Watkin to engage Joseph Creswell to supply further pieces. Creswell seems to have sub-contracted the dessert service to John Carter who made these pieces in 1774–5. The designs survive in the Sir John Soane Museum but an embellishment was the addition of the Williams Wynn arms impaled with those of Lady Charlotte Grenville, Sir Watkin's second wife. Dessert services were normally porcelain and Sir Watkin possessed several of those, but this rather spectacular service may be indicative of Sir Watkin's predisposition to style over economic sense.

Plate 15B. Silver sauceboat. John Carter. © National Museum of Wales.

By 1771 Sir Watkin's spending had begun to escalate. He began to assemble one of the largest silver dinner services an architect (Robert Adam) ever designed. This sauceboat, dated to 1773/4, is an indication of his lack of restraint in domestic matters. An otherwise quite obscure artisan, he may have been employed because Sir Watkin's preferred silversmith, Thomas Hemming, was demanding payment for previously supplied items for the service and Sir Watkin was temporarily embarrassed.

Plate 16. *The Society of Dilettanti*. Print after Sir Joshua Reynolds. © Trustees of the British Museum.

The Society of Dilettanti was founded in 1732 as a convivial dining club for young gentlemen who had made the Grand Tour. Sir Joshua Reynolds became its official painter in 1769 and this painting represents the reception of Sir William Hamilton into the society in 1777. On the extreme left is the figure of Sir Watkin, wearing the 'toga' as President for the evening and seated at the table, wearing the Order of the Bath, is Sir William himself. Open, on the table, is a copy of Sir William's *Antiquities*, the book which Sir Watkin loaned to Josiah Wedgwood in 1769. Sir Watkin is pointing to a vase on the table which is the subject of the illustration visible in the opened book. Of the society, Horace Walpole rather sniffily observed that the nominal qualification for entry was having made the Grand Tour, but the real one was for having been in a state of thorough intoxication throughout.

Between pages 128 and 129

Plate 17. *Sir Watkin Sketching*. Paul Sandby. © National Museum of Wales.

Paul Sandby's official relationship with Sir Watkin was that of drawing master. He not only taught Sir Watkin and his eventual children, but also the royal children and the students of Woolwich Military Academy. He was undoubtedly friendly with the baronet and this sketch seems to have been made during an open-air drawing session. The dog accompanying Sir Watkin appears in several of the north Wales aquatints and it may be that the drawing is earlier than its inscribed date. Another version survives in the Royal Collections at Windsor which is undated and which shows Sir Watkin facing in the opposite direction. It is possible that the Windsor sketch is the original and the Cardiff one is a copy made in 1777.

Plate 18. *Francis Cotes*. (Print after Paul Sandby. © Trustees of the British Museum.

Francis Cotes, Richard Wilson and Paul Sandby were all founder members of the Royal Academy. This portrait of Sandby, painted in about 1760, shows him sketching at the window of his house in Bayswater. He seems to have been urbane, witty and highly esteemed by his clients and pupils and was at the height of his fame when he came to north Wales in 1770 and 1771 as a guest of Sir Watkin. He had a particular interest in printmaking and pioneered the develop-ment of the aquatint in Britain. His sets of views in Wales, although not cheap, were responsible for disseminating an informed vision of the landscape of the country and were in the vanguard of an advance in taste towards the romantic and sublime. The inscription below the image reads '*Ruralium Prospectuum Pictor;*, which is how his contemporaries regarded Sandby.

Plate 19A. *An Iron Forge.* Paul Sandby. © Trustees of the British Museum.

The two-week tour around north Wales may have left Mr Sandby a little confused. He had to deal with Welsh place names and a very unfamiliar countryside, and when he began to prepare his work for publication some of the confusion creeps through. One of the published aquatints (Plate 27A) is inscribed a *Forge between Dolgellau and Barmouth* but is, in fact, a view of the forge at Dôl Gun on the road from Dolgellau to the Cross Foxes. In the National Library of Wales there is a pencil sketch (the only one which survives) with a similar inscription but of a quite different view. This watercolour appears to have been worked up from that sketch and has the same inscription. It seems likely that this is a view of a forge between Dolgellau and Barmouth and is of one located in either Cwm Mynach or at Bontddu where Sir Watkin owned land and where gold was eventually found. The general topography of the view may support that suggestion.

Plate 19B. *A View of the Traeth Mawr.* Paul Sandby. © Trustees of the British Museum.

Clearly the same view as in Plate 28B, this delicately-coloured watercolour shows the crossing where the baggage cart was loaded on to the ferry to make the crossing to Penmorfa and thence to Caernarfon, whilst the gentlemen carried ou up the Aberglaslyn Pass towards Beddgelert. The aquatint of the Traeth Mawr was published in 1777, a year after the first series and it is impossible to say whether the print or the watercolour came first. Although the prints were noted as being very expensive, Sandby normally seems to have charged about twenty guineas for a finished watercolour and perhaps this example represents a specific commission.

Plate 20A. *A View of Conway Castle.* Paul Sandby. © Trustees of the British Museum.

The short stay in Conwy was very productive for Sandby and several large-scale watercolours and gouaches of scenes around the castle exist. Although he is not known to have visited the town after 1771, he continued to produce finished works based on his sketches until 1800. This watercolour may have been intended as the basis for a print as the view has been reversed; a normal practice to assist the engraver.

Plate 20B. *A View of Snowdon.* Paul Sandby. © Trustees of the British Museum.

Labelled on the mount as a view of Snowdon, this is in fact a view of the church at Dolwyddelan and is related to a highly-finished watercolour in the Fitzwilliam Museum, Cambridge, which shows the same scene with more incidental detail. The mountain in the background is Moel Siabod which features frequently in Sandby's views of the area, at least six of which survive. To aid confusion, Sandby, by heightening the mountain and making its outlines more jagged, does contrive to make it resemble Snowdon.

Plate 21. *XII Views in North Wales*. Paul Sandby. © Trustees of the British Museum.

This is the frontispiece and dedication of the twelve views which Sandby first published in 1776. Other series of prints followed and altogether he published some twenty-five aquatints of views in north Wales. Some were withdrawn from sale because of technical difficulties and some were re-worked for subsequent editions. All of the surviving views (a reputed view of Castell Dinas Bran I have been unable to trace) derive from the itinerary of the 1771 tour and they are here presented in the order on which each location was visited and not in the order of their publication. I have ignored prints, the original of which were drawn by Sandby but engraved and published by others, but have included prints made by Sandby and possibly based on sketches by someone else. I have also ignored a flimsy view of Conwy, which is probably unfinished and yet another view of the Eagle Tower at Caernarfon. Otherwise, as far as I can ascertain, all of the known views are presented here.

The frontispiece is notable for describing north Wales, for the first time, as a 'Fertile and Romantick Country'. Gone is the infamous 'Fag End of Creation' of an earlier generation.

The spelling of various place names on the title of the print is Sandby's own. The anglicised eighteenth-century names have today been rendered into modern Welsh.

Plate 22A. *Overton Bridge*. 1776.© Trustees of the British Museum.

This view is substantially the same today. The bridge was replaced by a single-arched span, which promptly collapsed. Its replacement reverted to a double arch. The road by the river is much higher up the bank due to the regularity of flooding on this stretch of the Dee. In the distance, a man driving a fashionable curricle up the hill may be Sir Watkin himself. Sandby could have sketched this and the following four views on his 1770 visit to Wynnstay.

Plate 22B. *Wynnstay from above Newbridge*. 1776. © Trustees of the British Museum.

Newbridge was the main entrance to Wynnstay from Oswestry and here the immense extent of the park can be gauged from the far-distant mansion perched on the horizon. The figures on the lower right may be intended to represent Sir Watkin's second wife and their first two children. The marriage happened after the 1771 tour, but before the publication of the print, and Sandby, who knew Lady Charlotte, may have included her and the children as a simple homage

Plate 23A. *Chirk Castle from Wynnstay Park*. 1776. © Trustees of the British Museum.

Although Sandby labelled this aquatint *A View of Chirk Castle from the Park at Wynnstay*, the castle is hardly visible. Nor, in reality, is it easily visible from the park today. A situation which may have been welcomed by the Williams Wynn's who probably could not have regarded the castle as an ornament in the view, occupied, as it was, by their political rivals, the Myddletons. A prominent ornament is the same carriage as in Plate 22A and probably with the same driver. Sir Watkin was not a natural horseman and seems to have preferred his conveyance.

Plate 23B. *The Vale of Llangollen*. 1776. © Trustees of the British Museum.

This immediately attractive view is a composite of several viewpoints compressed together into a poetic vision of the main route from Wynnstay into the heart of north

Wales. Sandby has made the valley narrower, moved the church back from the riverbank on which it stands, straightened a curvaceous stretch of river and placed the sun in an almost north-westerly position, all of which has distilled the essence of the scene is a masterly way. The effect of sunlight cutting through air left damp by recent rain is vividly realised. See the notes on Plate 13B for a comparison between this view and Richard Wilson's version of the Vale of Llangollen and which Sandby may have used as a basis for the present print.

Plate 24A. *Abbey of Valle Crucis*. 1776. © Trustees of the British Museum.

Taken from much the same viewpoint as Turner was to use in 1794 (when he adopted the same expedient of moving Castell Dinas Bran into a more harmonious and visible position), Sandby's view is, on close inspection, highly detailed. In the field to the right of the abbey, he includes a finely drawn and minute group of haymakers working their way through the crop; presumably having just filled the cart which is making its way towards the Horseshoe Pass. Sandby and Sir Watkin had picnicked by the abbey ruins in 1770 and Sandby may have based this aquatint upon sketches made then. An oil painting in the National Library of Wales shows the abbey from the other side and although dated roughly to 1800, may well be a product of the same sketching trip.

Plate 24B. *Conwyd Mill*. 1776. © Trustees of the British Museum.

This slightly sooty view of the mill situated up a narrow valley behind Cynwyd was withdrawn from publication after the first edition and may have caused Sandby some difficulties in its production. The exact method of making the plate for an aquatint was still a matter of some experimentation and here the experiment may have misfired. Sandby's inclusion of boys fishing in the stream is pure invention. The strength of the torrent, which cascades over rocky drops, would prevent even the most foolhardy fish from swimming up it. The mill still exists and, modern extensions apart, looks much the same today.

Plate 25A. *View of the River Dee*. 1777. © Trustees of the British Museum.

Just after crossing the bridge at Llandderfel the road rises high upon the side of the valley and this scene is of part of the river at Bodweni before it curves to the west and enters the lake at Bala. The mountain in the distance is Arenig Fawr and not Cadair Idris as Sandby labels it. That mountain is not visible before the bend in the river towards Bala and the broadening of the valley. Sandby was paid for his attendance as Sir Watkin's drawing master and here he seems to show a lesson in progress although the figures are 'stock' and re-appear in other works. A watercolour version exists in the National Museum of Wales.

Plate 25B. *Pimble Meer* 1777. © Trustees of the British Museum.
Pimble Meer (or Bala Lake or Llyn Tegid) extends for four miles south west of Bala town and is the largest freshwater lake in Wales. The fishing rights and most of the surrounding land belonged to Sir Watkin and the dark promontory on the right hand side of the lake is where the main property, Glan-Llyn, was situated. Glan-Llyn was responsible for supplying a great deal of the comestibles for the 1770 coming-of-age celebrations at Wynnstay. On the tour, after a very convivial night enter-taining the tenantry in Bala town, Sir Watkin took to the water the next day and they all took a little voyage upon the water but only after consuming some tincture of rhubarb. Sandby charged Sir Watkin twenty guineas for a watercolour of the lake.

Plate 26A. *The Iron Forge.* 1776. © Trustees of the British Museum.

The grindings of early industry were beginning to be viewed as picturesque in their own right and Sandby was not alone in recording such scenes. The works at Coalbrookdale and what William Blake was to later christen those 'dark satanic mills' fascinated painters of the time. This print probably shows the crushing mill founded by Abraham Darby upon the lower slopes of Cadair Idris, a few miles south of Dolgellau. The confusion caused by Sandby's title (see Plate 19A) is lessened by the unmistakable profile of the mountain in the background. The whole valley of the fast-tumbling river Clywedog (now known as the scenic Torrent Walk) was devoted to iron workings and various remains are still to be seen. A watercolour version of the print is in the Metropolitan Museum of Art in New York.

Plate 26B. *Harlech Castle.* 1776. © Trustees of the British Museum.

Harlech Castle must have held a special place in the heart of Sir Watkin. It was the seat of the Merioneth Assize and he was to be appointed lord lieutenant in 1775 by a somewhat reluctant George III. Sandby's very accurate view is supplemented by a watercolour in Leeds City Gallery, which suggests that the sea may have still occasionally crept up to the castle rock. As in so many of the aquatints, Sandby includes some delightful details and the shepherd lad and his flock (absent from the watercolour) provide a lovely group on the path up to the castle.

Plate 27A. *Pengwern Corn and Fulling Mills.* 1776.© Trustees of the British Museum.

Although roughly accurate, this plate of the mills belonging to Owen Wynne is a somewhat strange composition. The point of it may be in the right-hand foreground where a slightly portly and recognisable figure, is slowly nodding off over his fishing rod, whilst an ebullient youth proffers him yet another bottle; the consumption of a previous one presumably being the cause of the gentleman's slightly sorry state. This may be a private joke between the artist and his patron. The accounts for the previous evening would suggest that not many of the party woke that day with a completely clear head.

Plate 27B. *The Traeth Mawr.* 1777. © Trustees of the British Museum.

See the notes on Plate 19B.

Plate 28A. *Pont Aber-Glaslin.* 1777. © Trustees of the British Museum.

The old road to Pont Aberglaslyn, along the Traeth Mawr, must have been an absolute nightmare to traverse. Many travellers complained about its rockiness and the impossibility of driving a carriage along it. That might have been the reason why the luggage cart was sent through Penmorfa on the easier route to Caernarfon. The bridge became a favoured subject of later painters and the pass between it and Beddgelert, now heavily wooded, was regarded as an archetypal 'romantic' scene.

Plate 28B. *Carnarvon Castle.* 1776. © Trustees of the British Museum.

A technical triumph, this view of Caernarfon at night shows celebrations of some sort happening around the castle. Fireworks are exploding overhead and there is a bonfire on the quayside beside the old Custom House. Although Sir Watkin paid for bonfires in Bala and Conwy, Caernarfon did not benefit in this way and the celebrations must have been unconnected with the baronet's visit.

Plate 29A. *Carnarvon Castle*. 1777. © Trustees of the British Museum.

This view and that of Plate 29B are variants on the same theme. Further versions of the view exist in an oil painting in Southampton Art Gallery, and a finished watercolour recently acquired by the Pierrepoint Morgan Library in New York. For some reason Sandby was dissatisfied with this particular print and withdrew it and, in a letter, asked Thomas Pennant not to mention it in his publications. On the rock upon which the boy sits in the foreground Sandby has engraved his initials and the date 1774, thus indicating that he may have contemplated publication well before its eventual release. There are many other variants of the Caernarfon views published as engravings by Sandby and others, but all are based upon the same set of sketches made during the two days he spent in the town.

Plate 29B. *Carnarvon Castle*. 1786. © Trustees of the British Museum.

On the rock in the foreground, over which the harpist leans, is inscribed 'Twelve Views in North and South Wales' and this represents the last collection of aquatints Sandby was to produce based on his visits to the Principality. After Thomas Grey published his poem *The Bard* in 1757, a positive mania for Welsh harpists developed and tourists felt deprived if they did not have one or two play for them during their visit. Sir Watkin's own harpist, John Parry, was the leading virtuoso, but each town seems to have had several available. By the time this print was published the routine was established and Sandby depicts a fashionably rustic scene. Indeed the type of scene he himself had made fashionable.

Plate 30A. *Llanberris Lake*. 1777. © Trustees of the British Museum.

Sandby first drew a view of Llanberris and Snowdon in 1764 (Birmingham City Art Gallery) but in all probability he copied the scene from a pre-existing work by someone else, as there is no evidence of him ever having visited north Wales before 1770. Curiously, that earlier drawing is from the same viewpoint as the present print and also includes a boating party upon the lake. However, this aquatint is thoroughly based upon experience. Sir Watkim's party visited the lake on 29 August and paid the boatmen 10s 6d for ferrying them over it. Sandby must have had local help in identifying the peak of Snowdon (which he has greatly exaggerated) because it is not immediately obvious from the side of the lake and the towering pinnacles of Crib Goch are often mistaken for it.

Plate 30B. *Bangor*. 1776. © Trustees of the British Museum.

This view, taken from the south side of Bangor, is roughly from where the railway station now stands. Sandby shows the town sparsely inhabited with only the cathedral standing out. In contrast to his usual practice of exaggerating for dramatic effect, here he seems to have eliminated to increase the scenic effect. Bangor was a little more populated than he shows and a later watercolour in the National Museum of Wales shows far more houses. In the far distance is the promontory of the Great Orme jutting out to sea and nearer the headland of Penmaenmawr, which generally caused terror to the eighteenth-century traveller traversing its elevated and unfenced road.

Plate 31A. *Conway Castle.* 1776. © Trustees of the British Museum.

Views of Conwy Castle survive in collections in Manchester, Liverpool, Aberystwyth, California, New Haven, London and several other places and Sandby produced watercolours and gouaches into the 1800s based on the sketches he made within the two days they spent in the town. This view of the castle is taken from near Benarth, which was to become the holiday home of Sir George Beaumont – part founder of the National Gallery in London.

Plate 31B. *Llanrwst Bridge.* 1786. © Trustees of the British Museum.

The bridge at Llanrwst is ascribed by local tradition to Inigo Jones; that tradition also claiming him as a son of the locality. The town and Gwydir Castle, formerly a seat of the Wynn's are on opposing sides of the Conwy river and the bridge links them. Sir Richard Wynn was widely believed to be a patron of Jones and the elevation of the designer into the pantheon of Palladian architects gave the bridge a celebrity which may not have been entirely warranted. Unaltered, it still causes lengthy traffic jams and the cottage at the end is now a National Trust tearoom. This print, although engraved and published by Sandby, may have been based upon a drawing by T. Nixon.

Plate 32A. *Pont-y-Pair.* 1776. © Trustees of the British Museum.

The famous bridge of Pont-y-Pair is now subsumed by Victorian Betws-y-Coed but in the eighteenth century stood quite alone. Sandby must have followed the Conwy river from Llanrwst and makes the pardonable mistake in thinking that he was still on its banks. It is in fact the Llugwy which tumbles through the arches and which is the subject of the last print. Careful observation of the second arch from the right will reveal two shadowy figures who seem to be sheltering, one of whom might be Sir Watkin himself. A watercolour version of the same view exists in the Yale Centre for British Art.

Plate 32B. *Rhaidr-y-Wennol.* 1777. © Trustees of the British Museum.

In this final print, of the Swallow Falls, the figure of Sir Watkin is quite unmistakable. His sits on the steep bank, close to the same noisy youths who have appeared in other views, and appears to be enjoying the view. Some commentators have suggested that Sandby has greatly exaggerated the flow of water over the falls, but the river flows directly from the slopes of Tryfan and the Glyderau and would, at times, be difficult to exaggerate. The effects of vapour and water mist sometimes fill the steep-sided gorge the river flows through after its quick descent.

INTRODUCTION

Sir Watkin Williams Wynn, 1749–89

IN EARLY JUNE 1768, THE NINETEEN-YEAR-OLD SIR WATKIN WILLIAMS WYNN began his Grand Tour of France and Italy. Most young men of his class looked forward to their tour as an excuse for a gentle bit of debauchery away from the family and most of their families were anxious that their wild oats should be sown well away from home. But Sir Watkin, who may not have had many wild oats to sow, seems to have been slightly reluctant to undertake the tour. This may have been because he had recently become engaged to Lady Henrietta Somerset, daughter of the late Duke of Beaufort, and plans were well in hand for the forthcoming marriage. The late Duke had been a political ally of Sir Watkin's father and the Dowager Duchess was a close neighbour to the Williams Wynn's town house in Grosvenor Square. The marriage seemed inevitable. A private Bill[1] was about to be submitted to Parliament to enable the under-age Sir Watkin to make a financial settlement upon his intended bride and he was anxious about its progress. Another possible cause of his reluctance, especially in view of his later development, was that he had just commissioned Robert Adam to design a new mansion for him at Wynnstay, the family seat,[2] and he was eager to watch the progress of the work. His surviving letters stress his eagerness to return home as quickly as decently possible.

When he came into his majority he also became a very rich man indeed, although his contemporaries generally exaggerated the extent of his wealth. His father, the 'Great' Sir Watkin had died on 26 September 1749 when his horse stumbled over a molehill in the park at Acton Hall near Wrexham – previously home to the notorious Judge Jeffreys. Our Sir Watkin was a mere five months old and his mother, Lady Frances, was pregnant with her second son, William, who was unfortunately to contract smallpox and die in 1763. Lady Frances (1717–1803), born Miss Shackerley of Gwersyllt, was Sir Watkin's second wife, his goddaughter and, at thirty one, considerably younger than him. She had fulfilled the purpose of the marriage and produced an heir, but also proved to be an astute and capable manager of the estates. Through shrewd acquisition and careful investment she increased their value to an extraordinary extent, adding some 100,000 acres to the family holdings. In partnership with her son's trustees, William Owen and Edward Kynaston, local and dependable worthies, she built up one of the biggest land holdings in Wales with a reported annual income of over £20,000, in spite of the considerable debt bequeathed by her late husband.

Sir Watkin's father was a highly political figure[3]; a dissipated youth who fell under the influence of High Church Anglicanism and became a staunch Tory. His grandfather (Speaker Williams) had served Queen Henrietta Maria and, after the Restoration, became Solicitor General and was knighted in 1687, thus bringing a title into his branch of the family. Fifty years later, his descendant continued the family devotion to the hopeless Stuart cause and became deeply involved in various Jacobite plots to bring the gentlemen of north Wales to the assistance of the Young Pretender during the insurrection of 1745. Sensing the incompetent way things were going, he wisely decided on a course of studied inaction, thus preserving both his head and his estates but at the same time, doing some amount of damage to his reputation. His condition that the Prince 'arrive at the head of a French Army' not being met, he felt justified in his desertion of north Wales for London at that crucial time. He had, in 1744, visited Versailles and met with Louis XV even though a state of war between Britain and France existed at the time but, wisely, committed nothing to paper. That same year, he was offered an earldom which he declined on the grounds that no honour could be higher than that of being 'Sir Watkin' in Wales. Consolation for the failure of the '45 was provided by the 'Cycle of the White Rose', nominally a subversive political society but practically a gentlemen's drinking club which he had joined whilst at Ruthin School in the 1720s and by the establishment of a Masonic lodge at Wynnstay. He also began rebuilding Wynnstay itself (previously known as Watstay but renamed by his father when he added Wynn to the family name) and engaged Francis Smith of Warwick to execute the work. A new (still surviving) stable block (1738/9) was completed, but the new house which was to replace a half-timbered mansion was only partially built by the time of his death and building work was suspended. A cultured and genial man, he was the acknowledged leader of the 'London Welsh' and it was reported that when he visited the capital, gentry would ride out to Finchley to escort him to his house. His opposition to Prime Minister Walpole was implacable but, as a politician, he was no leader and contented himself with being a thorn in the flesh of the ruling administration. His death was reported in the *Gentleman's Magazine*.

Saturday Oct. 3

At Rhewabbon in Denbighshire, was interr'd late in the night, in a private manner, the body of Sir W. W. Wynne, Bart. The herse was attended by his domestick and menial servants, amounting to a very great number. At the park gate of Wynnstay the corpse was solemly received by multitudes of people, whose outward gestures of affliction pathetically represented the inward sentiments of their hearts. Few men have ever deserv'd so general a lamentation! In his publick character, he was resolute and immovable; in his private character, he was generous and of exceedingly good nature. He lov'd his country with a sincerity which seem'd to distinguish him from all mankind: His morals were untainted: He had an utter detestation of vice: His manners, like his countenance, were open and undisguis'd: He was affable by nature; he knew how to condescend without [?] : He was munificent, without ostentation: His behaviour was so amiable, as never to create a personal enemy; he was even honour'd where he was not beloved: In domestick life, he was the kindest relation, and truest friend: His house was a noble scene of regular, yet almost unbounded, hospitality: His piety towards his creator, was remarkable in his constant attendance on the service of the church: he revered religion, he respected the clergy, he feared God, the whole tenor of his conduct was one continued series of virtue: So prepared, he had little reason to be afraid of sudden death; every day of his life was a preparation for heaven; and the loss of him will be a lasting calamity to his country.[4]

That rather partial eulogy (culled by the *Gentleman's Magazine* from the *Chester Journal*) was perhaps balanced by the different perspective displayed by the local Methodists whom he persecuted relentlessly and who were holding a prayer meeting at the time of his death. Their petition to the Lord 'O Arglwydd cwympa Ddiawl Mawr y Wynnstay' (O Lord, cast down the Great Devil of Wynnstay) thus being answered in an entirely satisfactory manner, the meeting was brought to a close. It was rumoured that several antagonistic local gentlemen adopted a more conciliatory attitude to the Methodists thereafter.

It is perhaps fortunate that the fourth baronet never had to exist under the shadow of such a paragon of political and religious excellence. 'Munificence without ostentation' was certainly not within the catalogue of virtue which he bequeathed to his son. His legacy took the form of estates with a rent roll of princely dimensions which his son managed to transform into a debt of over £100,000 in the course of nineteen years of slavery in the service of art, music and architecture. Considerately, the fourth baronet also died prematurely and gave the estates time to recover before his heir came into his majority, but the Williams Wynns seem to have given high art an increasingly wide berth thereafter.

Born in Wales, the fourth baronet's early years, and those of his brother, were probably spent at Llangedwyn, one of the Williams Wynn properties in the Tanat valley. He was educated at Westminster School although when he entered is uncertain but he was there by 1760 and was remembered as a pupil by William Hickey,[5] who was the same age and had entered in 1757. Whilst he was at the school, on 22 September 1761, the coronation of George III took place which seems to have been a slightly chaotic affair. The scholars of Westminster School fulfilled their allotted role and shouted *Vivat*, in schoolboy Latin, at appropriate points (Sir Watkin amongst them) but, during the slightly inappropriate and very boring sermon by the Archbishop of Canterbury, the assembled gentry took it as a signal to enjoy the collation which they had brought with them. The voice of the sermon was drowned by the clatter of cutlery upon china plates whilst the assembled multitude relieved the tedium of religion with a jolly good lunch of cold meats and alcohol. The King gave a discreet signal and the combined forces of choirs and orchestra launched into Handel's anthem *Zadock the Priest* (sung during the actual crowning) although at the behest of the wearisome archbishop, all of the other music had been newly composed by William Boyce. The effect this must have had upon a thirteen-year-old boy is probably responsible for Sir Watkin's later partisan passion for the works of Handel and one of the few passions he shared with the new king. Unfortunately there is no evidence for a persistent local story that Handel himself stayed at Wynnstay whilst on his way to Dublin for the first performance of the *Messiah* although such a visit would have been quite possible as his embarkation point was at Parkgate close to Chester and the presence at Wynnstay of John Parry, the virtuoso harpist, would have been a reason for the composer to visit.

Whilst at Westminster, Sir Watkin was to suffer his first serious fever caused by erysipelas (St Anthony's Fire), an event which was to recur throughout his short life. At first, it affected his legs and eventually his face. Curable today by penicillin, it often proved fatal in the eighteenth century. Queen Anne, Princess Amelia, Charles Lamb and John Stuart Mill all succumbed to the disease as ultimately did Sir Watkin. Various causes have been advanced but it seems that the bacteria gains access through broken skin; dog scratches have been suggested as a possible cause and in Sir Watkin's case, a likely one as he seems to have been quite attached to his various canines. Ironically, his eldest son was to suffer the same fate.

After public school, Welsh gentry usually went to Jesus College, Oxford but Oriel seems to have been chosen because that was the college his mother and trustees preferred for some reason (Thomas Pennant, the Welsh naturalist, and the duke of Beaufort had also attended Oriel). Thomas Apperley, a Wynnstay neighbour and ten years his senior, matriculated as a gentleman commoner at much the same time and seems to have acted as Sir Watkin's guardian whilst at the college.[6] Apperley's father, a doctor, had been a friend of Sir Watkin's father and the two families were on intimate terms. Perhaps Lady Williams Wynn felt reassured to know that a scholarly and solid man accompanied her son and it would be reasonable to presume that the Wynnstay trustees covered his expenses whilst at Oxford, although there is no documentary evidence for this presumption. They both left the university without graduating, although Sir Watkin was subsequently awarded a DCL when the college became the happy beneficiary of his gift of a (still existing) set of silverware for High Table. His premature departure from Oxford was probably because of the approaching tour, which was generally undertaken in a bachelor state, and needed to be completed before the banns were read out and the subsequent nuptials took place. It must be admitted that the parlous state into which both of our ancient universities had fallen was hardly a guarantee of a good education and that most gentlemen left before they graduated – no particular compliment or honour being derived from completion of a worthless degree.

Sir Watkin and the Grand Tour

The idea of Italy and the Grand Tour would not have been foreign to Sir Watkin. His distant cousin Richard Wilson, whose mother was a Wynne, had returned to London from Rome in 1757, after six years in Italy, and established himself in a splendid studio in Covent Garden where his Roman canvases were on display and new 'souvenirs' were being constantly manufactured or re-worked. It is almost unimaginable to think that Sir Watkin did not visit his kinsman and see Italian scenes glowing from every wall. If anything could have excited an eager anticipation of the glories of Italian landscape and antiquity, surely the sun-drenched views of Wilson would have fulfilled that role. Wilson's most gifted pupil, Thomas Jones, had already left his pupilage and was becoming established as an artist himself although his journey to Italy was to be delayed until 1776. Given the smallness of the artist circle in London, it is unthinkable that the Welsh baronet and the two greatest Welsh painters of the eighteenth century were not equally acquainted.

Whilst it was not particularly 'gentlemanly' to be especially good at any artistic endeavour, Sir Watkin seems to have taken two of his interests very seriously indeed. He was dedicated to both his cello and to his sketchbook. It is probable that, in the case of the latter, he was already having drawing lessons from Paul Sandby and in the case of the former; the accounts record a devotion to his instrument which was not strictly 'amateur'. The celebrity of his instructors may indicate that he was slightly better than that.

Preparations went ahead for his tour but not before he took a lease on number 2 Grosvenor Square in 1768 as a suitable town house.[7] The 5th Duke of Beaufort, his future brother-in-law, lived at number 7 and the dowager duchess, his future mother-in-law lived at number 8, whilst Sir Thomas Wynn, shortly to become Lord Newborough, lived at number 9. Apart from St James' Square, Grosvenor Square was quite simply the best address in London. The nineteen-year-old Sir Watkin was utterly confident in his social credentials.

His departure could not be delayed and around 2 June he set off from his new town house upon a journey which was to have a profound influence upon his artistic development and eventual financial ruin.

On the tour, Thomas Apperley took the place of tutor and they were accompanied by Captain Edward Hamilton, an officer in the 15th Light Dragoons. A military man in uniform was something of a necessity in some of the parts they were to visit; especially those near Naples. Apperley may not, in retrospect, have been a wise choice as he made a complete disaster of bringing up his own son, the sportswriter 'Nimrod', proving himself incapable of exerting any kind of discipline either fiscal or moral upon his errant child. Although, fifty years after Sir Watkin's death the errant Nimrod remembered him as follows:

> *I have yet to see a more aristocratic looking person – a person more truly coming under the denomination of the highly bred Englishman [sic]. I think I see him now standing with his back to the fire in the great room, after breakfast, as was his usual custom in the winter months, his attire of the neatest possible description a light pepper and salt mixture coat, a white dimity waistcoat, nankeen breeches, silk stockings and ... top boots. The fineness, whiteness, and beauty of his linen, a distinguished mark of a gentleman in all ages, ruffled as it was both at the breast and wrists, I have never since seen equalled; and he must have prided himself upon its appearance, for it was changed three times within the twenty four hours, to which some of the old women in the country attributed his days being cut short, the said frequent change being considered inimical to health ... His manners were bland in the extreme and he had a very harmonious voice.*[8]

The sweetness of Sir Watkin's disposition was frequently commented upon by his contemporaries and, strangely for such a sociable man, so was his shyness. His travelling companions seem to have been chosen for their efficiency and amiability and presumably their ability to ease the young baronet's launch into an European society very different from that at home.

Samuel Sidebotham, the London steward, kept the accounts and acted as paymaster and some of the Wynnstay servants, Mr Morris and Sam Stephens, made up the party. Binding the group together was Antonio Carrara who acted as valet to Sir Watkin and who had been recommended by David Garrick[9] after he had accompanied him on his tour of Italy in 1763. There is an implication here that even at the age of nineteen, Sir Watkin was moving in circles deeply connected with the arts and letters.

Sir Watkin seems to have been an affable youth who allowed considerable latitude to his companions and whilst he was acquiring social polish with dancing, fencing and language lessons, the rest of the party became avid sightseers, play-goers and opera buffs — all at his expense.

Whilst on the tour, Sir Watkin was to develop from a sometimes diffident, slightly gauche schoolboy into a gentleman of refined and unfortunately expensive taste, which his fortune, however immense, could not possibly sustain. Profligacy was not wholly to blame for the financial catastrophes which eventually overtook him, his generous and trusting nature and his genuine social conscience were equally to be held responsible.

During the time they were abroad, an event of great significance happened in London. A group of leading painters including Richard Wilson, Paul Sandby, and Sir Joshua Reynolds, and several other eminent artists, founded the Royal Academy. Sir Watkin's close acquaintance with and patronage of many of the founder members conspired to make him a leading social figure in the London art world almost by default and on his return from Italy, he was to capitalise energetically upon that connection.

The Grand Tour lasted a little over a frantic nine months during which time they managed to see the major cities of France and Italy, pass through parts of Switzerland and Germany, commission works of art and architecture, buy books, prints and paintings, establish valuable social connections and, in modern terms, part with slightly over half-a-million pounds (that is in addition to artists' fees paid by agents and bankers and re-imbursed later). Nine months was an indecently short time in which to undertake the tour. Two years was not an uncommon length of time and some gentlemen, finding Catholic Italy more indulgent to their tastes than Protestant England, managed to dawdle for five years before the inevitable summons to 'return home immediately' arrived.

On his return in March 1769, Sir Watkin seems to have taken leave of his senses and his spending was prodigious by any standards. His indulgent mother abdicated any responsibility for restraining his impulses and although his approaching wedding was a reasonable occasion for extra expenditure; his dalliances with architects, painters and musicians were bound to start draining his resources.

Sir Watkin's other tour

The only other extended tour which Sir Watkin made was to be the one he completed in 1771 through his own landholdings in north Wales. Accompanied by Paul Sandby, who sketched throughout, the tour was to have an influence which went far beyond its intentions. Though often quoted as the first scenic and therefore romantic tour of the British and especially Welsh countryside, the truth is rather more prosaic. Sir Watkin had inherited a good part of north Wales and he had never seen it – more importantly, it had never seen him. The route of the tour through the Dee Valley to the coast at Barmouth, up through Harlech to Snowdonia and thence, by way of Bangor, along the north coast and home, took on something of the nature of a royal 'progress' as he passed his tenants and political allies. Church bells were rung as he approached and bonfires lit as he entertained his allies and drank unwise amounts of alcohol.

The inclusion of Paul Sandby in the party caused the landowner's visits to his holdings to acquire an almost mythical status. When, in 1776, he published twelve aquatints drawn from sketches he had made on the tour he not only dedicated the work to Sir Watkin but, on the handsome title page, describing north Wales as 'that Fertile and Romantick Country', he made explicit something which had been implicit hitherto. Wales was indeed as he had described it and its scenic beauty was worthy of inspection. The landscapes of Salvatore Rosa, familiar to an audience accustomed to perceiving nature through a glass tinted with the classical past or a romantic crag-fringed and *banditti* inhabited present, could be found on our own soil. Sandby's means of distribution through the medium of aquatint meant that his work was widely accessible (although expensive) and British tourism to celtic Britain took off apace. He was, of course, not alone but laid the foundations for the next generation of artists who were to flood the Cambrian alps. By association, if nothing else, Sir Watkin must be regarded as a founding member of Welsh tourism.

Some contemporaries

Our sources for both his Italian and Welsh tours are the meticulous accounts kept by Samuel Sidebotham and now deposited with the Wynnstay Papers in the National Library of Wales.[10] For the tour to France and Italy, Sidebotham used an octavo, vellum-bound notebook to record his expenditures. Missing from the collection are the individual bills and receipts which he would have gathered on the tour. The bald entry 'Pd the road bill from _____ to _____.' would have been supplemented with the appropriate dockets, which are now missing. The disastrous fire at Wynnstay in 1858 is probably responsible for the lacuna. The Welsh tour however does retain all of its receipts and is therefore easier to reconstruct. Of course Sidebotham was primarily concerned with keeping a close account of the costs incurred but occasionally the ghost of a narrative can be detected behind his businesslike entries.

In order to elucidate his bare account of the Italian tour it has been necessary to turn to various other writers who made the journey at much the same time. Social and economic conditions changed so much both at home and abroad during the course of the eighteenth century that, whenever possible, a writer has not been included who would not have had a similar experience as Sir Watkin and his company.

Chief amongst these supplementary sources are the writings of the music-ologist and father of the novelist Fanny, Dr Charles Burney; both those he published himself and those published in relatively recent times. Although Burney was primarily concerned with the 'present state of music,' he was an intelligent and often entertaining observer and followed closely in Sir Watkin's footsteps and had a lot in common with the young man. Educated in Shrewsbury and Chester, he actually saw Handel embarking for Dublin, where he was to first perform the *Messiah,* in 1741 and called Handel, Geminiani and Corelli 'the divinities of my youth'; divinities to whom Sir Watkin was to stay constant and pay expensive homage. Burney made his main tour of Italy in 1770, one year later than Sir Watkin, to collect material for his *History of Music*, but the material he collected in Italy was so rich that friends, including David Garrick and the Earl of Holdernesse, persuaded him to publish a separate volume in 1771. This appeared as *The Present State of Music in France and Italy: or The Journal of a Tour through those Countries undertaken to collect Materials for a General History of Music*. The publication was gratifyingly successful, was admired by Dr Johnson and Sir Joshua Reynolds, and preceded the first volume of his history by five years. However, the published journal was very much 'prepared for publication'. The actual manuscript travel journal is much more colloquial, indiscreet, opinion-ated and generally more engaging. It was published, edited by H. Edmund Poole, from the manuscript in the British Museum in 1969 and it is that version which has been used here.[11] Burney was privileged, whilst in Rome, to inspect the designs for the proposed re-building of Wynnstay, long before the gentleman who had commissioned them, which he thought 'a noble one indeed'. He must therefore enlist our sympathies and be thought a worthy gloss on Sidebotham's account book. Burney and Sir Watkin were certainly acquainted and worked together on the Handel commemoration of 1784 in Westminster Abbey; Sir Watkin as treasurer and Burney as the musical expert: although, unlike Sir

Watkin, Burney was not recognised upon the commemorative plaque.

A Denbighshire neighbour of Sir Watkin was Mrs Hester Lynch Piozzi, otherwise more simply known as Mrs Thrale. Confidante of Dr Johnson and a writer and observer of no mean ability, she not only took the irrascible doctor on a tour of north Wales in 1774, but also toured Italy with her second husband in 1784. Mrs Thrale had been born in north Wales and eventually inherited estates near St Asaph. After Mr Thrale's demise in 1781, she shocked London society by marrying Gabriele Piozzi, her children's music master. Together, they built a beautiful neo-classical house upon her estate, afterwards known as 'Brynbella' (thereby compounding both Welsh and Italian), and lived there, much to society's dismay, in entire happiness for the rest of their lives. She had a sharp pen and was occasionally ill-judged but her account of her Italian tour with her Italian husband, together with her account of her Welsh tour with her difficult friend are useful in expanding Sidebotham's account book. A further point of connection is that Burney became music instructor to the Thrale children and that he and his daughter, Fanny (Fanny D'Arblay) became intimate in the social circle which revolved around Dr Johnson and Mrs Thrale at the latter's Streatham house. A circle which was broken upon Mrs Thrale's marriage to Mr Piozzi which was generally regarded as unfortunate. To save confusion, she is referred to her as Mrs Piozzi throughout. Her political observations are slightly prim, middle-class, sharp and occasionally tart. One would never think that she had shocked society by marrying a Catholic Italian musician for love.

Economic matters on the Grand Tour

Calculating the cost of a grand tour through France to Italy was like measuring the length of a piece of string. Some, like Dr Burney, took the public diligence, shared costs whenever possible and gladly accepted hospitality wherever offered. Sir Watkin with his party of nine, his private transport, his expensive inns and the necessity to cut 'una bella figura' in the courts he attended found it considerably more expensive.

Sir Watkin's tour cost him £8,643 12s. 9d. according to the summation in the accounts. But, as he continued to pay for artworks which arrived several years later, having only given a deposit upon their commission, the actual cost must have been very much higher. On one memorable page of the account book (62) Piranesi was paid for his complete volumes of prints, Hamilton for further prints, Byres for cameos and other items, Batoni paid in part for a full-length picture of Sir Watkin, Apperley and Captain Hamilton and for a history painting (*Bacchus and Ariadne*) and Jenkins for further antiquities. On the next page, Mr Hewson

[sic] was part paid for a 'bust in clay' of Sir Watkin. These part payments were generally redeemed after the completed works arrived in London; 1773 in the case of the full-length portrait. No mention is made in the account book of the commission given, through a third party, to the absent Raphael Mengs but it must have been an expensive one. Whether or not the finished work (*Perseus and Andromache*), which was intercepted by a French privateer en-route to London and ended up in St Petersburg, was paid for in full is a matter of speculation.

Sir Watkin was away for nine months, which was a relatively modest amount of time to spend on the tour. It was generally reckoned that a gentleman could, without undue privation, undertake the tour at that time for about £150 per month. Unfortunately, status was very expensive to maintain and Sir Watkin was very conscious of his.

The annual rent roll from the Wynnstay estates was about £20,000 in the late 1760s. This was a very tolerable income and one that allowed a high degree of comfortable living. The 5th duke of Devonshire, who joined Sir Watkin in Florence and continued with him to Rome and the immediate countryside around, was in receipt of twice that amount. Yet there was no question but that they should share the costs. The duke was likely to have spent about one quarter of his yearly income on his tour whilst Sir Watkin expended about one half of his.

When discussing the cost of living, it must be borne in mind that all sums involved are relative. In 1769, Sèvres porcelain was very expensive, as it is today, but in relation to average income, the price of a pig, once the standard for gauging the value of things, has declined steadily. Holy Week in Rome and the carnival in Venice, then as now, are costly times to stay in either city but otherwise, food and accommodation in 1769 were a great deal cheaper in Italy than in England. Luxury goods were exactly that but, questions of artistic worth aside, Lucien Freud has been relatively a great deal more expensive than Pompeo Batoni.

In the late 1760s, £1 sterling would have equated to approximately £68 in modern values,[12] accordingly the £8,463 12s 9d recorded in the account book translates into more than £550,000 against an annual income of about £1.3 million in current money. Those sums may not seem excessively grand until we put them against the incomes enjoyed by others. Captain Hamilton would have expected an annual salary of some £210, which makes his fee of £1,000 for accompanying Sir Watkin hugely generous and even in modern terms £64,000 is a lot of money for nine months 'protection'. However, an ordinary barrister[13] in 1780 could expect an annual income of about £2,420, which would equate to approximately £15,000 and an agricultural labourer on £21 would equate to £1,300. Although these figures clearly demonstrate the impossibility of direct conversion they do illustrate the unbridgeable gulf between the rich, the emerging middle-class and the labouring classes. Sir Watkin's spending power was twenty thousand times greater than that of the labourers who worked his estates. A modern agricultural labourer could expect to be paid around £18,500 and if we apply a proportionate relationship to Sir Watkin's income, we can see that in relative terms, his translated modern £500,000 becomes a more reasonable £6.5 million, a sum that is probably nearer the truth.

In pleasing contrast to all of the above, it may be noted that the Welsh tour cost a very modest £117 7s. 6d. (£7,475.61) and must have represented extraordinarily good value for an alcohol-fuelled, two-week jaunt around Snowdonia.

Sidebotham's life was not easy and was about to become considerably more difficult. In France, the currency of *livres* and *Louis d'Or* was easy to handle as for most of the late-century a *Louis d'or* was worth £1 sterling and a *livre* about 10d (Sidebotham obtained a slightly better rate in Paris). But when he crossed the Alps into Piedmont, his worst nightmares were to become manifest. One cannot read parts of the account book without feeling deeply sorry for the man and his impossible task. Leaving out the German-speaking lands they passed through on the way home, he was facing the prospect of travelling through nine or more different jurisdictions each with its own currency. Sometimes sharing similar names but with different values; sometimes having several systems concurrent with each other and sometimes refusing to accept the value of the coin of another previous state on the route. International banking was in its infancy but the international bankers had already learned how to fleece the trusting tourist with infinitely variable rates of exchange; usually weighted in their favour.

In France and Switzerland, Sidebotham kept the accounts in sterling but on page 34 the heading 'Here begins Piedmontese' is followed by an ominous note 'Errors Accepted'. He survived Turin but converted his headings into *lira* and *soldi*. Piedmontese coinage was acceptable in Genoa, their next destination, but he does not seem to have been informed that Genoese money, because of the parlous state of the economy there, was unacceptable in Milan, their next stop. The Genoese economy may well have been close to collapse but no-one could have guessed it from the sumptuous state kept up by the very rich merchants of the maritime republic. Lombardy and Milan followed, both with a stable economy, but he no longer bothered to record the different denominations in his account book simply contenting himself with entering the rounded figures of the sums expended. Surely Antonio Carara would have been aware of the problems but, if he was, he gave no particular help or advance warning. After Milan, Parma and Modena, they entered the Papal States by way of Bologna. Finances here were chaotic but Sidebotham recorded the expenses as being in *paoli* and *solidi*. The older Marquis Girolamo Belloni, the father of their banker in Italy, had attempted to rectify the situation and had published a learned treatise on fiscal prudence and was the recipient of much Papal gratitude, acquired his marquisate, but effected very little reform.

After arriving in Tuscany Sidebotham made another embarrassing entry 'Oct 12 I pray to be allowed what I can't account for'. But worse was to come.

In the Papal States, there were *scudi, baiocchi, paoli, zecchini* and a few others. The relative value of one to another sometimes changed and the various coinages represented two different systems which had enjoyed a very unhappy forced marriage. His difficulty must have been compounded by later events back in London when he needed to pay outstanding Roman bills. Several pages of the account in Florence and Rome are covered with calculations and conversions and may indicate a certain degree of frustration. Naples was relatively straightforward although on page 76 he has another page of calculations in *duckats* [sic] *carleens, crowns, pauls* [sic], *biocchi* and Venetian *leons*. Back to Rome and *sequins, paoli and baiocchi* before spending eight days on the road to Venice and *zecchini* and *leoni*. He must have been grateful, when over the Alps he had a draft from Child's Bank, which he drew upon a Mr Gulman of Augsberg in *Louis d'or*. From then on, it was plain sailing although on page 85 he had to indulge in some creative accounting to make the figures reconcile. He lost £1 14s. 1d. in exchanging Venetian money for French in Augsberg, but finally managed to bring the whole lot together and had it signed off by Sir Watkin once they were back in London. It must have been quite uncomfortable having to ask a nineteen-year-old employer to acknowledge and forgive his deeply felt mistakes and slight incompetences.

Sir Watkin's bank account in London was held by Child's Bank in the City and through the emerging system of bills and drafts, the traveller to foreign parts could equip himself with the means of access to funds whilst abroad. Ready cash was an absolute necessity but to carry any large sum would have been foolhardy indeed. The expensive Captain Hamilton was always ready with his sword and guns to protect the party from highway robbery but even so, it was prudent not to carry liquid assets. Child's Bank had a network of well-placed agents and other bankers throughout Europe who would honour a draft. The system depended upon trust and sometimes broke down when a draft from an unknown or suspect source was refused and the tourist had to resort to borrowing money. Such cases were plentiful but Child's Bank had credit and so, importantly, did his agents.

Before they left London, Sidebotham was issued with funds of £100 cash by Francis Chambre, the Oswestry solicitor and land agent to the family, which he converted into 2,285 *livres* and one imagines that expenses from London to Paris were thereby covered. Thereafter, he was dependent upon the services of a network of agents who could honour drafts or advance cash upon the security of

Child's Bank. The European bankers he called upon made a very distinctive group and it is worth observing that nearly all of them had some connection to the family and descendants of James III, the Old Pretender; Sir Watkin's father would undoubtedly have approved.

In Paris, almost upon arrival, Isaac Panchaud was called upon and relieved of £200, which he gave at a good rate of exchange, and Sidebotham pocketed 4,450 *livres*. Panchaud was an enigmatic character. Usually called a Swiss banker, there is reason to believe that he was actually born in London – he certainly admired British economic systems – and that his father was the Isaac Panchaud who was declared bankrupt by the Chancery Board in the 1740s. Panchaud the younger was a man of the utmost rectitude and later in the century, in partnership with Mirabeau, tried to institute serious economic reform in France. A similar history attaches to the Torras brothers in Turin whose father was naturalised at much the same time as the elder Panchaud.[14]

Sometimes, as in Lausanne, Sidebotham exchanged cash at a bad rate of exchange and most British tourists complained bitterly about the rates they were given.[15] In Geneva, a Monsieur Gaufoan [sic] provided funds, presumably by draft, but once they reached the Papal States, and thereafter, the Marquis Belloni became their means of funds. Belloni's Bank, which had been founded by the marquis's father, had originated in Bologna and was the bank of Mary of Modena, and thence that of her husband and children. Indeed, the exiled Stuarts were housed in that city in a palazzo which belonged to the Belloni family. Eventually their bank failed, which might be thought an invalidation of the much-published economic theories of Belloni senior. In Bologna, a Signor Giovardi acted for Belloni whilst the latter was resident in and acted in Rome. In Florence, the services of the Marquis Frescobaldi were called upon, although I am not sure whom exactly he acted for. In Naples, Signor Tiernes [Tierney] exchanged money for them and in Venice, Mr Watson (who was to become the last British Consul to the Serene Republic on the eve of Napoleon's invasion) did the same. Thereafter they were back in the safe hands of Panchaud.

Back in London, letters and bills kept arriving, mainly from Panchaud, and Sidebotham went so far as to write an apology on page 100 of the account book concerning his dealings with the gentleman and probably intended for Sir Watkin's eyes.

In some ways Sidebotham was a bit of a fusspot, but his devotion to Sir Watkin and his absolute integrity shine out from the pages of his sometimes arid accounts and the Williams Wynns no doubt realised their good fortune in having him on their staff. He coped with at least nine currency systems, and who knows how many languages or dialects, and yet managed to keep his head above water yet still enjoyed seeing the sights and going to the opera and the playhouse – all of which Sir Watkin paid for.

Politics and religion

European society in the late 1760s was beginning a momentous period of change although no-one, at the time, could have predicted how profound that change was to become. Some British visitors, confident in the excellence of their own country, viewed continental manners with some degree of condescension. Some, in Jeremy Black's delightful phrase, 'returned to Britain as better informed xenophobes.'[16] The perceived dangers of Catholic and Absolutist Europe had waned slightly, although European politics were still very dangerous and discretion needed to be exercised whilst abroad. The Williams Wynns were, after all, tainted with suspicions of Jacobite leanings. France was still the traditional enemy and the Seven Years War which had involved most of Europe had only ended in 1763. There was to be an uneasy peace until 1775 when the American War of Independence began. Enlightenment did not shine evenly into every corner.

Paris occupied an ambivalent position in the perceptions of the British. It was the capital of fashion and the seat of Britain's traditional enemy. The city was the place to acquire social polish, to learn to dance and to master elegant swordsmanship, but although the Parisian might have had clean linen, he certainly kept a dirty house. The British, as the Parisians remarked, were the opposite. The French king was a libertine in shocking contrast to the homely version who resided in St James' Palace. But, stereotypes and national prejudice aside, there was certainly something which the French had and which the British lacked in terms of social polish. A month in Paris would put that right; or so it was believed. It was noticeable, however, that the higher up the social scale one ascended, the less those differences showed. War was hardly a matter for civilians and, for the moment, was hardly allowed to interfere with the pleasures of visiting nobility of either country; cross-channel traffic went both ways. For every Rousseau who found refuge in Britain, there was a Wilkes in Paris. The Catholic Irish nobility were particularly thick underfoot and many of them had their daughters educated there. Protestant sensibilities were no longer as offended by aspects of Catholicism as much as they had been earlier in the century. Better acquaintance had modified some opinions although Mrs Piozzi, married to a Catholic, was not alone when she noted:

... and surely I never knew till now that so little religion could exist in a Christian country as in this, where they drive their carts, and keep their little shops open on a

Sunday, forbearing neither pleasure nor business as I see, on account of observing
that day upon which their Redeemer rose again. They have a tradition among the
meaner people, that when Christ was crucified, he turned his head towards France,
over which he pronounced his last blessing; but we must accuse them, if so, of being
very ungrateful favourites.[17]

She might have been pining, already, for a Welsh Sunday. However, the Continental
assault upon Anglican morality had begun much earlier in the century. Lady Mary
Wortley Montagu wrote to Alexander Pope in 1716:

Don't fancy, however, that I am infected by the air of these popish countries; though
I have so far wandered from the discipline of the Church of England, to have been
last Sunday at the opera, which was performed in the garden of the Favorita; and
I was so much pleased with it, I have not yet repented my seeing it.[18]

Apropos of which it must be recorded, however painful the task, that Sidebotham
and Morris regularly attended the theatre on a Sunday. French Catholicism had
a distinct aura of its own. Louis XIV had dreamed of a French national church,
Catholic in name, but with the Pope in an advisory capacity and the mandate of
Rome was always subject to national interest. It was true that the ceremonies,
superstitions and practices which most shocked the easily shockable Anglican
visitor continued unabated whatever the state of relations between Versailles and
the Vatican. Those visitors who were able to see beyond the comforts of an ill-
treated peasantry wisely adopted a laissez faire attitude. Those unable to do so,
often gave genuine offence with their unbending attitudes and absolute certainty
that theological truth had been revealed to them but hidden from others – for
'others' read 'all of Southern Europe.' Joseph II of Austria was to adopt a similar
position against the hierarchy of the church and was to confiscate church property
and usurp the power of reforming the institution to himself. His brother in
Tuscany was set upon a similar course. Monarchs were not enamoured of
institutions which were above national boundaries and the Roman Catholic
Church, if nothing else, was certainly supra national but an account of the
squabbles between the Jansenists and the Molinists, whilst endlessly amusing,
will delay our narrative. There were visitors who were able to observe the state of
things with a well-balanced and intelligent perception. Dr John Moore was one,
he wrote:

That in all Roman Catholic countries, and particularly in Italy, the clergy are too
numerous, have to much power, too great a proportion of the lands, and that some

of them live in great pomp and luxury, is undeniable. That the common people would be in a better situation, if manufactures and the spirit of industry could be introduced among them is equally true; but even as things are, I cannot help thinking that the state of the Italian peasantry is preferable, in many respects, to that of the peasants of many other countries in Europe. They are not beaten by their ecclesiastical lords, as those of Germany are by their masters, on every real or imaginary offence. They have not their children torn from them, to be sacrificed to the pomp, avarice, or ambition of some military despot; nor are they themselves pressed into the service as soldiers for life.[19]

The king of Prussia, Frederick the Great, with whom Dr Moore had private conversations and the Duke of Würtemburg, a militaristic nonentity draining his state for the upkeep of his toy armies, may have been his targets. He went abroad as the companion of the Duke of Lauderdale and spent five years travelling. His son was General Sir John Moore of Corunna fame.

For our visiting British, the veneration of relics appears to have been a chief sticking point, but then the British had established a national institution in 1753, for the scientific veneration of relics. The British Museum could be deemed a secular version of the charnel houses and their holy bones which dotted the Catholic south; only the London version claimed to be objective and certainly did not house anything with connotations of holiness. There was a perceived connection between the elaborate ceremonial of the Court and that of the Church. Ritual in all its forms was foreign to most of the British and participation was often interpreted as capitulation. Visitors with more than a smattering of sophistication went through the motions, rose and sank at appropriate moments, preserved their dignity and had a good laugh about it all back at home.

Sir Watkin does not seem to have been presented at the French court. Sightseeing excursions were made to the royal palaces at Versailles, Marly and St Germain but formal presentations seem to have been suspended in view of the imminent death of Queen Maria Leczinska. Although not much loved by the king who preferred to patronise the private establishment he had set up at the Rue St-Médéric in Versailles (the notorious Parc de Cerfs), proper form still had to be observed upon her death and the theatres were closed and Paris became dull. Sir Watkin's party, after being amused by her funeral at St Denis (they had previously been amused by Benediction at Notre Dame), left to continue their tour.

France and Britain were enjoying a temporary truce although Louis XV was still meddling in the matter of the Stuarts. The Old Pretender, James III had died in 1766 and the matter of the recognition of his successor was still up in the air. The Pope refused recognition absolutely because he did not wish to offend George

III and, in any case, had little personal sympathy for their cause. Louis XV would have liked to offend George III, but it was probably not politic to do so and in any case, Louis was a chronically indecisive politician.

The danger of the Stuarts, still regarded by some (who may not have had the somewhat dubious pleasure of actually meeting them) as the lawful kings of Britain, had subsided into a gentle farce.[20] Ejected from France by a king who found him a political millstone, Charles Edward Stuart, formerly known in Britian as 'Bonnie Prince Charlie', was a bibulous, ill-tempered old man. Subsiding in a fug of alcohol and kingly frustration in the Palazzo Muti in Rome, dependent upon a pension from the Pope and only recognised by him as the count of Albany, he was an unfortunate item on the tourist list. The knowledge that he was being ticked off that list, as an interesting relic, did not aid his equilibrium. His brother, the Cardinal Duke of York, knew the game was up but would not yield one iota of his royal dignity, much to the embarrassment of the then current Pope Clement XIII. That uneasy pontiff being further mortified by the cardinal duke's irregular behaviour with certain young clerics in his entourage. Mrs Piozzi affected to be shocked by his antics.[21]

Can the stories told by Suetonius be all true? I scarce believe it possible ... I might have heard similar stories in Italy all day, had I not hated lewd conversation as I do, Old Cardinal de York kept a catamite publicly at Rome while I was there, tho' a man of the best character possible, for piety and charity – with which as a person said to me – that vice has nothing to do. They consider'd it as a mere matter of taste'

Mrs Piozzi's loathing of lewd conversation was no impediment, it seems, to her retailing it widely.

All in all, the dangers and alarms of the '45 had evaporated into an easy *modus vivendi*. For the British visitor, things had calmed down and even the matter of kissing the Pope's toe could be addressed with equanimity, logic and total self-interest.

'All this fuss of being presented first at one Court and then at another is not very agreeable to me' are words which sit oddly on the pen of a very wealthy Tory landowner but Sir Watkin's sentiment was not unique. During the course of his tour, he was to travel through twelve or thirteen separate jurisdictions (today it would be four) each with its own pretensions to political power, cultural identity and religious certitude and each convinced of the superiority of its own ways. Whereas the British visitor knew, without doubt, that he was the representative of the most reasonable system of government yet devised by man; a sentiment only contradicted by some misguided American colonialists. The flummery and scraping of the continental courts was not only undignified it was also very un-British and it was with genuine reluctance – a partial and polite exception sometimes being made for the Pope's toe – that our countrymen would bend their knees to anyone.

If ever there were an argument against the hereditary principle, the crowned heads of the Italian States would have given more than adequate fuel to that argument. Inbreeding and its concomitant of mental instability and low intellect, combined with an absolute belief in a God-given right, were not easy foundations upon which to build a progressive modern political system. But a modern political system was probably the last thing in the world which the anointed heads of Europe, and particularly those of Italy, would have desired. Unfortunately, presentation to the local potentate, was a very necessary social ritual for the young grand tourist, otherwise their social credentials could not be regarded as having been established.

King Carlo Emmanuelle III of Sardinia was a gloomy, religious obsessive, devoted to the hunt and the veneration of relics. His palaces of Stupinigi and Venaria Reale were devoted to the wholesale slaughter of the stag and boar but the Royal Palace in Turin had, as an annex, the Capella della Sacra Sidone where the Holy Shroud itself was kept; an object of singular devotion. The king's father, Vittorio Amadeo II, had been equally obsessively devout and paid agents to effect the conversion of his Protestant subjects in Savoy to the disciplines of Holy Mother Church. Ensnared in his net was the teenage Jean Jacques Rousseau who converted from Calvinism in the church of Corpus Domini in 1728, perhaps attracted by the doctrine of the forgiveness of sins. He renounced his Protestant-ism whilst in Turin but later, to be allowed back into Geneva, he renounced his renunciation.

Dominating Turin, on its hill to the north, is the Basilica of La Superga, the masterpiece of Filippo Juvarra. Modern visitors may descend into the crypt below, where the remains of the house of Savoy are interred, and experience some hint of the religious morbidity, which was customary in eighteenth-century Turin. It is quite ghastly.

Visitors to that elegant capital admired the architecture but complained about its social dullness. Turin had an academy to impart superior manners and it was an essential part of the Grand Tour to enrol there and be improved, Sir Watkin included. Our party spent three weeks in the city and Sir Watkin seems to have been presented to the unimpressive king at Venaria Reale; hence perhaps, his burgeoning aversion to court ceremonial. Turin was one of the great centres of opera in Italy and had a magnificent theatre. Sidebotham and his friends became assiduous attendees. Fortunately it was noted that the king rarely stayed beyond halfway through a performance and upon his departure the audience relaxed and enjoyed the spectacle for which the theatre was famous. In spite of their marriage alliances, the kings of Savoy (or Sardinia) were committedly pro-British and anti-French and Turin was a reasonable and sensible introduction to the confusion of the Italian States. A senate and an elected *doge* ruled Genoa, but for over three hundred years the same handful of family names appear as the elective head of state. The highest office appears to have been hereditary by circulation but, in any case, seems to have had no power or influence whatsoever. Genoa was effectively ruled by an oligarchy of merchant families who had plundered the state coffers and built themselves palaces which prompted Rubens to christen the city 'La Superba'. Some visitors mocked the fact that whilst the ducal palace was frescoed with depictions of Genoese naval power, the reality was that their entire fleet consisted of a few mouldering galleys.

> *It seems in some degree ridiculous that the Genoese should abound in pictures and statues commemorating their former heroes and victories in the Great Council Chamber of the Ducal Palace, at a time when their navy is reduced to a few galleys – Corsica lost – and their very existence at the mercy of the Court of Sardinia.*[22]

Genoa was in a sad state of corruption and suffered from bad government. The Senate had secretly sold Corsica to the French in 1764 and when the sordid bargain became public in 1768, it provoked outrage, especially in Britain where the patriot Corsican General Paoli was in exile. But, all in all, it was a delightful city and Sir Watkin was most impressed with it. Mrs Piozzi most definitely was not.

> *The streets of the town are much too narrow for beauty or convenience – impracticable to coaches, and so beset with beggars that it is dreadful. A chair is therefore, above all things, necessary to be carried in, even a dozen steps, if you are likely to feel shocked at having your knees suddenly clasped by a figure hardly human; who perhaps holding you forcibly for a minute, conjures you loudly, by the sacred wounds of our Lord Jesus Christ, to have compassion on his.*
>
> *Such pathetic misery, such disgusting distress, did I never see before, as I have been witness to in this gaudy city.*[23]

Later she contrasted Milan under the governance of Austria with the Genoese republic:

> *The certainty of their irrevocable doom, softened by kind usage from their superiors, makes, in the mean time, an odd sort of humorous drollery spring up among the common people, who are much happier here at Milan than I expected to find them:*

every great house giving meat, broth, &c. to poor dependants with liberal good nature enough, so that mighty little wandering misery is seen in the streets; unlike those of Genoa, who seem mocked with the word liberty, while sorrow, sickness, and the most pinching want, pine at the doors of marble palaces, whose owners are as unfeeling as their walls.[24]

In Lombardy, an imperial fiefdom, the Duke of Modena, Francesco d'Este III, imperial governor of Lombardy, ineffectual and a man of high, self-applied colour, left governance to his deputy, Count Firmian. The count, providing possibly the only example of enlightened rule in the entire peninsula apart from that of Tuscany, was very pro-British. After enduring his presentation to the duke, Sir Watkin sensibly seems to have spent the greater part of his twenty days in Milan in the count's company. The latter was liberal to the extent of encouraging an Italian version of the *Spectator* (*Il Caffe*) to be published and of encouraging the great Italian jurist Beccaria to publish his proposals for the wholesale reform of the penal system – including the abolition of the death penalty. The contrast seen when passing from the poorly-managed lands of Piedmont into the highly productive fields of the Lombard Plain was often commented upon to the discredit of King Carlo Emmanuelle.

The king of Naples, Ferdinando IV, was an ill-educated, boorish and highly superstitious man, who whilst not in rut or out hunting, enjoyed kicking the backsides of his courtiers. He was an eternal embarrassment to those courtiers who had been given charge of his education whilst he was a minor and were faced daily with the evidence of their abject failure to discharge their duty. Married to Maria Carolina, sister of Marie Antoinette and a woman of excessive appetites, he came to an early accommodation with his wife when they each agreed to pursue their personal viciousnesses separately. His description of her after their first night of connubial bliss 'She sleeps like she'd been slaughtered and sweats like a pig'[25] gives a general clue as to the delicacy of feeling prevailing at the Neapolitan Court although Ferdinand did manage to father eighteen children with Maria Carolina. She eventually relieved the king of the burden of ruling his country and interfered in every aspect of state policy.

Sir Watkin seems to have been presented to this paragon of regal virtue on 29 December, probably in the Royal Palace in Naples itself (the only trip to Caserta, the usual royal seat, seems to have been that of Apperley and Hamilton as tourists). The Neapolitan nobility were a very welcoming class of people, especially to British tourists, and Prince Francavilla gave weekly dinner parties to the visitors. Princess Francavilla was equally welcoming, although those who welcomed her embraces, in lieu of her uninterested husband whose tastes leaned in another direction, had much reason to regret it several weeks later when a visit to a discreet physician in Paris on the way home was often necessitated. There was, however, a silver lining to the court of Naples in the person of the cultivated British envoy, Sir William Hamilton.[26] He had no illusions about the state of affairs in Naples and wrote to the British Secretary of State Lord Weymouth:

> *... his Sicilian Majesty is trifling away his time in a continual round of dissipation. In short, a general corruption prevails in this country which has infected every class and the disease is so rooted that it must require a great length of time and very wise measures to bring about any essential alteration.*[27]

Mrs Piozzi found the king able to 'charm every one with his kindness and affability'[28] although those virtues did not necessarily rule out dissipation. Sir William smoothed the way for visiting compatriots, had influence, could effect important introductions and obtain permission for visitors to see the jealously guarded excavations at Herculaneum and Pompeii. All of this he did for Sir Watkin and the two seem to have become quite friendly. They met again in London much later when Sir William was admitted into the Society of Dilettanti of which Sir Watkin was president at the time. The musical evenings at the Palazzo Sessa, the British Residence, were particularly fine and Sir William's first wife was not only Welsh but was, by all accounts, a most brilliant harpsichordist. Dr Burney wrote that 'Mrs H. has a very neat finger and plays the harpsichord with great delicacy, expression and taste. Mr H. is likewise a pretty good performer on the violin'.[29] Burney's private notes had no reason to be obsequious and his musical assessment is probably true. Sir Watkin bought another new cello in Naples.

The adage that 'Naples is a paradise inhabited by devils' was nowhere so true as in matters of religion. Catholicism there was a syncretic mix of death-obsessed obscurantism and an exuberant paganism.[30] Not for the Neapolitan the reasonable religion of Enlightenment Europe – they preferred it red of tooth and claw and nail, much to the dismay and embarrassment of the Roman Curia, a deal of whom were closet *philosophistes*. What northern European, of whatever religious persuasion, has not viewed the shenanigans associated with the liquefaction of the blood of St Gennaro (conveniently on set dates) with a confused mixture of repugnance and fascination?[31] Even Turin would have seemed reasonable after this.

Religion was a confusing issue to the British visitor. At home, the Established Church held mild principles, mildly enforced and mildly believed in. *Fox's Book of Martyr's* had left no doubt in the British mind that the rule of Rome was that of a theocratic tyranny enforced by a ruthless inquisition. Thumbscrew, rack and dark, dark dungeons (imagine the *carceri* of Piranesi) were widely held images in the popular imagination. What could they make of a France where the shops were open on Sunday, or of a Rome with witty and urbane cardinals, of an obsessive king of Sardinia, a Florence which confiscated Church property or of a Venice which seemed to possess no religion, or at least no priests, at all? Mrs Piozzi was put out in Florence when she was introduced to Cardinal Corsini who said, in English, 'Well madam! you never saw one of us red-legged partridges before, I believe; but you are going to Rome I hear, where you will find such fellows as me no rarities'. Cardinal Andrea Corsini was the great nephew of Clement XII, chamberlain of the College of Cardinals and vicar general of Rome – from the horse's mouth as it were!

Venice had given up, except in the matter of virulent anti-clericalism, and vied with Naples for the sobriquet the 'Brothel of Europe'. The once feared Council of Ten, the Inquisition and the relentless machinery of the state were broken and the great officers of state were mostly piddling geriatric old men. The Lion of St Mark occasionally snarled, as Casanova discovered to his cost, but otherwise it preferred to sleep. The only *doge* of note was the one who gave the republic away to Napoleon. Venice was dancing her way into oblivion and cared not one whit about it. She was sinking into a sea of glorious depravity but in all honesty there seemed little alternative. Economically broken, tired after one thousand years of splendour, she welcomed the tourists and tried her best to fleece them whilst about it.

Leopoldo I, grand duke of Tuscany and an anti-clerical product of the Enlightenment and Clement XIII, pontiff of Rome, an enlightened clerical man, stood out as rare exceptions to the general rule in Italy. Clement, a member of the Rezzonico family from Venice had been elected at a time of great stress for the papacy. A kindly, intelligent and understanding man, he clearly had no time for sectarian strife or bigotry. After the death of James III, he abandoned the Stuarts completely as a cause, whilst remaining reasonably indulgent to those members of the family who had invited themselves to Rome to live on his munificence. George III was the legal king of Britain and that was that. He privately commented that were he British, he would also have thrown out the Stuarts. He had other, more weighty problems in that the European Powers were intriguing for the abolition of the powerful and socially enlightened Jesuit order. As an ex-Jesuit himself, he was torn between sentiment and realpolitik. Early in 1769, he signed the order for abolition and then, at the moment Sir Watkin was making his way home, died disillusioned and broken-hearted. He was not unaware that Cardinal Albani, papal secretary of state, was in regular contact with Horace Mann, British envoy in Florence, and that the cardinal supported British interests whenever he could. But as there were no official diplomatic relations between Rome and London, the cardinal was a useful channel. When Edward Augustus, duke of York (the Hanoverian one not the Stuart one) visited Rome in 1764 as a tourist, he was the first member of the British royal family to visit the city and the Pope rolled out the red carpet and gave him a reception in the gardens of the Quirinal Palace, much to the chagrin of the Stuart duke who flounced off to Frascati in a high rage. The duke, although the respectable king's brother, came with the intention of enjoying carnal pleasures wherever he could find them. He was very successful in his quest and it is reputed that many women of the Roman nobility enjoyed the satisfaction of aiding him in his enterprise. Other members of the British royal family followed and in 1772 the Duke of Gloucester, tactlessly accompanied by his mistress, arrived. Four years later, he came once again but with the legitimate duchess this time and Pompeo Batoni, who had painted his portrait the first time he visited, added her to his catalogue. The papacy was quite able to see beyond the foibles of men, especially where politics were concerned. Rome thus had the royal seal of approval and thereafter no British visitor need worry about the machinations of the 'Scarlet Woman' or even the 'Whore of Babylon'; Rome was officially friendly. Forty-five years later the rapprochement was completed when Sir Thomas Lawrence painted the portraits of Pope Pius VII and Cardinal Consalvi to be hung in the Waterloo Chamber at Windsor Castle.

Leopold I ruled Tuscany, a vassal state of Austria, as grand duke. Gian Gastone, the last of the Medici, had died without issue, which was hardly surprising given the tastes which he flaunted through Florence. Unfortunately, his 'mere matter of taste' had political ramifications and the grand duchy became subject to the house of Lorraine through endlessly complicated manoeuvrings between the same European powers who had caused Clement XIII such grief. When Tuscany came under Austrian influence, Francis Stephan of Lorraine, husband of Maria Teresa, became its grand duke but he never resided there. On his unlamented death, his third son Leopold inherited the duchy and set to reform its institutions with a zeal which would brook no opposition especially from the clergy – one of his particular targets. When young he had been intended for the priesthood but his theological education seems to have backfired completely.

His reforming zeal did not necessarily apply to himself, however, and although possessed of a charming wife, he saw no reason to restrict himself to only one. Other men's wives, including that of the long-resident Earl Cowper, allegedly, were added to the grand ducal menagerie. Otherwise he was a model of enlighten-ment and abolished the death penalty (the first such abolition in Europe), reformed prisons, confiscated conventual properties, abolished the ancient duties and privileges of the nobility, reformed agriculture, reformed the judiciary, abolished clerical privilege and exemption from taxes, irritated the Church and everyone else with a vested interest and generally proved himself the very model of an enlightened despot. Only the death of his brother, Joseph II, and his own translation to Vienna as emperor prevented his promulgation of a written constitution. He was not only missed by the Florentines but also by the British colony to many of which he had been particularly partial. He was said to have brains instead of a heart and when he returned to Vienna became increasingly reactionary and returned the previously freed Hungarian serfs back to servitude. Mrs Piozzi, sharp as ever, made some very pertinent observations.

> *Our Grand Duke lives with little state for ought I can observe here; but where there is least pomp, there is commonly most power; for a man must have something pour se dedommager, as the Frence express it; and this gentleman possessing the solide, has no care for the clinquant, I trow. He tells his subjects when to go to bed, and who to dance with, till the hour he chuses they should retire to rest, with exactly that sort of old-fashioned paternal authority that fathers used to exercise over their families in England before commerce had run her levelling plough over all ranks, and annihilated even the name of subordination.*
>
> *When they appeared to complain of this behaviour to me, I know not, replied I, what to answer: one has always read and heard that the Sovereigns ought to behave in despotic governments like the fathers of their family.*
> *'Yes, Madame' replied one of my auditors with an acuteness truly Italian; 'but this Prince is our father-in-law'.[32]*

Whatever Mrs Piozzi may have thought, at least the Grand Duke did not pry into his subjects' or residents' bedrooms. Had he done so, Sir Horace Mann, Mr Thomas Patch, the Earl Tylney, reputedly the Earl Cowper and many other British ex-patriots would have been embarrassed for their reputations. Perhaps the Grand Duke took the sensible course and thought it 'simply a mere matter of taste', one, it must be noted, which was known in Germany as 'the Florentine vice' and elsewhere as the 'Italian'. Peccadilloes which meant the death penalty in Britain, were merely part of the scenery in Florence. To some Britons, Catholic Italy had a lot to commend it and the scenery was quite lovely.

So there we have it; a liberal despot in Florence, an illiberal one in Turin, an ill-educated and dissipated one in Naples, a committee of despots in Genoa but the very cynosure of despotism in Rome had other things to worry about and was very uncomfortable with the label. The Church's despotism could be counted an historical inheritance. Venice was not despotic although it tried very hard to keep up the pretence that it was, but mostly could not be bothered and Lombardy and Milan were suffering under liberal and sensible rule but one which was imposed by the uninvited Austrians.

Italy, considered an expression of geography by Metternich, was considered as an expression of something else by the British *literati*. Gothic horror romances were, almost by default, set there. Only in the Italian peninsula were the requisite conditions for the truly dreadful and exquisitely awful to be fulfilled. Mrs Radcliffe, the doyenne of the English gothic horror story, lived in an Italy of the imagination, viewed through the eyes of Salvatore Rosa and Claude Lorrain, where Udolfo and its mysteries needed Catholic Italian soil to flourish. The reality in some aspects was worse but was perhaps modified for the visiting tourist by the arts of living which the Italians had substituted for political improvement and which they had brought to a degree of perfection which was to be envied and if possible copied. It is remarkable to consider that within twenty to thirty years of this particular tour, the fabric of society had not just unravelled but had been comprehensively torn apart and trampled upon.

The complexity of the situation should be remembered with the proviso that family loyalty, especially Bourbon loyalty, was above national loyalty. The Austrian Hapsburgs were not quite as self-interested as the Bourbons but were bad enough. The Bourbon family pact could be broken in the case of extreme self-interest such as in 1779, when the Spanish Bourbons declared war upon Great Britain, the Neapolitan Bourbons resolutely refused to support them. The Hapsburg queen was pro-British and the Bourbon king was allowed no say in the matter other than to deliver a warm encomium, probably written by his wife, to Sir William Hamilton celebrating the warmth which existed between Naples and London. Fortunately, Sir Watkin had no need to travel through the wastes of the Hohenzollern lands where mismanagement had become an exact science. The Bourbons knew that God, who had given them a mandate to rule, had neglected to specify where. Ferdinand of Naples was the son of Charles III of Spain who was the son of Philip V and grandson of Louis XIV of France. Charles was another 'enlightened despot' whose reforms in Spain were swept away upon his death. Ferdinand was only in position because his elder brother had been certified as an idiot. A streak of morbid melancholia ran through that branch of the family and stories of Carlo Broschi (Farinelli) singing the same three arias nightly to relieve Philip V's melancholy are, alas, all too credible. Ferdinand's wife was the daughter of the Hapsburg Maria Teresa of Austria and therefore the sister of Leopold of Tuscany and Marie Antoinette of France and of the future Joseph II. Her eventual loathing of the French state had more to do with the fate of her sister than political realities. But the queen was incapable of detaching family from state interest. The 'insipid' daughter of the duke of Modena married Ferdinand Karl, archduke of Austria, and brother of the emperor thereby becoming an Austrian archduchess. The king of France and the king of Spain were cousins and they mostly loathed each other. Family squabbles escalated into wars, often exploited by the British, for which the general populace paid the price. This was a tangled undergrowth which needed cutting down. It was a pity that the means of pruning proved so barbarous and destructive of just sensibilities.

The bloodbath of Paris engulfed the rest of Europe and the cultural milieu within which our young connoisseur spread his wings was destroyed forever in the year of his death. Insurrection in Naples, brutally and shamefully put down by Horatio Lord Nelson, with the tacit agreement of Sir William Hamilton, the British minister and with the encouragement of the notorious Emma, Sir William's second wife and the admiral's paramour, failed and thus allowed the devastatingly corrupt and intellectually challenged Bourbons to survive for another forty-five years of misrule. Elsewhere, the myriad small states which comprised the Italian peninsula were either swept away or reformed into a different existence.

The then pope, Pius VII, was virtually kidnapped and forced to attend Napoleon's coronation in Paris, although denied the right of placing the gilded wreath on the conqueror's brow, never really recovered and his successors retreated behind the walls of the Vatican and theological intransigence. The Venetian republic, after a thousand years of shimmering upon its magical lagoon, was abolished with the wretched connivance of its last *doge*, Lodovico Manin. The republic of Genoa, the duchies of Lucca, Parma and Piacenza, the duchy of Milan, the duchy of Massa and principality of Carrara the grand duchy of Tuscany and the duchy of Savoy were all either abolished or under new management. Only the kingdom of Piedmont/ Sardinia survived and that was in a form which was to see the emergence of Italy as a political entity as well as a geographical expression.

The Mechanics of the Grand Tour

A tour from London to Naples was a tremendous undertaking and there were as many means of accomplishing it as there were tourists. Choices depended upon income and for some it was an undoubted delight whilst for others, it was a misery to be endured. We may surmise that Sir Watkin's income insulated him from the myriad inconveniences which lesser, and less fortunate, gentlemen experienced at every stage of their journey. However, before examining the means by which the tour was undertaken, it might be useful to identify the persons who were on it.

Sir Watkin, Mr Apperley and Captain Hamilton comprised the gentlemen and thereafter the social categories become less distinct. Antonio Carrara, Sir Watkin's valet and most probably general *cicerone*, may have been the only member of the party who had been on the tour previously and his help with the route, negotiations with accommodation and general linguistic abilities made him absolutely indispensable. The handsome gratuity which Sir Watkin gave him upon their return to London is perhaps some measure of the esteem in which he was held. He seems to have occupied an intermediate position between that of a gentleman and that of a servant. Samuel Sidebotham, however senior, seems to have counted himself amongst the servants. His elevation to steward at Wynnstay was not to happen for another ten years. Seemingly equal to Sidebotham was a Mr (Thomas?) Morris with whom Sidebotham and Carrara made frequent visits to the opera and various tourist attractions. Presumably when Sir Watkin was occupied and unneedful of their services they were left to their own devices to spend time as they wished. Sidebotham mentions six servants altogether, but they are mostly recorded by their initials in the accounts. A Sam Stevens occurs several times and we can presume that he accompanied the whole of the tour. On page 18 of the account book[33] we have TM, SS, CB & LMG, and on page 42 we have TM, SS, SS, NL and CB. I surmise that TM was Morris; that the SSs were Samuel Sidebotham and Sam Stephens. Page 36 makes things a little clearer. The servants are listed as being Morris, Carrara, Sam Stephens, Louis Mark Comte, Christo Bremer and Sidebotham. Carrara joined the party in Paris, as did Louis Mark Comte and Christo Bremer, and it may be that the two lesser servants were hired upon Carrara's recommendation as being people with experience. Someone seems to have been mislaid because on 5 January 1769, in Rome, the board wages were paid for five servants. Several days later, however, we are back to six when six pairs of gloves were bought for them in Venice. Several weeks after that, in Strassburg, a John Davies makes an appearence and the wages bill was paid for six servants. It might be that either 'NL' or 'CB' did not complete the tour and was substituted with Davies. In Paris, on 9 February, the hired servants were dismissed but given an extra gratuity and Sidebotham's mention of a 'Savoyard' who did 'sundry messages' might indicate that Christo Bremer or Louis Mark Comte were natives of that region.

In general, the party seems to have consisted of nine individuals. In Naples, five caleshes were hired to go to Pozzuoli. Each vehicle being a two-seater, we not only have confirmation of the total number involved but also of the fact that Sir Watkin treat his servants with a great deal more consideration than did many in his position.

This was an unusually large party; most tourists scraped by with a valet and perhaps one other servant. Sir Watkin was, after all, a gentleman rather than an aristocrat and the splash which he must have made was perhaps partly responsible for the rumours which abounded in London and which greatly exaggerated his wealth, but which put him upon an easy footing with the Devonshires and Beauforts of the world.

The first stage of the journey from London to Paris by way of Dover seems to have been made by Sir Watkin, Hamilton, Apperley, Stephens, Morris and Sidebotham. The driver and postillions, if there were any, must have been household servants from Grosvenor Square who could take the coach back to London when the party had embarked at Dover.

The question of who sat where is an intriguing one. Coaches were not generally very capacious and could only carry four passengers inside with any degree of comfort. Remembering that there must have been a lot of luggage strapped to the back and roof of the vehicle, there was always the danger that passengers on the roof could overbalance the coach and send the whole lot sprawling. Legislation was passed[34] to regulate the numbers and placing of passengers on public transport precisely because of the number of accidents which had happened. Stephens, who seems to have been a handyman and general factotum, was especially concerned with the horses and equipment on the tour and Sidebotham and Carrara seem to have ascended the Mont Cenis Pass on horseback and it would not be unreasonable to think of them on horseback and the others inside, or on the coach.

Having abandoned their coach at Dover, a new one needed to be acquired at Calais and the normal method was to buy one from someone returning to England. In this case, Lord Leigh of Stoneleigh Abbey, an old boy of Westminster School, had one to dispose of and Sir Watkin took possession of it. Thus, they travelled to Paris in the remarkably short space of seven days.

In Paris, coaches and horses were hired for excursions into the countryside and to Versailles, Marly and St Germain and eventually Lord Leigh's coach was part-exchanged for a new one.[35]

The gentlemen were lodged in one of the better establishments and hired a *valet du place* to look after them there. Meals were supplied by a *traiteur* and could therefore be eaten in private rather than in a public dining-room. The servants were paid 'board wages', something which we would recognise as a *per diem* and lodged in a cheaper establishment where meals were provided for them. This was the common arrangement throughout the tour.

Two more, but French speaking, servants were hired in Paris for the duration of the journey and when the time came to continue south a new coach and a chaise were hired from *Monsieur* Pascall, the coachmaker. Later Sidebotham described the coach as a 'Berlin' and we may presume that that was intended for the luggage and servants whilst the gentlemen travelled in a faster but more constricted chaise.

The party, now nine in number, made fairly good time towards Dijon and Besançon until they arrived at Lausanne where a long stay was intended. Here, horses were hired for various excursions and a mare was bought for Sir Watkin and possibly Captain Hamilton. The probable reason would be that the driver (*voiturine*) and postillions had been dispensed with and, according to normal practice, would have offered their services to anyone returning to Paris. Until other men were hired to get them to Lyons, the coach was impractical to use.

Unusually, Sir Watkin, who had an egalitarian sensibility, often included all of the servants in his excursions and expeditions. To view the glaciers at Sallanches (Chamonix), eleven horses were hired so that everyone could enjoy the sight; Sir Watkin demonstrating that both his artistic taste and his social awareness were of the most advanced order. Glaciers, rather like the mountains of north Wales, were not yet romantic and conformed too well to the idea of the horrid and primitive.[36] Generally the journey seems to have been very smooth and only once did they have serious trouble with the *voiturine* and postilions. The man they hired to get them from Grenoble to Turin, the most difficult and terrible part of the journey, was obviously very unsatisfactory and Sidebotham withheld part of his fee until he had had satisfaction for some mismanagement on his part.

Once in Italy, presumably mud-spattered and worn, the travelling coach was not suitable for the young baronet to be able to cut '*una bella figura*' at the several courts he was to be presented at and other more splendid equipages were hired. Thus, he made three visits to Venaria Reale just outside of Turin and the summer seat of King Carlo Emmanuelle of Sardinia. In Milan, two postillions and six horses were hired to make a splash when he visited Count Firmian, the imperial governor and was presented to the Duke of Modena. A stay of any length in a place was always taken as an opportunity to have their own coach repaired and overhauled and Sam Stephens seems to have come into his own by supervising the purchase and installation of new equipment. The hire of local carriages and drivers was a common practice somewhat akin to our notion of the use of the taxi (or hackney cab), although in the case of a two-day excursion the driver was expected to be responsible for his own accommodation.

The cost of horses was a huge part of the expense of such a tour. Horses needed to be changed and especially in France, regulations stipulated the number needed to draw each category of coach. There were over thirty-three post houses between Calais and Paris alone;[37] all in theory state-regulated, but often with widely differing ideas of what constituted fair payment. In England, post horses usually went for twelve miles, or two hours, before being changed but the roads were gradually improving with the introduction of the turnpikes. In large parts of Italy, the roads were atrocious and twelve miles could hardly have been accomplished in the two hours it would have taken near London. Apart from the good road from Susa to Turin, Piedmont had awful tracks, Milan and Lombardy was slightly better but, because of the sandy soil, those around Bologna and from there to Florence were shocking and slow. Rome veered between the patchy to the north and the unspeakable over the Pontine Marshes to the south but the main road to Naples from the border was excellent and had been built recently to welcome the king's new bride. Some roads wore out both the traveller and his horses. Floods were frequent, tracks boggy and impassable, clumsy ferries substituted for decent bridges and there was always an imperative to reach the next destination before nightfall when the gates would be locked. Tired horses were of no use to anyone and it was in the traveller's interest to ensure their well-being and stop them from being over driven. In those few parts of Italy, which did have good roads, the opposite problem presented itself and drivers needed to be frequently restrained from going dangerously fast and it was difficult to restrain the Italian spirit, a pattern clearly reflected in modern-day Roman traffic.

The differing currencies presented Sidebotham with some problems but the various monetary systems also represented political divisions. From France until their return there the party crossed over some fourteen state boundaries and for each of them a passport was required. Usually they were to be obtained from the Secretary of State in the jurisdiction they were in, to get them into the next one, and they needed to be held onto in case of difficulty. The notion of a British passport in which 'His Britannic Majesty's Secretary of State could request and require all of those whom it may concern to allow the bearer to pass without let or hindrance' was not yet established and a travel document was a local affair. Mr Sidebotham was not beyond greasing the slow machinery of state with the occasional backhand offering to expedite the issue of a passport (Turin to Genoa). He also realised that customs officials could be circumvented by a letter from an appropriate dignitary (Rome to Naples) and became quite adept at the mechanics of foreign travel.

Domestic arrangements were well-organised and the washing of linen occurs throughout the accounts as does the tacking in of shirt ruffles. Ruffles, especially lace ones, could be very expensive and could not be expected to last for very long under the ministrations of a local washerwoman. They did not need to be worn all of the time and were, therefore, tacked into the wrist and neckband of a shirt when needed. I presume that the gentlemen wore theirs most of the time but Sidebotham and his friends would have needed them to be in place only for their frequent evenings at the opera and not during the working day. Although the south of Italy is normally reasonably pleasant in the winter months, it can suddenly change. Naples can be warm and almost hot on one December day and icy cold the next and Sir Watkin seems to have taken it upon himself to correct the deficiencies of the servant's wardrobe. As has been said elsewhere, the winter of 1769/69 seems to have been a particularly severe one and gloves, nightcaps, travelling cloaks, muffs, flannel linings for coats and anything else which could mitigate that severity was supplied without hesitation throughout the tour. Venice can be uncomfortably and bone chillingly cold and the short time of five days they spent there may, in part, be blamed on the weather.

When they returned, the French coach was surrendered in Paris and another hired to take the reduced party back to Calais. That being left behind, another was hired at Dover to take them back to London and James Rowland, a Wynnstay servant, took it back to the port. Lord Leigh's agent, Daniel Graaf, who had provided them with his coach when they had first arrived in Calais, was now repaid with the money Sidebotham had obtained through selling it in Paris before they left for London. A veritable flood of packing cases and other miscellaneous items then began to arrive, all of them accompanied by a Mr Jones of the Customs House with a hefty bill for import duties in hand. A total of £123 was charged on the pictures and books from Rome alone.

For several more years, Sir Watkin's purchases continued to arrive by which time his financial affairs were beginning to arouse concern in the minds of some of his retainers.

The Arts in Italy

The one thing, which most Grand Tourists expected and looked forward to was to be entertained with music, either instrumental or vocal, but they were by no means an undiscriminating audience. Italian musical artists of any note regularly performed in London and the standard of the capital's performances was probably higher than that of most Italian centres. Dr Burney, travelling around Italy collecting notes for his History of Music recorded, with regret, that the great days of the conservatories seemed to be over. He found much to please him. Galuppi, Jomelli, Paisiello and Piccinni were, he conceded, writing attractive music but the teaching and achievement of the conservatories of Naples, formerly outstanding in Europe, were at a very low ebb. Only in Venice, he thought, were standards still maintained. The standards, which Italian singers had set in London thirty years previously, were sadly a thing of the past in their own country. He was equally disappointed with the oratorios in Rome where he found the music reasonable, but without the grandeur or complexity of that shown by Handel in his great choruses. It must be said, regrettably, that the appreciation of Handel became a dead hand over English music for the next hundred years and was perhaps responsible for suffocating most attempts at a native musical culture, which was always compared to that of the great German master and always found wanting.

Music was a commodity in Italy and impresarios were careful to deliver what the public demanded and very little more. Although the great theatres of Naples and Turin had the status of Royal Opera House, their funding was largely supplemented by income from the box-office. In Germany the theatres in Munich, Stuttgart, Mannheim and so on could rely upon direct and total funding from the crown and could be slightly more experimental than the public theatres of eighteenth-century Italy dared allow themselves. It must be admitted that the music was often subordinated to the demands of the star performer and that the opera house itself was more akin to a public drawing room than a temple of high art. Visitors noted, often with indignation, that the audiences talked all the time and that their attention to the stage could only be assured during a favourite aria or vocal pyrotechnics. Otherwise they chatted, played cards, ate, made the social round and disported themselves as though they were at home. In many ways they were, because the system of subscribing to a box for the season encouraged proprietorial attitudes and the private boxes were decorated to the taste of the owner. When La Scala in Milan was built in 1778, the boxes each had a little private salon attached where food could be prepared or to which bored auditors could retire. Some still exist on the opposite side of the access corridor to the door to the box itself. This was by no means an unusual arrangement but it tended to reinforce the idea of the theatre as a social drop in centre rather than as a purely musical venue.

Mrs Piozzi visited the theatre shortly after it was built –

It is now time to talk of the theatre; and surely a receptacle so capacious to contain four thousand people, a place of entrance so commodious to receive them, a show so princely, so very magnificent to entertain them, must be sought in vain out of Italy. The centre box front, richly adorned with gilding, arms and trophies, is appropriated to the court, whose canopy is carried up to what we call the first gallery in England; the crescent of boxes ending with the stage, consists of nineteen on a side, small boudoirs, for such they seem; and are as such fitted up with silk hangings, girandoles &c ... An immense sideboard at the first lobby, lighted and furnished with luxurious and elegant plenty, as many people send for suppers to their box, and entertain a knot of friends there with infinite convenience and splendour ... across the corridor leading to these boxes, another small chamber numbered like that it belongs to, is appropriated to the use of your servants, and furnished with every conveniency to make chocolate, serve lemonade &c ... but we

must not be partial. While London has twelve capital rooms for the professed
amusement of the public, Milan has but one; [next to and part of the theatre] there
is in it, however, a ridotto chamber for cards, of a noble size, where some little
gaming goes on in carnival time; but though the inhabitants complain of the
enormities committed there, I suppose more money is lost in one club in St James's
street during a week, than here at Milan in the whole winter.[38]

Italian towns generally lacked alternative accommodation for public events and the sheer size of the theatre auditoria ensured that everyone who mattered in a town could assemble there. The Teatro Reggio in Turin (1740), the San Carlo in Naples (1737) the Teatri Communale in Padua (1748) and in Bologna (1763) La Scala in Milan (1778) and La Fenice in Venice (1792) could all hold several thousand spectators. The San Carlo, the oldest such working theatre in Europe (according to its modern management), had a capacity of 3,300 when it was first opened in 1737; modern safety regulations and notions of comfort have reduced that number by half.

In Britain, by contrast, the main social centre of any town of note was usually the Assembly Rooms where a completely different attitude prevailed in that attendees could be vetted for respectability and subscriptions withheld from those deemed socially unacceptable. Management committees were fiercely protective of the privileges of their own class. Rooms proliferated towards the end of the century but Lord Burlington's rooms in York (1732) led the way, to be followed by Derby (1752–5) Norwich (1754) Almacks in St James's (1765) Bath (1769) the Pantheon (1772) Newcastle-upon-Tyne (1776) and Edinburgh (1783) amongst many others.[39] Newcastle is an interesting example of a regional capital in the period. There was a vibrant musical life led by the native composer Charles Avison (1709–70) who gave fortnightly subscription concerts in the winter, organised oratorios, wrote very good music himself and supervised musical life in the town. His orchestral concerts were at first held in the church of St Nicholas and then transferred to the magnificent Assembly Rooms after his death. A pupil of Geminiani, he was visited by his master in 1760 who paused in Newcastle as he made his way to Edinburgh. Interestingly there was no permanent theatre building until 1787. Orchestral and choral music were of prime importance and opera must have been an exotic beast indeed and William Shield (1748–1829), also born on Tyneside, needed to travel to London in order to establish his career as a stage composer.

The situation in London was complicated by the conditions set for licensing a theatre. Drury Lane (1663) and Covent Garden (1732) were the two 'patent' (i.e. established by Royal Charter) theatres and had the monopoly of the spoken word.

Others tried to evade the conditions by charging for a short musical work and throwing in a lengthy drama as a free entertainment. Covent Garden staged opera as well as plays and oratorios and served Handel particularly well. The King's Theatre in the Haymarket was the nearest thing London had to a purpose-built opera house. It did not possess a patent and therefore could not stage straight drama. Italian opera and Italian opera singers became its *raison d'être*. Supported by the nobility, frequently insolvent, plagued by absconding impresarios, it nevertheless staged work to an exceptionally high standard and its audience by contrast to those of Italy, mostly listened to the music throughout because of interest and not reverence. In size it approached the Italian model; audiences needed to be large to ensure adequate income. Another means of ensuring income was by what we would call 'star casting'. Farinelli (Carlo Broschi), Senesino (Francesco Bernardi), Guadagni (who made a memorable appearance in Ruabon Parish Church), Faustina Bordoni, Francesca Cuzzoni (the last two were such rivals that they descended to fisticuffs during a duet performed before the Princess of Wales and ripped each others' wigs off) and most other luminaries of the Italian opera made guest appearances. Although the audiences were mostly quiet during the music, when applause broke out so did partialities and rivalries, abuse of one party by the other was frequent. It was against this model that British tourists measured their experience of Italian opera in its homeland.

The musicality, or musical ability, of the tourist was quite surprising. Sir Watkin played the cello to as high a standard as a gentleman should aspire to. Captain Hamilton played the flute and Mr Morris played the French horn and appropriately, Mr Carrara had a fine singing voice. When they were not visiting the opera or the playhouse, musical evenings seem to have been the norm and represented a surprisingly high proportion of the expenses. In Rome and Naples particularly, musicians were hired to supplement the numbers and in Florence, Sir Watkin bore part of the expenses incurred in mounting Handel's *Alexander's Feast*. We need to remember that most gentlemen undertaking the grand tour were hardly more than schoolboys, but it does seem that most of them packed an instrument with which to while away the evenings. Dr Burney, whilst in Rome, seemed to flit from one soirée to another and the Duke of Dorset also, staying in Rome at the time, earned the gratitude of a number of his countrymen for his regular musical evenings.

New music in Italy was in temporary decline although there were new and interesting works by Galuppi, Jomelli, Hasse (Faustina Bordoni's husband) Piccini and Sacchini, there was nothing as sensational as the works of the next generation were to be. The Germans were now the innovators and Gluck, the young Mozart, Dittersdorf, Bach (Johann Christian) and Salieri (Italian but resident in Vienna) were taking opera into different directions. In Italy, rising stars such as Cimarosa were yet to shine although when they did most went off to Vienna or Paris for better fulfilment of their careers.

Architecturally there was also a war of styles being fought. The last great days of the baroque exemplified by the work of Guarini (d. 1683), Borromini (d. 1667). Juvarra (d. 1736) and above all Bernini (d. 1680) seemed to have drained the creative wells of the country. Architectural innovation was in the hands of the colony of foreigners who had either settled permanently, or made long residence, in Rome. Gian Battista Piranesi was a rare exception but his few completed works made the exception more theoretical than practical – he was better known as an extraordinary printmaker.

In Paris, the visitors could have seen some of the most innovative architecture in Europe. Ange-Jacques Gabriel (1698–1782) had completed the Place Louis XV (Place de la Concorde) by 1763 and the École Militaire was already dominating the Champ de Mars. At Versailles he had completed the Petit Trianon (1768) and the exquisite Opera Royale (1770) was under construction. These cool, classical, rational and entirely beautiful buildings were the precursors of an entirely new direction in architecture.[40] Paris was a city which the king did his very best to keep away from but in which the arts were thriving. What hopes could Italy hold, where kings, princes, dukes, doges and assorted clergy were omnipresent? They were to find out.

The first Italian town that Sir Watkin saw was Turin and it was an extraordinary piece of town planning. It was also virtually the only piece of large-scale town planning that he was to see. Dominated by the late Baroque buildings of Guarini and Juvarra, it seemed most agreeable to English taste. Its regularity reminded the tourist of St James' and Grosvenor Square – it was also very clean; a tribute to absolutist rule? Of independent mind, as usual, Mrs Piozzi found the arcades 'polluted with smells that poison all one's pleasure'. Oddly, Sir Watkin preferred Genoa whose painted palaces were not to everyone's taste but after Turin it must have seemed the apogee of gayness.

The largest *modern* building project in the peninsula was the Royal Palace at Caserta. Designed by Vanvitelli (1700–73) in a late baroque style, with aspects of neo-classicism struggling to get out, its vastness, if nothing else, was overwhelming. The theatrical splendour of the royal staircase and rotunda aroused expectations which simply cannot be met and the rest of the building peters out into a slightly dispiriting and lengthy sequence of boring interior spaces. The theatre is delightful and the gardens, into which initial efforts were concentrated, are very ambitious. The central axis of over three kilometres does, however, tend to drain enthusiasm from the feet. Vanvitelli called other architects to help him and Ferdinand Fuga (1699–1781) fresh from respected work in Rome (e.g. the front of Santa Maria Maggiore) came to his aid. Fuga designed the exquisite court theatre in the royal palace in Naples for the king's wedding celebrations in 1768 and it is a delightful building but one which sets its face firmly against any kind of innovation. Built in a glittery late roccoco style, it is an exemplar of the difficulties which Italian architecture was facing.

Alessandro Galilei (1691–1732) was an interesting exception. A mathematician, he was an early exponent of a form of anti-baroque neo-classicism. Much esteemed by visiting British gentry he was invited to England in 1714. Although occupied with minor projects, his most interesting design was that of the monumental Castletown House built for Speaker Conolly just outside of Dublin in the 1720s. The house, in its massing if not its detail, has resemblances to the new Wynnstay designed by James Byres for Sir Watkin. Galilei returned to Italy in 1719 and with papal approval designed a new facade for San Giovanni in Laterano – a design which shocked the baroque sensibilities of the Romans unaccustomed to neo-classical purity.

The hiatus was to last several years until a new generation, which embraced neo-classicism, was ready to make its mark. Interestingly, Piermarini's neo-classical theatre of La Scala in Milan (1778), which represented advanced taste, was not to be replicated in the delightfully gaudy rococo interior of La Fenice, in Venice, ten years later.

Architectural innovation did not particularly happen in Rome but rather through it. Piranesi's faltering attempts at a kind of neo-classicism in the Church of the Order of Malta (Santa Maria del Priorato, 1764) were eclipsed by the theories and practices of the foreign architects who came to the city to drink at the fountainhead, as it were. In the forefront of these must be accounted Robert Adam who gained the sobriquet 'Roman Bob' for his troubles but who was to be responsible for a revolution in taste after he had assimilated his Roman experiences. Sir Watkin's ruin may be associated with Roman Bob's assimilation of Roman style. A man famous for his 'ruin room' at Santa Trinita dei Monti at the top of the Spanish Steps was Charles Louis Clerisseau (1721–1820) who Adam met in Florence and accompanied to Rome in 1755. Clerisseau, who was a friend of Piranesi, had studied under Pannini and became an early theoretician of the neo-classical. Under his tutelage, Adam learned the essence of the antique and adventurously set off to Spalatro (Split) to survey the ruins of Diocletian's palace. His eventual publication of the measured drawings he made of the remains was an event of European importance in the development of a 'modern' style. Other British architects followed and the new taste, which had its roots in ancient Rome, flowered everywhere from St Petersburg to Pennsylvania but hardly in the city of its rediscovery.

Apart from music and architecture, painting and sculpture were the bait which drew the tourist. A souvenir portrait by Pompeo Batoni,[41] some Venetian views by Guardi or more probably by Canaletto (d.1768) or Pannini, easily portable prints by Piranesi, a lot of very dubious 'old masters' and as many pieces of antique statuary as could be decently exported were on the tourist shopping list and there were plenty of agents willing to supply them. Here, the British preyed upon their own and men such as Thomas Jenkins, James Byres, Gavin Hamilton and James Forester in Rome and Consul Smith in Venice were very happy to supply the desired articles and if unable to lay their hands upon the genuine relic were equally happy to manufacture 'new' antiquities. It was a thriving trade. The *vedutisti* of Rome were kept very busy satisfying the tourist taste but, in truth, the number of serious native artists could be counted upon the fingers of one hand. Here again the foreigners dominated a market which they were determined to keep to themselves. Richard Wilson, Raphael Mengs, Jakob Philip Hackert, Anton von Marron, William Pars, Hugh Douglas Hamilton, Jacob More and John Robert Cozens among many others, became indissolubly associated with *modern* Roman view painting.

The appreciation of art was a difficult issue. Many tourists came from homes which had old masters hanging on the walls but the appreciation of colour, form, line and composition may not have been imparted to them. There were several self-help guides published which sought to correct that deficiency and works could be viewed, guide in hand, and checked for conformity with the rules established well after they were painted. To be admired were works of the Bolognese School and the Carracci brothers, the 'divine' Guercino, Guido Reni and Domenichino were admitted into the ranks of the worthy. Gaspard Dughet (1615–75) and his paintings of the Roman Campagna and Salvatore Rosa (1615–73) and his proto-romantic views of rocks, caves, storms, *banditti* and not so innocent shepherds were admitted into the ranks of the collectable. Sir Watkin seems to have owned works by Guercino, Domenichino, Veronese, Poussin, Rosa and Sebastiano Ricci. Some he may have bought on his tour although, as Ricci had worked in London, the three canvases which were sent off to Sotheby's in 1947 and 1965, may have been acquired at home.[42] The baroque had become unacceptable. Carravagio was hardly mentioned and Bernini, whose sculptures were unfortunately 'all of a flutter' was not rehabilitated until relatively recently. James Byers loathed the baroque and lost little time in trying to 'correct' the taste of the gentlemen he guided around the city.

Modern artists, particularly in Rome, were usually categorised by their fees and obviously, the more fashionable the artist the higher the fee. Pompeo Batoni, known as the 'Prince of Painters', was very fashionable. Many gentlemen settled for lesser and cheaper artists when commissioning their grand tour souvenir but Sir Watkin, as we might have come to expect, was the only British visitor to commission a full-length portrait to include three figures. He also paid Batoni to paint a 'history' picture, which was to materialise as *Bacchus and Ariadne*[43] several years later. The Wynnstay collections included two other portraits by Batoni but how and when they were acquired is unknown. Presumably guided by James Byres, with more than half an eye to his commission fee, Sir Watkin patronised other living artists. Anton Raphael Mengs was in Madrid in 1768 and Sir Watkin's commission to him must have been funnelled through a third party. The resultant canvas of *Perseus and Andromache* was intercepted on its way to Britain and was eventually bought by Catherine the Great and now resides in the Hermitage Museum.[44] The work of Mengs was further represented by a portrait of Richard Wilson which he had painted for, and given to, his sitter. The probability is, however, that Sir Watkin had it from Wilson during that artist's sad decline in the 1770s. Other instances of his patronage in Rome were to the Irish sculptor, Christopher Hewetson, for a portrait bust in terracotta, to James Byres himself for designs for a new mansion at Wynnstay and to a Mr (Gavin?) Hamilton for several pictures. In the account book, there are tantalising entries such as that for 4 November – 'Pd for Drawings £50'. A not inconsiderable sum but can it represent payment for the drawings by Magnasco, Guercino, Tiepolo, Veronese, Poussin, Palma Vecchio, Castiglione or Domenichino, which were in a portfolio in the Wynnstay sale of 1947? An intriguing possibility but one which will probably remain simply that. If only Sidebotham had had an informed interest in art added to his list of virtues, we could have profited much more from his account book.[45] In Batoni's portrait, Sir Watkin is holding a chalk drawing of the Raphael fresco of Justice in the Stanza della Segnatura in the Vatican, obviously his own work. The above slight list of drawings certainly reveals an eye for fine draughtsmanship on the part of whoever collected them and it would be nice to think that our young baronet was assured enough in his own taste to have the confidence to buy what *he* wanted and not that which a guide for the uninformed pointed out as being worthy.

When he returned to London, his Italian spending did not stop. Payments to Maron for a copy of a Raphael, to Hugh Dean Primrose, who was about to set off to Rome, for a landscape, and disbursements to Byres and others for other unrecorded additions to the collection suggest that the named pieces in the accounts are the tip of a large iceberg. William Parry, the artistically gifted son of John Parry, the harpist, was given an allowance and packed off in the footsteps of his patron to study in Rome with the proviso that he supply copies of notable works back to London. The accounts for 1777 record the arrival of '... the

Transfiguration [after Raphael] a Galatea, *The Charity of Allano, The Holy Family* after Corrigeo. Originals – *The Dwarf, The Artist* and 2 more to be done.' Parry certainly seems to have kept his side of the bargain! *The Transfiguration* was hung on the staircase at St James's Square and the rest went to Wynnstay. Other works in the Wynnstay sale included a pair of Neapolitan coast scenes by Pietro Fabbris (sometimes Fabris), signed and dated 1773. Fabbris was the main illustrator of Sir William Hamilton's publication concerning the *Campi Phlaegri* and the two scenes may represent the fulfilment of an earlier commission although Fabbris was known to have exhibited in London in 1768 and 1782.[46]

For some people the point of going to Italy was precisely that of returning as a well-informed connoisseur in the visual arts as well as the musical. Sir Watkin fulfilled all of those expectations.

NOTES

1. Private Act, 9G. III, c.11 HL/PO/PB/1/1769/9G3n 43.
2. Dated to 1770, the designs are in the Adam Collection in Sir John Soane's Museum. Sir Watkins letter from Rome (Wynnstay 122 p5f) mentions his eagerness to see them.
3. See Peter D. G. Thomas, *Dictionary of National Biography*, Oxford, 2004.
4. *Gentleman's Magazine*, 1749, p.473, 'A Dirge addressed to Edward Kynaston'; p. 475, 'A Poem upon Sir Watkin's death; p.480, 'An account of the Circumstances of his death and a Eulogy'.
5. Quoted in Pritchard, op. cit., p. 3.
6. Charles Lancelot Shadwell (ed), *Registrum Orielense*, vol. II, London & New York, 1902. Sir Watkin is recorded as matriculating on 8 May 1766. Thomas Apperley on 6 June 1766, where he is noted as being from Leominster.
7. *Survey of London*, vol. XXXIX.
8. J.C. Apperley, *My Life and Times*, 1927, pp.47–8. Quoted more extensively in Pritchard.
9. David M. Little and George M. Kahrl (eds), *The Letters of David Garrick*, 1963, p.693.
10. National Library of Wales/*Llyfrgell Genedlaethol Cymru*, Wynnstay Papers: France & Italy, box 115/1 and MS 122; Wales, box 115, bundle 22.
11. Charles Burney (ed), H. Edmund Poole, *Music, Men, and Manners in France and Italy, 1770*, London, 1969. Reprinted, 1974.
12. National Archives, www.nationalarchives.gov.uk/currency. The National Archives have an easy to use interactive calculator on this site which converts eighteenth-century costs to modern values and is indeed a blessing for the non-mathematicians amongst us.
13. Jeffrey G. Williamson, 'The Structure of Pay in Britain 1710–1911', research in *Economic History*, 7.
14. Private Acts of Parliament, 29 April 1728, (2 Geo) C 32P, 'Naturalisation Of John Julian and Isaac Panchaud', 1729, (3 Geo 2) CiP, 'Naturalisation of Paul Torras and others'. For some reason the Acts were later repealed.
15. J. Black, op. cit., quotes Norton Nicholls thus '[the banker Leonardi] endeavoured to practise a little dirty deceit on me of which an English banker would have been ashamed'. This was not an uncommon sentiment.
16. Jeremy Black, *The Grand Tour in the Eighteenth Century*, p.256, Stroud, 1992.
17. Mrs Hester Lynch Piozzi, *Observations and Reflections made in the Course of a Journey through France, Italy and Germany*, vol. I, 1789, p.28.

18. Lady Mary Wortley Montagu, *Letters*, Vienna September 14 to Mr P., London, 1906.
19. Dr John Moore, *A View of Society and Manners in Italy*, vol. II, 5th ed, 1790.
20. James Lees-Milne, The Last Stuarts, New York, 1984.
21. Charles Hughes, (ed), *Mrs Piozzi's Thraliana*, London, 1913 (Hereafter referred to as *Thraliana*).
22. Charles Abbot in 1788, PRO 30/0/40, p.149.
23. Piozzi, *Observations*, p.60.
24. Ibid, p.109.
25. Sir Nathaniel Wraxall, *Historical and Posthumous Memoirs*, London, 1836, p.173.
26. Brian Fothergill, *Sir William Hamilton – Envoy Extraordinary*, London, 1969.
27. B.M. Egerton, MSS 2636, f.195.
28. Piozzi, *Observations*, p.267.
29. Burney, Journal, Friday 26th October 1770.
30. There has been a practice in Naples, until late, of a family adopting an unclaimed skull from the catacombs, particularly those of San Gennaro, and treating it as one of the family. Encased in a glazed display cabinet, the skull is asked to intercede with the heavenly powers to grant small favours to the adoptive family. The Church, at first uneasy, then appalled, forbade the practice. It still continues. After all, the Roman Church, a relatively modern institution, does not understand Naples where the household Gods are an absolute necessity.
31. The one occasion that I witnessed the Liquefaction (1968), I might have shared those feelings of religious fascination and repugnance were it not for the fact that, at the time, the extreme discomfort caused by the impatient, exited and very vocal congregation had distracted my reason.
32. Mrs Piozzi, *Observations*, p.300/301.
33. Wynnstay 115/1.
34. 28 Geo. III, c. 57.
35. For transport generally see Jeremy Black, *Italy and the Grand Tour*, New Haven, 2003.
36. P. Toynbee & L. Whibley (eds), *Correspondence of Thomas Gray*, 3 vols., Oxford, 1935; revised edition by H. W. Starr, Oxford, 1971.
37. Anon, *A Gentleman's Guide in His Tour through France*, 1770.
38. Mrs Piozzi, *Observations*, p.87.
39. A point which has been made before, is that the designs which James Byres made for the unbuilt new house at Wynnstay have more in common with the needs of public assembly rooms than the character of a private house.
40. Alan Bramham, *Architecture of the French Enlightenment*, London, 1980.
41. Bowron & Kerber, *Pompeo Batoni*, National Gallery Exhibition Catalogue, New Haven, 2008.
42. The well-known paintings by Ricci of an opera rehearsal, one of which Sir Watkin certainly owned, were executed in London and exist in about nine versions. Sir Watkin's version is now in the Yale Centre for British Art, New Haven. See Richard Leppert, 'Imagery, Musical Confrontation and Cultural Difference in Early 18th Century London', *Early Music*, vol. 14, Nº 3, 1986.
43. Sold in 1947 and now in a private collection in Rome.
44. The interception of HMS *Westmorland* and the dispersal of the art treasures it held was the subject of a major exhibition at the Ashmolean Museum, Oxford between May and August 2012.
45. In the Wynnstay Inventory of 1790 there are over one hundred portraits and thirty landscapes and other subjects listed as being hung in the house. Nº 20 St James's Square was another matter.
46. For Fabbris and the exquisite Lusieri see Nicola Spinosa & Leonardo Di Mauro, *Vedute napoletane del Settecento*, Naples, 1993.

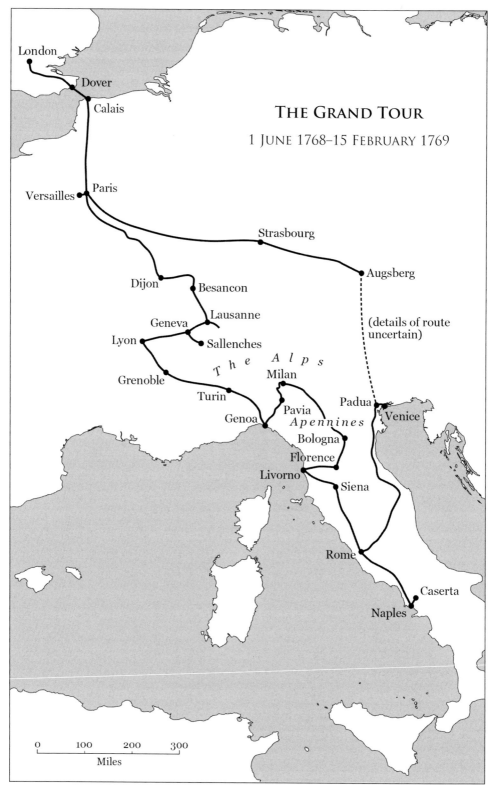

THE GRAND TOUR

1 JUNE 1768–15 FEBRUARY 1769

London

Dover

Calais

Versailles

Paris

Strasbourg

Augsberg

Dijon

Besancon

Lausanne

Geneva

Lyon

Sallenches

(details of route
uncertain)

The Alps

Grenoble

Milan

Turin

Padua

Pavia

Apennines

Venice

Genoa

Bologna

Florence

Livorno

Siena

Rome

Caserta

Naples

0   100   200   300

Miles

THE GRAND TOUR

London to Paris

HESITATIONS ABOUT THE TOUR HAVING BEEN PUT ASIDE, the party left the rented town house in Grosvenor Square on 1 June and proceeded to Dover. It was normal to leave in the very early hours and the cobbles of Grosvenor Square must have rattled as the coach drew up at the front door. It was still dark in the streets but there was a flurry of excitement as the party lined up ready to board and start the adventure. Candles burned in the house and *flambeau* lit the road outside as the chest of silver was finally packed.[1] Lady Williams Wynn stood upon the doorstep, perhaps wondering what state her son would be in when he returned. Would he become affected, or modish, or even perhaps Italianate? Sir Watkin, slightly hesitant about the whole business, was thoroughly out of his depth. Mr Apperley, a classical scholar, was excited at the prospect of seeing those places of which Virgil had written and Captain Hamilton, sophisticated but penurious, was very likely glad of the chance to undertake a very well-paid commission. Mr Morris and Sam Stephens were thoroughly enjoying the experience which was probably an unforeseen bonus for them. Finally, the worthy Mr Sidebotham was worried about his ability to cope with the demands which would be made upon him, wary about the difficulty of coping with the translation of various foreign currencies and nervous about foreign languages, knowing full well that he was on trial for the future.

On the day they left London, Sidebotham received £100 from Frances Chambre, an Oswestry solicitor who managed the Wynnstay finances, who, several years later, was to be dismissed for suspected financial mismanagement. Sidebotham calculated this sum to be equivalent to 2,285 livres (on their arrival in Paris they would spend 2,599 livres which, in modern values, would have been close to £7,000). Travel in the eighteenth century was indeed only for the very rich. Farewells made and an anxious mother reassured; promises were made to Mr Chambre about restricting their expenditure and general good wishes were expressed to all before the coach trundled off towards Westminster Bridge and the Old Kent Road, bound for Dover. Somehow the modern traveller's early morning taxi to St Pancras seems a little less epic.

All in all, it was an oddly assorted company. For Sir Watkin, who appeared not to have had any kind of father figure in his youth, it would have been quite normal to have gone away with a respectable elder, such as a clergyman[2] or senior tutor. The choice of Thomas Apperley, who was only ten years his senior, as his temporary guardian seems almost too cosy. There is sufficient evidence to show that Lady Williams Wynn was particularly close to her son but her apparent trust in his ability to comport himself decently whilst abroad would have been thought by many of her contemporaries, to be verging on the foolish. Perhaps we should simply accept that she knew him best and had every faith that his sense of morality and decency would not desert him whilst subjected to the myriad temptations which most boys of his age surrendered to gladly. To visit Italy was the final polishing stage in the education of a gentleman and Lady Williams Wynn, who seems to have ambitions for her son, desired him to shine in the best company. There was no choice, Italy it had to be.

A man who has not been in Italy, is always conscious of an inferiority, from his not having seen what it is expected a man should see. The grand object of traveling is to see the shores of the Mediterranean .... All our religion, almost all our law, almost all our arts, almost all that sets us above savages, has come to us from the shores of the Mediterranean.[3]

London to Naples is 1,973 miles by the most direct route, but the road they opted for was certainly not that. One cannot but wonder if any of them had the slightest concept of what an epic journey it was to be. Sir Watkin would have been well acquainted with gentlemen who had made the journey, but the experience of listening to travellers' anecdotes is not quite the same as carrying out the journey oneself. They were about to find out the truth behind the tales.

The first stage was to Dover, a two-day journey at least. The seventy-three miles to the port were relatively well-paved and were probably the fastest part of the tour. European visitors coming in the opposite direction were often amazed by the convenience of the route and, incidentally, by the cleanliness of the houses lining it. The first night was likely spent in or near Rochester from where a very early start could get them to Dover for a second night's stay. The Channel crossing to Calais was fraught with difficulty. Both harbours were relatively shallow and boats could not dock until a favourable high tide but if wind prevented access to the harbour, the traveller had no recourse but to pay exorbitant charges to the local boatmen to be rowed out to the packet ship. Under favourable conditions the crossing could be made in three hours but, under adverse conditions, could take several days. Many gentlemen had never even seen the sea before embarking upon it and making the crossing in a wildly bobbing boat, not much bigger than a modern lifeboat, was possibly one of their worst experiences ever. Even in fair wind, as Dr Burney noted,

On Thursday the 7th I embarked with a fair wind and arrived at Calais without any other accident than the very common one of being intolerably ill throughout the whole passage.[4]

Most travellers spent the night at Calais and the two decent hotels, the Silver Lyon of *Monsieur* Grandsire and the Hotel d'Angleterre of *Monsieur* Dessin were well-used to dealing with the ill or apprehensive tourist, depending upon the direction of the journey. It was there that negotiations were begun over obtaining a coach in which to proceed to Paris. Gentlemen returning home had a coach to spare and those setting out needed one and bargains were struck. Sir Watkin acquired one from Lord Leigh, an acquaintance from both Westminster School and Oriel College, and shortly to be declared insane. He appears to have refused money for the coach until after Sir Watkin returned to London. Having furnished themselves with the means of transport, the luggage would be released from the rapacious customs house and loaded on board. A trunk went missing, a not uncommon occurrence, and all of Mr Sidebotham's efforts failed to locate it. He was still fretting about it a month later when they were preparing to leave Paris for Dijon. The other horror which revealed itself at Calais was the French postillions. Truculent, frequently ill-natured, generally obnoxious and altogether exploitative (their descendants now drive taxis in Paris), they nevertheless needed to be endured. A deal was generally struck with the *voiturine* to provide accommodation and food on the journey to the capital, which could take three days, during which the innocent Briton was in the hands of the gods. Sir Watkin and his companions must have been fortunate and they entered Paris seven days after leaving London which was very good going indeed. It may have been that the troubled Lord Leigh had handed over to them his entire equipage thereby saving them from being fleeced in negotiations with which they were unfamiliar. It is probably correct to presume that the gentlemen in the party had at the very least some smattering of French, but they were yet to meet up with their cicerone and were, for the moment, on their own.

As has been noted previously there were in the region of thirty-three posts stages between Calais and Paris and travel on the road was strictly regulated. It needed goodwill on the part of the persons responsible for driving the coach to make decent progress and Sir Watkin seems to have been lucky. There is no mention of where they spent the night on their way, and the bills have been lost, but Amiens was a favoured and well-appointed place to break the journey.

The weariness brought in by the journey must have been forgotten on the 7 June when the travellers entered Paris through the Porte St Denis and made their way across the river to the Faubourg of St Germain where they were to stay for a month.

Paris

Once settled in Paris – Sir Watkin and the gentlemen at the Hotel de Saxe on the Rue des Petits Augustins, and the servants with *Madame* Simoneh at the Hotel Park Royal around the corner – no time was lost in acquiring a veneer of sophistication. It may be that upon his arrival there, Sidebotham acquired the small, vellum-bound, account book which was to serve him for the rest of the tour and upon which the present narrative is based. Glued inside of the front cover is a tradesman's notice, which suggests that the book was purchased at a shop specialising in artists' materials, situated on the Rue de Seine in the Fauberg Saint Germain. There are ten identical books in the Wynnstay Papers,[5] which take the Williams Wynn accounts up to 1780, the year in which Samuel Sidebotham was appointed steward at Wynnstay. The first several pages are filled with currency calculations, but on page seven the account proper begins and the heading tells us exactly what the book was for – 'Expenses & Disbursements in Sr Watkins Expedition into foreign Parts by Saml Sidebotham'.

Previous to page seven it is recorded that, as well as receiving £100 sterling from Mr Chambre in London, Sidebotham had negotiated an advance of £200 from M. Panchaud, the banker. Altogether, he had £1,600 from him whilst in Paris to fund the costs of sophistication. The following day, a barber was summoned to cut and curl Sir Watkin's hair. Interestingly, he seems to have invariably had his own hair powdered and curled and there is no mention in the account of wigs, even at the various courts to which they were presented. According to Tobias Smollet, who seemed to have little admiration for anything foreign,

> *When an Englishman comes to Paris he cannot appear until he has undergone a total metamorphosis! At his first arrival it is necessary to send for the tailor, perruquier, hatter, shoemaker, and every other tradesman concerned in the equipment of the human body. He must even change his buckles, and the form of his ruffles.*[6]

PLATE 1

PLATE 2

PLATE 3

PLATE 4

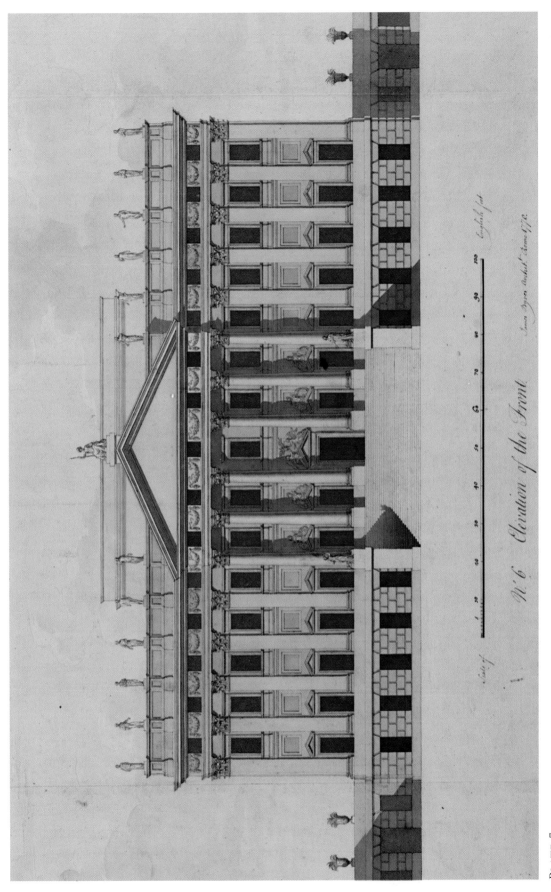

N.º 6.   *Elevation of the Front.*   *James Paine Architect Anno 1770.*

Scale of   English feet

PLATE 5

PLATE 6

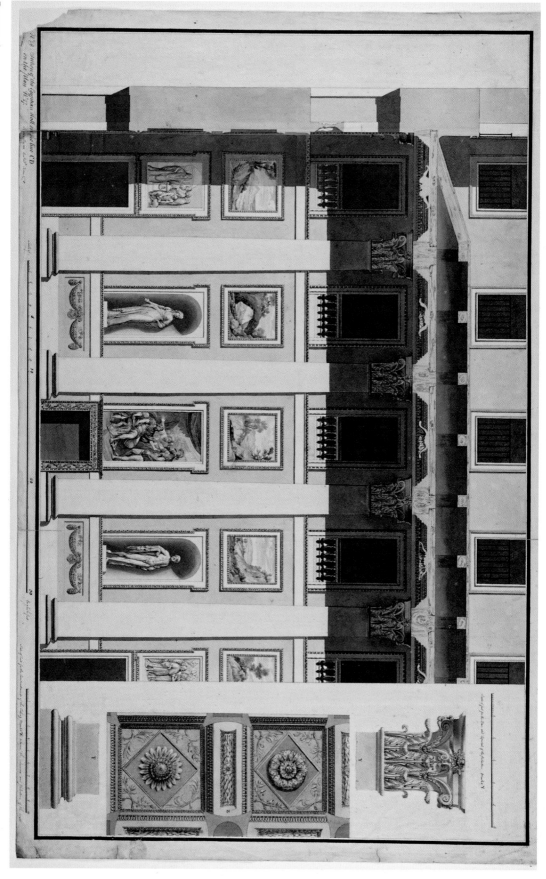

1760

Disbursements for
Prints Pictures &c

		D	B
Nov. 29	Pd Sigr Piranesi for his Work compleat in 1 Vol. of prints	1219	2
30	Pd a man for 4 Drawings in Stile Cafer after Raffael	61	5
Dec. 3	Pd Mr Hamilton the following 3 Prints from Homer 30:7½ 3 Prints at 5:0 — 15:0 3 Prints at 4 — 12:0	57	7½
	Pd Mr Byres a Bill for 2 Cameos a Ring Prints &c a sq Bill	297	7
	Pd Pompeo in part of payment of a large full length Picture of Sr Watkin Mr Hamilton by Mr Chytles 75 Sequins	1537	5
1769 Jan. 6	Pd Do in part for a History Picture he is to have for Mr 50 Sequins	1025	
7	Pd Mr Jenkins for 0 Pictures 2 Marble Tables Taylo a sq Acct 194	8140	
	carried to Page 63	14246	7

1769

	Disbursements for Prints Pictures &c br.t forward	D	B
Jan. 7		14246	7
	Pd Mr Hamilton for 5 Pictures a sq Acct 345	1431	5
	Pd Mr Byres for 9 Pictures a sq Acct which makes a sq Acct	35275	0
	Pd Do for Prints cutting a Seal &c a sq Acct	4742	5
	Pd Mr Wiseman a bill for Majse	1181	5
	Pd Mr Steuvon for a Bust in Clay of Sr Watkin borne Cast from it 20 Sequins	410	0
	carried to Page 90	70093	2

PLATE 7

Vaso antico di marmo adornato di finissimi intaglj ed arabeschi
Si vede in Inghilterra presso il Signor Egidio Earle Cavaliere Inglese
amatore delle belle arti

Al Signor Watkin William Wynne Cavaliere Inglese
amatore delle belle arti
In atto d'Ossequio il Cavaliere Gio. Batta Piranesi D.D.D.

PLATE 8

PLATE 9

PLATE 10

PLATE 11

PLATE 12A

PLATE 12B

PLATE 13A

PLATE 13B

PLATE 14A

PLATE 14B

J.W. W.Wynne   P.J. Taylor   M.Reynolds...   S. William Hamilton   M. Richard Thompson   M. Stanhope   M. Smith of Heath

PLATE 16

Sidebotham recorded 'June 8th. Pd a Barber for cutting and curling Sr Watkin's hair'.

Sir Watkin, Apperley and Hamilton were installed in the Hotel de Saxe, which was anything but cheap. It was the custom simply to hire rooms as needed and to make all other domestic arrangements separately. Thus their food was supplied by a *traiteur* who, from his centralised kitchen, could supply hot meals to his entire neighbourhood. They occasionally ate in the hotel but also employed *Monsieur* Brunet, the butter man, *Monsieur* Sejean, the wine merchant, *Monsieur* Jolli, another wine merchant, resident at the Quai de l'Union (whose firm was to survive the Revolution), and, most importantly, *Monsieur* Duboot [sic] a *valet du place* at the hotel who was there to satisfy every need not yet thought of.

The servants were living under a similar arrangement around the corner at *Madame* Simonet's establishment, the Hotel Park Royal. They were paid a *per diem* (board wages) whilst on the tour and their arrangements were their own business, but they seem to have opted for full board with their Parisienne landlady and thereby avoided the confusion of squabbling suppliers. They must have been satisfied and stayed there again, eight months later, when on their way home.

Four weeks were spent in Paris, time which was used as preparation for the epic tour to come. Sir Watkin was enrolled with a fencing master and also received lessons in dance from D'Auberville, the famous choreographer who was later to create *La Fille mal Garde*. Obviously, the quality of instruction was of prime importance and his fee of £120 was paid promptly; his apprentice was tipped a further £24.

A routine was settled into and most days Sir Watkin went to instruction in whatever subject was down for the moment and, once their duties were discharged, Sidebotham, Morris and Carrara went sightseeing, as did Apperley and Hamilton. We get an early insight into the latter's attitude to the tour and his duties on it when, four days after arriving, he receives re-imbursement for a ticket to the 'Comedy' – having attended by himself. Although he was earning a handsome fee, he seems to have had his general expenses refunded and, as time progressed, was to make frequent recourse to Sir Watkin's purse. Other demands became frequent and it seems that when extra servants (usually footmen or coachmen) were hired, they were also smartened up.

Jun 11th Pd for Powder and Pomatron	*4*	*10*
Pd for a Soap Box	*0*	*10*
Pd @ the Comedy for Capt Hamilton	*6*	*0*
Pd Allowance for bags & Silk Stockings for		
2 footmen and Coachman	*45*	*0*

The lower servants did not escape instruction however and, during their otherwise idle hours, French lessons were provided for the Welsh contingent, as were Italian lessons later in the tour. Oddly, although Sir Watkin was an enthusiastic cellist and had his instrument with him throughout the tour, there is no mention of music lessons whilst in Paris; a situation which was to be greatly remedied in Italy. Antonio Carrara, who had joined the party in Paris, seems to have been the possessor of a pleasant singing voice and several volumes of French songs were bought for him, presumably so that he could entertain the company during their frequent musical evenings. Garrick had certainly done Sir Watkin a great favour in suggesting his former valet as guide, cicerone and general whatever and Carrara fancied himself as a man of letters and supposed that his literary skills were equal to those of Goldoni. Whatever the truth of that, he certainly had a ready wit and an earthy sense of humour. Most of his English clients seemed to have liked him, but he offended some of his own countrymen by telling elaborate tall stories to gullible tourists, concerning sexual licence in Italy, and thereby perhaps raising their hopes to the unreasonable degree of fevered anticipation which Boswell was to suffer from in Turin.[8]

In the evenings, when Sir Watkin was practising his newly-acquired language and dance skills, the upper servants went to the Opera, the Italian Comedy and the Comédie Française. One imagines that the multi-lingual Carrara translated the proceedings for them until their own language skills had improved sufficiently for them to be able to follow the proceedings unaided; obviously not a prerequisite for the opera and possibly why they went there so often! Sometimes an entry recording the purchase of tickets for, say, the Italian Comedy, is followed by another entry recording the cost of the playbook. Playbooks for plays performed in English were common in London. Bell's *British Theatre History* printed a great number in the 1770s and 80s and it would seem that much the same custom pertained in Paris. The book, to be read slowly and at leisure the next day, would have been an invaluable help in acquiring fluency in the language.

A curious entry in the accounts is that for 15 June when Sidebotham, Morris and Carrara were equipped with short hunting swords (*cuttau de chasse*) There was obviously every intention of them being worn as belts and buckles were also bought. This entry is on the same page which records expenditure on silk stockings (6 pairs), snuff boxes (3), *valenciennes* ruffles (2 pairs), a tip to some comic singers and 2lbs of mustard. The exquisite, the mundane and the threatening – all necessary and all recorded!

Occasionally, the whole party joined forces and went on shopping expeditions for fabric, waistcoat pieces, tapestries at the Gobelins works, shoes for Sir Watkin, riding boots for Carrara, books and clothing for the coming journey for all of them. Either Carrara, or someone else with experience, guided them around the shops of the French capital and only the best and most luxurious establishments were patronised. Sir Watkin seems to have ordered or 'put aside' some extra-ordinarily expensive items such as a Sèvres dinner service and diamond shoe buckles, intended for his future wife and mother-in-law, and which he intended to collect upon his return from the south. Some things, however, were not to Sidebotham's taste – 'June 17th Pd for a Bottle of very bad Beer.'

One special expedition was a two-day excursion to Versailles, Marly and St Germain for which a four-horse coach, coachmen and postillions were hired. Marly-le-Roi was famous for its waterworks, St Germain-en-Laye was famous for having been the refuge of the exiled Stuarts, although the building itself was not much of a spectacle and Versailles was simply famous.

Unfortunately for them the Queen, Maria Lecsinska, was in mortal decline in the state apartments and therefore, probably not receiving. The palace was likely a gloomy affair, but the park and gardens could be inspected and the Petit Trianon, a decent distance from the dying Queen, and only just finished, was the only piece of advanced architecture which could have been inspected, although at that moment unoccupied as Madame Pompadour had preceded the Queen, as usual, and Madame du Barry had not yet moved in; so perhaps it could have been inspected.

The Opera Royale was in the process of construction and was to be inaugurated in 1770 on the marriage of the future Louis XVI and Marie Antoinette. One of the most beautiful theatres in Europe, it was one of the final extravagances of the *ancien régime* and exhausted ten thousand candles in an evening. There were only about ten recorded performances held in the eighteenth century – even in Versailles, economy sometimes ruled.

The palace, *Le Chateau* to the French, was an unmissable sight but was already nearly one hundred years old and mainly memorable for the egomania it embodied rather than for its architecture. Some British visitors were impressed but others, like Horace Walpole, thought it 'a lumber of littleness, composed of black brick, stuck full of bad old busts, and fringed with gold rails.'[9] Walpole had had the inestimable benefit of having been brought up at Houghton Hall and perhaps it is understandable that he could remain insensitive to the seductions of Louis XIV's vast political statement.

Upon their return to Paris, sightseeing continued and new sensations experienced, and Sidebotham and three others (names unrecorded) actually went to Benediction at Notre Dame. Sidebotham seems to have been generally charitable to begging monks and friars and exhibited little of the British atavistic aversion to Catholicism, but they took a speedy antidote to benediction and went to a playhouse immediately afterwards. The Gallery of the Palais Royal was visited at a shilling a head, but they would probably have avoided the arcades, which had a reputation as seedy and louche because of the pimps, prostitutes and revolutionaries who gathered in its shady corners.

Several days later Sidebotham, Carrara and Morris climbed to the top of the cathedral and must have related the experience to Sir Watkin as the next day he climbed it himself. At 387 steps, for the slightly overweight (some went so far as to have called him fat) young baronet, it was quite a feat.

The city was much more interesting architecturally than Versailles and the Place Louis XV (Place de la Concorde), the Ecole Militaire and other 'modern' works by Ange-Jacques Gabriel were beginning to embellish the capital and Sidebotham took himself off to see Les Invalides on the 21st.

June 21st			
	Pd for a silk Waistcoat	60	
	Pd for a Cheese & Bollogna Sausage	8	5
	Pd for a pr of black Silk Stockings	15	
	Pd for my self at hospital of Invalides	1	4
	Pd at the Italian Opera	12	

Several excursions were made into the countryside but the destinations have not been recorded, apart from the visits to Marly and St Germain.

On the 24th, the Queen, who had been gently expiring throughout their visit, gave up completely. Although she was not much lamented by the King, correct form still had to be observed and the theatres were closed. Versailles was only some twelve miles or so from Paris, but the news of the Queen's demise took a long time to reach the capital. On the same evening as her death, a spectacular firework display was held somewhere in the city which the travellers attended and hired a coach to take them home afterwards. The next day, Paris descended into gloom and the only entertainment to be had was at the Queen's funeral, at St Denis, which they duly attended.

July 2nd	*Pd for 3 Horses to see the Queens Funeral*

Whether the three horses were for Sir Watkin, Apperley and Hamilton or for Sidebotham, Morris and Carrara is frustratingly unclear. Paris was obviously wet and umbrellas were bought (as well as weatherproof travelling clothes for the servants when they arrived at Dijon).

Sidebotham negotiated with Pascall, the coachmaker, and acquired a new coach for 110 guineas, part-exchanging the one which he had acquired from Lord

Leigh at Calais for a 40 guinea allowance and hiring an extra chaise for 90 guineas; a complicated, but satisfactory negotiation which meant that their cavalcade now consisted of two coaches and a variable number of outriders. The splash which Sir Watkin was making was sufficient to announce at the gates of any town he cared to visit, that here was a gentleman of importance and furthermore a gentleman of means. This was not the best way to try and extricate reasonable rates from wayside inns, but Sidebotham seemed happy with his negotiations. Less satisfactory was his purchase of a travelling bed – presumably to spare Sir Watkin from the torments of the bug infested and flea-ridden bedding supplied by most of the establishments en route to Italy (leather sheets were also part of the sensible man's preparations). The vendor had tried to overcharge him by 153 livres. Sidebotham recognised him as a rogue and bought the bed for a less inflationary 850 livres.

July 6th	*Pd a great Rascal for a Travelling Bed which he*	
	at first charged	*1003*

Paying off their bills at the Hotel de Saxe (especially for broken crockery) and then the dancing master, the language master, the embroiderers, the tailor and the booksellers, they set out on 7 July. Sir Watkin's bill at the Hotel de Saxe had generally been settled by the week but, and to one's surprise, *Madame* Simonetz at the Hotel Park Royal had allowed her guests to run up a month's bill. Perhaps hers was a much jollier establishment. Sidebotham needed to pay 960 *louis* for the month and from that, one may be allowed to guess that the Hotel Park Royal was a very superior, inferior establishment.

July 5th	*Pd Fencing Master for 21 Lessons @ 8 pr Lesson & for Foils*
July 7th	*Pd Mr Durbervalle [sic] Dancing Master for 20 Lessons at 6*
	pr lesson

Expenditure in Paris had been relatively modest, but when they returned on their way home, the newly refined and artistically assured Sir Watkin was by then no stranger to objects of 'virtue' and his collecting instinct was unrestrained. His family and guardians had wanted him to acquire the instincts, taste and manners of a sophisticated gentleman and he discharged their trust splendidly, but I doubt that any of them would have been conscious of the awful cost it would entail. Inconvenient in the short term, but disastrous in the long.

Paris to Italy

The next stage of the journey was to take them a little over a month and they would pass through Dijon, Besançon, Lausanne, Geneva, Lyons and Grenoble until they reached the Alps at the terrifying pass at Mont Cenis. It is roughly 256 miles (411 kilometres) from Paris to Lausanne and they made the journey at a very good rate, had time for a little sightseeing on the way and arrived in Lausanne after seven days on the road. Although not recorded in the accounts, the likely route of the journey would have been through Fontainebleau, Sens, and Auxerre to reach Dijon; thereafter the route is noted. Perhaps fortunately, they were far too soon for the grape harvest whilst travelling through Burgundy and there was nothing to delay their progress.

Apart from the generally miserable state of the inns, it must have been an agreeable jaunt. Who would not wish to travel through mid-France in July? The heat may have been inconvenient but the country must have looked glorious. The weather took an unfortunate turn for the worse when they reached Dijon and the lesser servants may have been unprepared. Sir Watkin intervened.

July 10th   *Pd for 4 Travelling Capes for the Servants TM, SS, CB LMC at Dijon.*

After Dijon, they went to Besançon where Apperley did some private sightseeing and probably inspected the famous fortifications built by Vauban, Louis XIV's great military engineer. The Roman triumphal arch, the Porte Noire, would have been his first sight of a complete survival from the classical past. The Alps were now clearly in sight and this was probably the first time that most of them had seen mountains. Those which Sir Watkin owned he had not yet seen and it would be another three years until he did.

The next stage of the route is somewhat curious. Lausanne seems to have been a little off the direct route and must have been an intended destination. The road from Besançon would have taken them close to Motiers, where Jean Jacques Rousseau had lived before his enforced exile to England in 1765, and Lausanne was one of his favoured haunts.[10] Rousseau's publication in 1761 of *Julie, ou la nouvelle Héloïse* had caused a sensation throughout Europe. An instant best seller, it was immediately translated into English by William Kendrick. Primarily concerned with purity of feeling, its rhapsodic descriptions of the Swiss countryside in the area they were travelling through may have had some bearing on their choice of route. It would be mere speculation to suggest that Sir Watkin nursed an admiration for the philosopher but he was later to take up with a gentleman whose sister had been one of his closest English friends.

Lady Dorothy Cavendish, sister to the fifth Duke of Devonshire, and later Duchess of Portland, had been a stout defender of the philosopher's right to philosophise and visited him frequently during his exile at Wooton near Lichfield.

Lausanne was reached on the 14th and they put up at the Crown. Over three weeks were spent in the vicinity of Lake Geneva and, although language lessons continued, considerable time was made for sightseeing. Unlike the average eighteenth-century tourists they seemed to find the Alps fascinating. To make travel easier, the coach was temporarily abandoned and horses were hired for everyone, although the little mare acquired for Sir Watkin was purchased outright. They visited Vevey where one may still be shown the table at which Rousseau dined in his favourite restaurant and, in the church of St Martin, be shown the graves of some of the exiled signatories of the death warrant of King Charles I. Villeneuf and presumably the Chateau of Chillon, which lies between, were also included in a very busy schedule of visits. When they were not riding along the lake they went for excursions upon it and the servants were sent off by themselves on a fishing expedition and, it may be noted, they were amply supplied with wine for the trip. Although it was July, the alpine weather may have turned cold and nine pairs of 'very warm Winter Gloves' were purchased.

Lake Geneva (or Lac Leman) was bordered by the Swiss Confederation, the Duchy of Savoy and France. Oddly, there is no mention in the accounts of the usual passport difficulties although the normal customs duties applied when they re-entered French territory. An excursion across the lake to see the Carthusian House at Thonon-les-Bains near Evian, and in Savoyard territory, was evidently conducted in some style and Sir Watkin's silver plate was loaded onto the barque as well as apparently lavish provisions. The silver plate which Sir Watkin had seen fit to take with him, must have been quite heavy and men were paid to carry it to the lake.

July 24th	I gave a boy at Farnese	3	0
	Pd for a Barque on the lake of Geneva to go there	48	
	Pd for carrying the Plate Box to and from lake	1	10
	Pd a Bill for provision for Do	61	4

A destitute ex-Oxford man was encountered in Lausanne who was given more than £24 to aid his passage home. A poor Englishwoman encountered at Bea, also in difficulties, was given half as much. Vivay [Vevey] was stayed at for three days, although these little jaunts were not allowed to distract from continued 'improvement'.

July 29th	*Pd a Language Mas'r at Lausanne*
	Pd two Dancing Masters

Leaving Lausanne for Geneva a spirit of adventure was in the air and the coaches were sent ahead unoccupied whilst the entire party rode the 33 miles (53 kilometres) along the shores of the lake. The views to the south encompassed a dramatic panorama towards Mont Blanc and the Alpine chain and the peaks must have exerted some considerable allure to provoke an adventurous proposal.

This spirit of adventure continued when they reached Geneva on 2 August where they made preparations for the whole company to ascend to Chamonix and Mont Blanc. Eleven horses were hired to facilitate the ascent. Three days were spent on this diversion. Most tourists would have been glad to avoid the mountains and did so whenever they could – the taste for the sublime was an advanced one, but we can only assume that this side excursion was a deliberate and quite daring choice. There had been earlier British visitors to the glaciers, but it was not yet an established part of the tour. Even on horseback, this was hardly a ramble in the park. Geneva is 373m above sea level and Chamonix is 1035m and the simplest computation suggests that they ascended 662m up very rocky and insecure paths. There was an element of 'roughing it' as inns or hotels were few and far between. It must have proved enjoyable, however, as the ascent of Mount Cenis, a week or so later, seems to have been made by several of the company on horseback. They stayed with a local priest at Sallenches and climbed further to view the actual Glaciers. Three years later, Sir Watkin's tour of his north Wales possessions, with much of the same company, but with the addition of Paul Sandby, resulted in the publication of views of the sublime which were most influential. Perhaps the Chamonix excursion is evidence of an advanced taste indeed. Between 1775 and 1800, under the influence firstly of literature and then of painting, mountainous landscapes slowly became rehabilitated. At best an inconvenience, and at worst a severe danger, mountains were to be endured and crossed as quickly as possible; usually with half-closed eyes. The thought of climbing a mountain to experience a delightful frisson of awe and excitement would probably not have occurred to Sir Watkin's father. Times had become less rational in matters of the imagination, in spite of its appellation, 'The Age of Reason' and visions of the sublime were now to be pursued. Our 1768 expedition puts its members in the very vanguard of advanced taste.

Back in Geneva, the horses were surrendered, the coaches retrieved, Sir Watkin bought a gold stopwatch from M. Fulga, and they set out on the 6 August for Lyons. It is interesting how often, buried in the general account and amid very mundane purchases, odd little items such as silver knee buckles, a subscription for books, a fan for Sir Watkin, a knife for Sir Watkin, artificial marble eggs etc, can almost slip by unnoticed.

After the exertions of the Alpine jaunt and the Swiss Confederation were left behind them, five days relaxation in the second most populous city of France was enjoyed. The most difficult stage of the journey was fast approaching and, after visiting the glaciers of Chamonix, there could have been no limit to the horrors they were imagining on the state of the road ahead.

The best accommodation to be had in Lyons was at the Hotel de la Croix de Malthe and therefore that was where they stayed; to assuage his conscience, Sidebotham gave alms to a begging friar. Boswell had stayed there in 1766 and Mrs Piozzi followed several years later. *Monsieur* le Blanc was the proprietor and close by a *Monsieur* Minet ran a restaurant which supplied their meals. The hotel was slightly unusual in that it had a bathing establishment attached and most visitors were extremely grateful for the chance to become slightly less than filthy. Obviously, Lyons was a place where retail therapy was incumbent upon the rich and fashionable visitor and Sir Watkin succumbed to temptation whilst Sidebotham and Morris went off to see a puppet show. The firm of Camille Pernon was one of the best and most expensive manufacturers of silk and velvet in France and a flowered velvet suit and waistcoat pieces (to be made up later) were bought from him – 'August 9th. Pd the Mercers Bill at Lyons for a flowered Velvet Suit & Waistcoat pieces, 552'. That bald entry in the account book does not quite reveal the entire truth. When they had returned to Paris more became clear – 'Feb 8th 1769. Pd Mr Pernon of Lyon for Sr Watkin's best suit, 1940 French or £84 17s. 6d.' In modern values, that suit had cost £5,405.60, a reasonable cost for a lavishly embroidered velvet suit.[11] Apart from the coercions of fashion, Sir Watkin may not have worn his new suit very often as he began to display a sad tendency to put weight on quite early in life. The coat was not generously cut.

After Lyons, two nights were spent in Grenoble at the Three Dolphins, and in anticipation of the next stage of the tour, an Italian grammar was bought. Grenoble was often known as the capital of the Alps and it was here that preparations were made for the crossing of the mountain chain. A new *voiturine* and two postillions were hired and Sidebotham and Carrara were equipped with new riding caps. There must have been an intention to travel part of the journey by night as wax lights had previously been bought for the coach and chaise whilst they were in Lyons.

The distance from Grenoble to Turin is not great (approximately 96 miles), but it took them six days to actually cross the Alps into Piedmont. After leaving Grenoble, they entered the territory of Savoy, since 1720 part of the kingdom of

Sardinia, and therefore their first official entry into Italian lands, apart from their brief excursion to Evian from Lausanne. Lanslebourg was the last town before they ascended to the pass and many a traveller found his nerves giving out on this stage of the tour. Some went up it on hands and knees, praying the while, and some preferred the moonlight when alpine peaks and crevices were blanketed in decent obscurity, whilst others thought fondly of Norfolk. Our intrepid travellers had already ascended to the Chamonix glaciers and perhaps were inured to Alpine terrors.

The normal means of crossing the Mont Cenis route was to hire guides and porters to carry one over. The carriages were dismantled and taken piece by piece and the gentlemen and servants were put into a curious legless wicker-chair slung between two poles, a kind of rustic sedan chair, and carried over by the guides. Many accounts survive of the fear and terror experienced by tourists on this route but given their previous alpine excursion, our redoubtable tourists may have enjoyed the experience. Equally, as it was August, the snow might have cleared, hence Sidebotham's and Carrara's acquisition of new riding caps which may have signalled their intention to ride the way. Evidently, the upper servants had nerves of steel.

At 7,000 feet, the pass was certainly agreeably vertiginous. Thomas Grey thought that Mont Cenis carried 'the permission mountains have of being frightful rather too far' [12] and this was the very place where Horace Walpole's King Charles spaniel was snatched away, and presumably devoured, by a wolf. The fact that the dog was called Tory adds a little piquancy to the tale. The length of time taken for Sir Watkin's party to reach Turin from Grenoble may well be in part accounted for by leisurely sightseeing and admiration of the views in order to satisfy their newly-acquired romantic sensibility.

One of the first things they did on reaching Turin was to have the kettle mended, perhaps it was worn out on the crossing through excessive testing of the altitude by timing how long water took to boil, an experiment recommended by most contemporary guidebooks.

Once the pass was crossed, they began to descend into warmer air and the rich country from Susa to Turin must have convinced them that they had indeed entered Mediterranean lands and were, at last, in Italy. Dr Burney wrote thus of his descent in 1770:

This is 10 times worse than ascending as you constantly see your danger, and besides it is much further down than up – 'Tis a dreadfully laborious trade for the poor men: they were obliged to rest 5 or 6 times ere we reached Novalese. In short this descent is both terrific and fatiguing. I was never more thoroughly tired in my life. But the rocks, precipices, cataracts and torrents amused as well as frightened us, so that I did not know how much I was tired till all was over.[13]

Most visitors remarked upon the ordered approach to Turin which came as such a contrast to the disordered crossing on Mont Cenis. Dr Burney again – 'From Rivoli to Turin which is 6 miles, is a strait, broad road planted on each side. As one approaches the city, the collini on the right hand afford a most beautiful prospect, being covered with villas and vineyards.'

But gratitude at having made the crossing safely must have been the overwhelming emotion. Sidebotham bought an ice cream and gave alms to begging monks. The first probably to revive his overheated spirit and the second likely in gratitude for a safely accomplished crossing.

Turin to Florence

On arrival in Turin, Sidebotham recorded the only real unpleasantness he seems to have encountered upon the entire journey.

Pd the Voterine in Part of 50 Guineas that he was to have for bringing us from Grenoble to Turin 30 Guineas. We stopt 20 till we had satisfaction for a mare, Saddle & furniture left in his hands at Geneva.

However the experience could not have been entirely bad and the postillions were given an extra tip for their work.

Turin was the most magnificent of cities and a mixture of despotic government and brilliant town planning gave it a degree of regularity and order which the British visitors could not have experienced before. The streets, laid out upon a regular grid plan and lined with palaces designed by Guarino Guarini and Filippo Juvarra, its two famous and favourite architects, paved, arcaded and swept were, (in spite of what Mrs Piozzi thought) at the time, unique. Guarini was a mathematical theoretician and architect of a mystical bent who, incidentally, was also a Theatine monk, whilst Juvarra, his successor, was a priest whose first success was as a theatre designer. There is a boldness and vitality about the baroque architecture of Turin which is very specific to it. Several Piedmontese designers had been employed in London and the Home Counties and the unveiling of the interiors of Norfolk House in St James' Square, by G.B. Borra, in 1756 had caused a sensation in London society.[14] Sidebotham and Morris joined forces to visit the great basilica of La Superga, (Juvarra) burial place of the reigning dynasty, but whether the ostentatiously magnificent hunting palace of Stupinigi was also viewed is not recorded.

From this point on, the account book provides a record of how they settled into an agreeable *modus vivendi* whilst in Italy. Mr Apperley and Captain Hamilton, when not accompanying Sir Watkin, made their own visits to places of architectural and archaeological interest during the day. At night, they must have accompanied the young baronet into 'society' and are rarely recorded as having gone out to plays or the opera by themselves. Sidebotham and Morris, sometimes joined by Antonio Carrara, went their separate way to the sights, but are frequently recorded going out to the theatre at night. The rest of the servants, whilst not on duty, were frequently sent off to see plays, although the more expensive opera was rationed. Sir Watkin's retinue was unnecessarily large and there may not have been sufficient things for them to do when they were not actually travelling. Their idle hours seemed to be occupied in learning Italian during the day and practising it at night. Only Sam Stevens, handyman and horse master, seems to have had his hands full, hiring coaches, horses, postilions and keeping the equipage in order. One is glad to note that in Rome (7 January) he actually managed to make time to attend the opera with the others.

The pro-British king of Sardinia, Carlo Emanuelle III, was residing in his summer palace of Venaria Reale[15] from where, on 5 September, eighteen days after arriving, the summons came and Sir Watkin went off to be presented to him. A suitable retinue of postillions was hired and that miniature, but infinitely more charming, version of Versailles was visited with suitable state. Although they had their own travelling coach, it must have been reckoned unsuitably dowdy as transport to Court and another equipage, presumably a more elegant one, was hired to make the short journey to Venaria. The king of France, being preoccupied with other things, had not been available for presentations and the king of Sardinia had to suffice for Sir Watkin's first *entrée* into European society. He seems not to have been impressed with the experience, although the time he spent at the Academy in Turin would have honed his social graces to an extent, which, in Britain, may have seemed excessive.

Venaria Reale was built as a hunting lodge, like most of the palaces which surround Turin, but it had slowly put out tentacles and spread into something quite extensive. Filippo Juvarra's spectacular gallery amply demonstrated the Piedmontese genius for interior design. Light filled, embroidered with stucco curlicues and painted white, off white, pale blue and the palest yellow, and with frescoed ceilings, it makes Versailles seem grossly overstated. Hopefully, it was in this glorious space that Sir Watkin was presented to its less than glorious monarch. Carlo Emmanuelle was the grandson of the martyred Charles I and upon the death of the remaining Stuart brothers in Rome, he became, in the eyes of any surviving Jacobites, the lawful king of Great Britain. His descendants, the dukes of Bavaria, hold that claim today.

The weather seems to have been hot and Sidebotham bought ice creams for himself and a fan for Sir Watkin. In summer, Turin can be very humid, sitting as it does on the banks of two rivers and encircled by mountain peaks, some of which they had recently crossed. Unfortunately, the heat seems to have had an ill effect upon Morris and Louis and they were both bled and the latter was prescribed 'Physic'. Louis seems to have been quite young and is always referred to by Sidebotham by his christian name. He bought a souvenir flag in Naples, but had the money he had paid for it refunded to him by Sir Watkin – an endearing gesture.

Turin had a great reputation as a place where the finishing touches could be put to a young gentleman's education in the refined arts and Sir Watkin's improving instruction continued. Some thought Turin society the most polite and refined in Europe, whilst others found it 'old and dull' (Gibbon).[16] Although Boswell arrived there in 1765 'with mingled sensations of awe and adulterous anticipation'[17] – the anticipations of which were satisfied. An academy, under royal patronage, existed in the city for the improvement of manners and gentlemanly conduct. It was to this establishment that Lord Chesterfield had committed his much put upon son – to absolutely no good effect whatsoever. As in Paris, Sir Watkin was not about to suffer alone and an abbé was engaged to teach the servants Italian and more grammars bought for them. Priests were usually employed to teach languages throughout the tour and encounters of the 'Catholic kind' were not avoided. Did anyone remember that the fifteen-year-old Jean Jacques Rousseau had abjured his Protestantism in Turin, if only temporarily? His re-admittance into Geneva depended upon his re-embrace of Calvinism, which he did with remarkable equanimity. Edward Gibbon did much the same at Oxford and was sent to Lausanne to rethink his new-found Catholicism. When he had re-thought and was re-embraced by the Protestant church, his father's threat of disinheritance was withdrawn.

Sir Watkin's 'improvement' must have been marked and he visited Venaria Reale twice more during his stay. Music lessons were at last started, a cello bought and an instructor hired to improve his technique.

Sept 5th	*I gave 2 postillions that went Veneri [Venaria Reale]*		
		3	*0*
	Pd the Coachmakers bill at Turin	*368*	*0*
	Pd for a Violincello at Turin	*480*	*0*
	Pd the Violincello Master	*48*	*0*
	Pd an Abbe for teaching the Serv Italian	*48*	*0*

Whilst Sir Watkin was being refined and improved, Sidebotham and his friends also began a course of self-improvement and seem to have begun to develop an obsession for the opera. Turin had a celebrated operatic establishment and the Teatro Reale was one of the great Italian centres for opera. Curiously, because of the theatre's royal status, there were halberdiers on each side of the stage throughout the performances, although whether they watched the King or ogled the dancers is a matter we can only speculate over.

Sir Watkin's time being completely spoken for, the servants were sent off to see plays, presumably at the still existing Teatro Carignano, and playing cards were bought to while away the time. More expensive clothes were bought at a cost of 849 livres and Sidebotham, who was a gentleman from north Wales, was becoming so assured in himself and his facility in Italian that he seems to have bribed the Secretary of State's servants to 'fast-track' his application for passports to Genoa. His assurance worked, and they left on the 6 September.

Genoa

No greater contrast could be imagined as that between Turin and Genoa. In the former, the architecture is bold and formal, but in Genoa, a vibrant port city with a medieval street plan, but with a spectacular collection of patrician palaces, it is light-hearted and almost frivolous. This republican city may have been responsible for implanting architectural ambition in Sir Watkin's heart.

Genoa was declining in international significance, but her ancient families still lived in great splendour, especially in the palaces of the Via Balbi. The decline of the republic was most seriously demonstrated in 1768 when, following the Treaty of Versailles, the Bank of St Giorgio admitted having sold Corsica, her last remaining colony, to the French on behalf of the government.

Genoa, unlike Turin, was coming to terms with the enlightenment, but only in as far as it did not relieve the ruling families of any of their powers. The Doge, Marcello Durazzo, had an outstanding collection of prints and drawings which his brother, Giacomo, ambassador to Vienna, presented to the newly-formed Albertina museum there in order that they might provide 'education and the power of morality rather than amusement and representation' - a rather chilling analysis of the power of beauty, especially from the city of Rubens and van Dyck.

The accounts for this leg of the tour are remarkably cursory. There is no indication of where they stayed, no accounting for food and drink and the only serious entry is for '12 Dozen of artificial flowers'. An ominous entry, however, is that which follows the artificial flowers 'Pd for a Messenger to a Violincello Player'; this is not a messenger to an instructor, it is to an instrumentalist. That entry, combined with one for the previous evening 'Pd for Music last night' suggest that Sir Watkin's soirées had begun and that he had started to hire musicians to play in the evening. That habit was to become an increasingly frequent aspect of the accounts and one which reached its apogée in Rome. One may presume that Sir Watkin was a very competent sight-reader and could, with minimum difficulty, play the music which he bought so often. Apart from time spent with his instructors, there seems to have been little other time left in which he could have practised the actual music as opposed to improving his technique. So, we may presume that he could play whatever was set before him and that, in joining in with professionals, he was quite able to hold his own. Musical summers at Wynnstay with musicians from the King's Theatre would seem to support that thesis.

The six days spent in Genoa are remarkably undocumented. As has been pointed out, there is neither indication of where they stayed, nor any payment for food or drink. There is, however, a possible explanation. The Genoese Republic had a novel practice of billeting important visitors in residences which passed muster (classification being decided by a committee) and these were inscribed upon a roll of honour. Known as the Palazzi dei Rolli, they were the most august of Genoa's palaces. Built to a reasonably common plan, with an atrium and double staircase to the main apartments, they all contained features which were present in the plans that Sir Watkin commissioned from James Byres in Rome, for the re-building of Wynnstay. Sir Watkin was looking at houses, which had been built by merchant families and the contrast between these glorious palaces, and his own rambling, partly Elizabethan, country mansion must have been painfully apparent.

The Prince Doria Pamphilji, whom Sir Watkin had possibly met the previous year when the prince visited London and stayed in Somerset House as a guest of the government, owned one of the largest of the Genoese palaces. The Palazzo dei Principe occupies an outstanding position with gardens once stretching to the harbour's edge (today to the motorway viaduct) and it was regularly used for housing visiting dignitaries. The guest book is extraordinarily distinguished and it may well be that this is where Sir Watkin and his party stayed. During his stay in Rome, he attended what we may presume was a rather grand popish ceremony when he was a guest at the christening of the Prince Doria Pamphilj's first born, at his palace on the Corso.

The coastline was explored a little and, on 10 September, the day before they parted for Milan, a *felucca* was hired to sail along the bay. After crossing the Channel this was only the second time at sea for most of them.

Genoa seems to have charmed Sir Watkin, although not all eighteenth-century visitors found the painted facades to their taste; some indeed found it all slightly ridiculous. Charles Abbot observed:

The painting of the outside of the houses at Genoa has certainly a very uncommon effect to an English eye. To see green, blue, and strawberry coloured walls, shocks at first sight, and with reason, as those colours resemble nothing that properly belongs to any known materials for the construction of building.

What I think must be universally condemned is the painting the outside of their finest palaces with columns, cornices and entablatures in imitation of real architecture.[18]

One may care to disagree with Abbot, certainly Sir Watkin did, and on a sunny autumn afternoon, when the city seems joyous and comfortable in its multi-coloured finery, one would have to be the dourest of men not to respond happily to it. Rubens' epithet of 'La Superba' is well-deserved. Architectural purists and their universal condemnation perhaps should stay well away and leave the city to those of a more levitatious disposition.

Milan

Sir Watkin's party arrived in Milan, by way of Pavia, on the 12th and lodged at the Three Kings. Sidebotham immediately contacted the bankers for a fresh supply of funds and Sir Watkin wrote to Chambre:

Milan, Sept 13th

We go on yet exceedingly well and happy but I own I had rather be in England than where I am. All this fuss of being presented first at one Court and then at Another does not please me much. We have seen several places very well worth seeing Particularly Genoa which I think is much the finest town I ever saw, but yet it has not the Charms of London.

We arrived here late yesterday evening after an exceedingly pleasant journey from Genoa. This is I believe a very fine place but we have seen nothing yet but what is to be seen from the window of our Auberge.

This evening we are to be presented to the Duke & Dss of Modena & all the principle [sic] people in the town. It is not very agreeable to me but we must go through it.

I am exceedingly glad to have by a letter from Jones that the new park wall is on at Wynnstay.

Although Sir Watkin was undertaking his Grand Tour to put a final gloss on his manners and education, he had not yet become acclimatised to the idea and purpose of travel, and his mind does not seem to have abandoned his parochial concerns. That slow transformation seems to have begun when they reached Florence. The park at Wynnstay is on the north bank of the river Dee and the wall, some ten feet high, was to encircle it from the river at Newbridge and back to the river at Erbistock. Some four miles in length, it was an enormous undertaking, but it enabled Sir Watkin to stock his ornamental grounds with deer and buffalo. He was already thinking on an extravagantly grand scale. It should also be admitted that a project so big would have provided considerable employment in the area. Sir Watkin's brand of Tory paternalism was to provide a degree of security for his tenants whilst he was actually in funds but he would gently bleed them when he was not.

After having been presented to the 'principle people' of Milan, although not to the duchess due to her unfortunate demise, he seems to have relaxed a little. Although Dr Burney's comment 'I am already tired of seeing the same faces and the same equipages, the Governor D of M's painted face and his insipid daughter's pale one' may give a hint as to the ossification of part of the society of the principal people. But Sir Watkin was taken under the wing of the Anglophile Count Anton Firmian, the governor general of the duchy. A man of singular enlightenment and deputy for the Duke of Modena, the count was a great collector of antiquities and prints and his collection of the latter was, upon his death, bought for the Royal Collections of Naples. It was he who initiated the building of the Teatro alla Scala and gave the young Mozart his first operatic commission (Mithridate Re di Ponto). He seemed to take quite an interest in the young tourist and they went off together to visit lakes Como and Maggiore and to visit the remains of Pliny's villa (26 & 27 September). A pleasant enough excursion in itself, the trip to the lakes was often made by the resident Milanese to enjoy the cooler air close to the Swiss mountains. They were also in the company of a mysterious Count Fideli, who may, or may not, have been the marquess of Kildare. The marquess described the excursion in a letter to his mother, the duchess of Leinster and records that through the kindness of Count Firmian they were enabled to stay on the Borromean Islands.[19] Unfortunately Isola Bella did not meet the marquess' approval. He 'expected to have seen the works of nature; instead of it we found the worst of art.' The marquess later became Grand Master of the Grand Lodge of Ireland and Mr Sidebotham's referring to him as Count Fidelis may well have been a private Masonic joke; *Semper Fidelis* being a common Masonic tag. Sir Watkin established a Masonic Lodge at Wynnstay in later years and gave furniture to the Oswestry Lodge. Count Firmian was most likely a Freemason; his closest friends were recorded as such, although he must have remained discrete in that matter as his uncle was the relentlessly zealous Archbishop of Salzburg.

Although Captain Hamilton had seen the Charterhouse at Pavia as the party made its way to Milan, Sidebotham and Morris took the excuse of a day off and hired a chaise and postillions to see that monumentally splendid building for themselves. It is a recurring feature of the account that the Captain took side excursions of his own and then presented the bill for payment by Sidebotham several days later. It had happened in Paris when Hamilton went to Versailles by himself and also in Turin and Genoa. The exact nature of his contract is uncertain, but he was paid £1,000 for his time accompanying the expedition and yet seems to have taken himself off at the slightest excuse, sometimes it may be admitted, accompanied by Apperley, but more often alone. Perhaps he found the company tiresome or felt that they were not in any physical danger which would have required his intervention.

Milan, in the eighteenth century was a violent, scurrying kind of place. Already established as a centre of fashion and tailoring, it seems to be the only place where Sir Watkin did not improve his wardrobe. The art collections were already famous, but they seem to have been ignored in favour of jaunts out into the countryside.

The weather may have been hot. In Turin, Sidebotham had bought his first ice cream; in Milan, he paid for an entire week's supply. The humidity, which they may have experienced in Turin, was nothing to the heavy mugginess which enveloped Milan in the summer. The city sits on a damp plain and can be quite intolerable at times.

They did the usual tourist things whilst there – climbed onto the roof of the Duomo, went to the opera (already of exceptional merit), saw various palaces and seemed to do an awful lot of sightseeing in the close environs.

On the 29th, the bill at the Three Kings was settled and, loaded in the newly-repaired coach once more, they made their way to Bologna by way of Piacenza, Parma and Modena.

Bologna

The roads in the valley of the Po were seriously awful. The sub-soil is sandy and damp, and tracks quickly became rutted, flooded and verging upon the impassable. Coaches were frequently overturned and damaged and, outside of the towns, there was no serious accommodation to be had. The gates of most towns were firmly locked at night and late entry was absolutely refused. Considering that the route from Milan to Piacenza, Parma, Reggio Emilia, Modena and Bologna was one of Italy's main highways, its condition was shocking. Our tourists may have been forewarned by Antonio Carrara and they seem to have hit upon a solution. From Milan to Bologna is a distance of about 125 miles (201 kilometres) and, according to the account book, they paid their final bill in Milan on 29 September and their first bill in Bologna on 1 October. They must have travelled by both day and night to have made the journey in that exceptionally short time. Another consideration would be that, in the cool of a moonlit night, they could probably travel a great deal faster. However they did it, they must have been exhausted.

Entering Bologna on 1 October, they were left in no doubt as to whose territories they were in. The Porta Galliera, one of the main gates, is positively festooned with Papal insignia. This northerly outpost of the Papal States had been where the Stuarts had first resided in Italy and the family of one of Sir Watkin's bankers, the Marquis Belloni, had sub-let their Bolognese palazzo to the Old Pretender. Sir Watkin's father, the 'Great Sir Watkin' had notoriously Jacobite sympathies and north Wales was still a seat of aristocratic nostalgia for the dispossessed 'King over the Water' and the Circle of the White Rose, which took its lead from Wynnstay, still existed though, to be frank, it had largely degenerated into a gentlemen's drinking club rather than a hotbed of revolutionary idealism. Sir Watkin, however, needed to exercise caution. King George III had a wary eye open and there were informers everywhere. Perhaps Bologna was a good place to practise blameless behaviour before reaching Rome itself.

At Bologna, they stayed in the Pellegrino – the best inn in town,[20] good enough for the King of Naples to have stayed there in 1782, much to the chagrin of Mrs Piozzi who was denied entry and had to settle for an inferior hotel. The Pellegrino was on the Via Venturini 86, now the Via Ugo Bassi and opposite to the Palazzo Communale, Palazzo di Re Enzo and the main square of that comfortable city. Its centrality was also its misfortune and it was comprehensively bombed in 1943. The site is now a modern shopping complex.

An event of great significance occurred on 6 October – Sir Watkin bought his first painting. Although the account details the cost, it records neither the artist nor the subject matter. Perhaps Sidebotham saw it as just another piece of baggage which he would have to cope with. Generally, he only noted the names of modern artists - that of Titian being the only exception in the entire account.

Messrs Sidebotham and Morris and the other servants were ostensibly accompanying Sir Watkin whilst he made his Grand Tour. However, an interesting sub-text would be the thoughts and experiences of the employees whilst they also made their Grand Tour. There is no particular reason to suspect that Sidebotham was artistic or musical, much less the other servants. But we can see through the misty narrative presented by the account book and surmise that they were all making the best of the opportunities on offer. Sidebotham's Italian spelling improved throughout the journey and he became a keen opera goer – as did his friends, the servants attend plays – immensely boring if they had no understanding of the language, and visits to architectural marvels increase. Too little has been noted of the effect a tour such as this one, could have had upon people unused to this degree of international sophistication. The servants from Wynnstay were, after all, drawn from the local community and were probably overwhelmed by their first glimpse of London. To become familiar with Paris, Turin, Genoa, Milan, Bologna, Florence, Rome, Naples and Venice, the delights of the opera and the wit of the playhouse could have turned their heads by the time they returned to Ruabon. Sir Watkin seems to have had an enlightened attitude to those who served him and displayed a liberal attitude in everything but his politics. In any case, his politics seem hopelessly confused and his support for the Tory party merely nominal. Support for the landed interest and support for the Tories, were not always two faces of the same coin. His concern for the physical and intellectual well-being of his staff cost him a great deal of money and he seems to have thought it incumbent upon himself to allow them to share some of his experiences. In spite of an English education, he seems to have retained a quite unstuffy and very Welsh sentiment towards those who served him. One must imagine that, several years later, there were employees on the Wynnstay estate, who could have spoken better French and Italian and have seen more great works of art than some of the 'educated' visitors to the great house. Educating the servants was not regarded as a wise thing to undertake – revolutions lie that way – but Sir Watkin, who died in 1789, appears to have thought differently.

Just to the south of the city is the hill upon which San Michele in Bosco is situated and we might assume that the party climbed it for the particularly splendid view of the city it affords. When they reached Venice, Sir Watkin bought a book of prints of the views and one can but wonder what he thought, on a cold wet winter at Wynnstay, staring at a book of black and white prints, whether it reminded him of the glorious autumnal light bathing Bologna in its gentle glow or whether it was just a sad reminder of a country he was never to see again.

In Bologna Sir Watkin's instincts as a collector began to emerge and he bought more prints, in addition to the previously noted picture, but culture did not reign supreme and one must regrettably record their attendance at a bullfight on 9 October. Morris, who seems to have been in poor health, recovered and the not inconsiderable bill for his restoration was paid.

Sir Watkin seems to have been an admirer of Guercino (G. P. Barbieri) and they made a brief excursion to Cento (7 October), his birthplace and where some of his works were still exhibited. Later in life, he acquired some drawings by him (perhaps auctioned at Sotheby's in 1947). His taste was beginning to take form and he even seems to have overcome his slightly schoolboyish aversion to being presented to the local bigwigs judging by his behaviour on the next stage of the journey to Florence.

They left Bologna on the 10th, after paying the bill at the Pellegrino, and arranged to have a masquerade costume forwarded from Milan although as to where it came from and why it had been left in Milan, we are given no clue. Sir Watkin seemed to be spreading his wings and in the next stage of his journey was to begin to emerge as a connoisseur and gentleman of note.

Florence

The journey from Bologna to Florence was generally reckoned to be the worst leg of the Grand Tour, apart from the crossing over Mount Cenis, and it took Sir Watkin's party two days to reach that city and they must have stayed en route at one of the notoriously squalid hotels on the Apennine pass. Only the inn at Mashere gained general approbation; the rest were little better than hovels with bad food, but which at least taught the tourist the wisdom of bringing his own sheets – usually of leather – to discourage the bugs. Overcharging was rife and banditry widespread. Captain Hamilton had become a necessity and the wisdom of including him in the party became apparent. On 12 October, when they reached Florence, Sidebotham had once again to record his inability to reconcile the arithmetic in his accounts but, by their arrival in Florence, he was dealing with his seventh monetary system and his problems were understandable and, in some cases, seem to have been caused by downright fraud.

In Florence, Sir Watkin was to mingle with a company of men who may have been socially elevated, but were not entirely respectable. Garlanded with titles they may have been, immensely rich they may also have been, but for each of them there was a certain associated vice which was not mentioned in polite company and, although one hesitates to mention it now, the English were always disinclined to accept human nature unless, of course, it accorded with their own. Seymour Conway, Horace Walpole's cousin, on quitting Florence in 1752, wrote 'there are but two things at all thought of here – love and antiquities, of which the former predominates'.[21]

Horace Mann, the British Consul in Florence, and the planet around which the others revolved, was described by some of his contemporaries as 'a finicky little man', whilst others described him as 'amphibious', an eighteenth-century code word loaded with meaning. It was widely rumoured that he had been on terms of extreme intimacy with Horace Walpole himself several years earlier, before they began their deliciously scurrilous correspondence together. His then current confidant was Thomas Patch, the painter, who, exiled from Rome by the

Holy Inquisition for making too free with Roman youth, found Florence entirely to his taste. Another associate, the Earl Tylney, a very rich Irish nobleman, had wisely departed Albion's shores after having been caught in a compromising position between two footmen and had been caricatured as Lord Strutwell by Tobias Smollet in 'Roderick Random', was in permanent residence. Then there was Earl Cowper, possessor of a pretty young wife and an immense fortune, both of which he seemed happy to lend to Grand Duke Leopold, to the entire satisfaction of all three; thus relieving the noble earl of marital duties, which may not have been to his entire taste, and relieving the Grand Duke of the necessity of finding a respectable mistress. On the earl's death, his family unwisely tried to sue a journalist for suggesting that he may not have been as other men. The case was withdrawn!

Zoffany's famous painting of the Tribuna in the Uffizi shows, amongst the many British visitors, the Earl Cowper, Sir Horace and Thomas Patch. The latter seems to be effusing over the luscious contours of the Venus of Urbino, although it has been unkindly observed that he is also pointing to other contours more to his taste (the buttocks of some distant wrestlers). Unfortunately, the Earl Tylney was excluded from Queen Charlotte's commission, wisely in view of the fact that the very prim queen was decidedly not amused by the inclusion of Patch and failed to appreciate the utter brilliance of Zoffany's canvas. The inclusion of Tylney, whilst delightfully bold, would have nailed far too many colours to the mast.

In Florence, that which was unmentionable elsewhere was virtually institutionalised, following the example of the last of the Medici, the Grand Duke Gian Gastone and his infinitely wicked boys, the Ruspanti;[22] and there were lots of British tourists visiting the institutions of Florence.

Sir Watkin now began to fulfil his proper role in society.

With the political influence of Walpole, the now Sir Horace was made a Knight of the Bath and, during his investiture at the Grand Ducal Court, was escorted by most of the gentlemen of distinction resident in Florence at that moment. The *Gazzetta Toscana*[23] records the presence of Sir Watkin, Mr Apperley and Captain Hamilton at the Pitti Palace for the investiture. Most of the witnesses to the ceremony were men of considerable means and although Sir Watkin was by no means poor, he was playing his part as an equal to the duke of Devonshire when, in fact, neither his title nor his income were equal to the duke's. Sir Horace wrote to Walpole ...

The Duke of Devonshire will condescend to thither; Earl Cowper, Earl Tylney, Lord Algernon Percy, Lord Fortrose, Sir Watkin W. Wynne, Sir Gregory Turner, and at least thirty more English gentlemen all as fine as the richest Peers accompany me.[24]

The company, recorded in strict order of precedence, extended the festivities for Sir Horace's elevation. The Earl Cowper, a fervent admirer of Handel, as was Sir Watkin, gave a performance of *Alexander's Feast* at his country villa and allowed our young baronet to share in the costs. Galvanised into action by this splendid gesture, Sir Watkin responded.

Sir Horace wrote further,

Florence, October 25th

The Ceremony was performed by the Great Duke on fryday last with all the marks of respect on his part for the King, whom he then represented, and with all the decency, nay, show, that we (I mean myself and a numerous body of English, many of whom of the highest rank) could exhibit on this occasion. The Gazette will inform you of the particular circumstances, which would even if I had time to repeat, but you must still excuse my Vanity, which has guided me in all this, and which indeed I have not attempted to conceal, if I add that the whole town has expressed a satisfaction on this occasion that has flattered that Vanity extremely, and that the English have done everything they could to show their respect to the King, by honouring his Minister on this occasion.

Next day, Sunday, Lord Tylney gave a dinner still bigger, the best and most magnificent I ever saw, and so said those of the Court who were there; he dressed all his upper servants in new laced cloaks. The Desert was very fine built on the occasion, and charged with the Ensigns of the Order, with Trophies and Emblems which Lord Tylney's good nature induced him to place there. Yesterday many of us dined at Court, and in the evening Lord Cowper had Alexander's Feast, by Handel, performed at his villa, about a mile from the town, and it was followed by a Ball.

To-day, Sir W. Wm' Wynne gives a great dinner at a country house belonging to the master of the Inn where he lodges (as ladies could not go to this latter), which is to be followed by a great concert of Musick and a Ball in the evening. This great compliment is the more extraordinary, as I had not the honour to know Sir Watkin till a few days ago; and I must add too my obligations to the Duke of Devonshire on this occasion, for having stayed many days longer here than he intended, to assist at this Ceremony, and to honour me by his presence at it.

Sir Horace was an appalling snob and he must have purred with delight at the recital of ancient titles present at his elevation into the lower ranks of the society he most wanted to be a part of.

Charles Hadfield, a Mancunian from a comfortable background, owned, as well as two hotels in the city, a country villa (Palazzo Bruciato) a short distance from the city walls. Sir Watkin hired the villa and gave a great dinner, concert and ball at the enormous cost of 8,617 *Paoli's*. His first grand gesture, but one which was to be repeated in various forms over the coming months.

> *Oct 26. Pd Mr Hadfield the Expenses of the Dinner, Concert &*
> *Ball given at his Country House by Sr Watkin yester Day as*
> *of accompt where In is included the Music & Singers.*   *8617. 4 [paoli]*

Had Sir Watkin known it at the time, Hadfield's daughter, Maria, having survived the lunatic ministrations of an imbalanced nursemaid, was to mature into Maria Cosway, the miniaturist, and was already beginning to show evidence of her great gifts.

Politics were beginning to creep into the accounts. On behalf of Boswell's appeal for the Corsican patriots, especially General Paoli, who were resisting French rule, Lord Fortrose was collecting funds for the cause. The previously noted sale of Corsica by the Genoese to the French had shocked liberal Europe and support for the insurgent islanders had become a cause célèbre. The *London Chronicle* reported that 'Three Englishmen at Florence – the Duke of Devonshire, Lord Algernon Percy and Sir Watkin Williams Wynn – are credited with £200 apiece and other Englishmen in Florence with £900'.

The accounts record Sir Watkin's contribution as being 200 Roman Sequins and we may notice that he was putting himself upon a level with the Duke of Devonshire and Lord Algernon who was the Duke of Northumberland's son and the Northumberlands were probably richer than the Devonshires. Apperley's guardianship seems to have been elsewhere!

The three weeks they spent in Florence appear to have marked an important turning point in Sir Watkin's development. His first tentative purchase of a painting in Bologna was to be as nothing compared to the acquisitions gathered in Florence. Books of prints and fine printed books, vases, marble knick-knacks, inlaid tables, mosaic work, an order placed for two tables with Florentine marble work tops from Lamberto Gori, more fine tailoring and a caricature portrait by the infamous Mr Patch (Sir Watkin, Mr Apperley, Captain Hamilton and Antonio Carrara) all appear in the accounts. Page 53 of the account book is a dreadful indication of things to come.

> *1769 (page 53)*
> *Books, Prints, Vauses etc etc at Florence*
> *Oct 15   Pd for Views of Florence & sundry counttry Palaces*
> *   bound in 2 Volls*   *117 0*

20	*Pd for 2 Books of Prints*	165	0
22	*Pd for 2 small Florentine work figures on Marble*		
	a Woman & a Turk	195	0
	Pd for 10 Vol of the Florentine Gallery &		
	Binding as of Bill	867	0
26	*Pd for Giustany's Gallery 16 Roman Sequins*	312	0
	Pd for a Virgil	19	4
	Pd for a copy of Tasso	156	
	Pd Mr Harwood of Florence for Vauses &		
	12 pieces of Marble made like Books as of Bill	1040	
	Pd in part of payment for a chequer Table of		
	all sorts of Marble valued at	205	
		600	
	Pd Lamberto Gori of Florence in part for 2 Sceoli		
	[scagliola] Tables that he is to make in 7 months	994	4

Music lessons started again with twelve lessons from Mr Piantanida and his son and a cello hired for the purpose. Piantanida was a distinguished 'cellist who had had connections with Handel in London; a connection Sir Watkin must have been aware of. He was sufficiently distinguished to be admitted into the ranks of the famous musical academy of Bologna in the same ceremony as the young Mozart. His fees were probably of an elevated order as well.

During Sir Watkin's junketings at the Mann festivities, the servants were sent off to the Playhouse – obviously their Italian lessons were beginning to have an effect. Sidebotham proved himself as voracious a sightseer as ever before and whether from the effects of heat or rain, another umbrella was purchased.

In all, over £600 was spent in the city. Sir Watkin picked up a travelling companion in the person of the fifth Duke of Devonshire, a gentleman only a year older than himself and shortly to become married to Georgiana Spencer. He also began to establish a name for himself as a connoisseur and gentleman of substance and also, regrettably, as a man with an open and deep purse.

On the 27th they set off once more. Unusually they did not take the direct route to Rome via Arezzo and Orvieto but chose to take the more indirect route through Lucca, Pisa, Leghorn (Livorno) and Siena. Perhaps Carrara, with his knowledge of the Grand Tour, was advising them of the more interesting, scenic and inform-ative routes, although the accommodation available on the stage between Siena and Rome was almost as dismally filthy as that crossing the Apennines from Bologna to Florence. The post-house at Radicofani, although built by the Grand Duke Cosimo, seemed designed to deter the tourist from venturing further and most tourists found, to their absolute horror, that there was no alternative but to stay there. Many a tourist noted the complete absence of both doors and windows in the establishment and, more importantly, the lack of any means of heating. However, if the route was of Carrara's choosing, he gave the right advice and Sir Watkin, unlike a lot of his contemporaries, seems to have admired the scenery they passed through.

Rome

Six months to the day from leaving London, their destination was reached and on 2 November, they entered Rome through the Porta del' Popolo. Staying at the 'Hotel Ville de Londres', Sig Rolland's famous establishment on the Piazza di Spagna, they were in the centre of the English colony. The hotel was a favourite with British visitors and the charms of the landlord's daughter, the delightful Teresa, seem to have been enjoyed by Casanova several years earlier, although she sensibly married his brother. The servants lodged with *Signor* Benedetto who lived close by and who seems to have been bereft of delightful daughters.

Opposite the hotel was the celebrated Caffe degli Inglesi, the social hub of the British, although Thomas Jones,[24] visiting a few years later, loathed the place. Attendance there by visiting artists was an absolute necessity if they hoped for commissions from the wealthy tourist. Richard Wilson was a frequent habitué during his time in Rome. Piranesi had decorated the café inside in such an advanced taste that it resembled an Egyptian Mausoleum. He resided in great splendour in the Via Sistina, at the top of the Scala di Spagna, whilst at the bottom, in Via Bocca di Leone, Pompeo Batoni lived no less immodestly. Our tourists were in the very heart of things; an area so colonised by people similar to themselves that it was known either as the 'English Ghetto' or as 'Little Westminster' and is still Rome's artistic quarter.

Ancient Rome has been estimated to have had about a million people living within the area defined by the still existing Aurelian walls. The population of eighteenth-century Rome had dwindled to some 100,000 and within those walls, farms and pasture co-existed with the ruins of its past Imperial grandeur. The ancient Forum was generally known as the Campo Vaccino because it was indeed a field where cows grazed. No visitor could have been unaware of the example, which the city displayed, of the transitory nature of human ambition. Deeply layered, with wave after wave of conquering tribes or changing cultures, the city was one of the most fascinating in the world. The collapse of the Western Empire, when the seat of Imperial rule was transferred to Byzantium, which endured a thousand years of ensuing theological squabbles and oriental conspiracies, had left the ancient capital bereft of the means to support itself. Squatting in the ruins was the new power. The Church of Rome, embryonic during the years of empire, was given hegemony over the decaying city by the disinterested Eastern Empire. Earthly ambition combined with spiritual energy began to resurrect the ancient glories. From a population of some 30,000 in the sixth century, the city began its slow recovery. The bishops of Rome began to occupy the space once reserved for emperors and the Byzantines, realising their mistake, gave up and abandoned the West to itself.

The ascent of the Roman Church is hardly a matter to be discussed in detail here, but the results of that ascent became manifest in the attempts by the newly-named Papacy, to beautify their city and restore to it some of its old glory. Thence lies the cause of the Reformation. More layers and more problems of objectivity. The determined efforts of the late Renaissance Popes to answer theological argument, not by counter-argument, but by an unanswerable argument in the form of beauty in the service of the Church was what had created the face of the city with which the grand tourist was presented and it was a compelling argument. It was also a very seductive one and the early eighteenth-century tourist needed to be resolute, despise the Catholic baroque and reject the blandishments of the proselytising Church. By the late eighteenth century, though, the Church had lost its vigour and had largely given up proselytising. It was exhausted by its squabbles with France and Spain and the matter of the Jesuit Order. It had tried to institute social justice in South America, but was frustrated at every turn and had attracted the enmity of well-placed politicians. To most European Catholic governments, the Church was all very well, as long as it knew how to remain in its place. To be the Pope in eighteenth-century Rome was more of a predicament than a position. With its layers of history, meaning, politics, sensitivities and occasional intransigencies, Rome was not to be taken lightly and help was needed to negotiate the rocks and whirlpools of its past, both ancient and modern.

Immediate steps were taken (presumably by Apperley) to engage the services of a guide and James Byres, the most eminent, and expensive of them, accepted the post. We shall meet Byres throughout this Roman period and his fellow antiquarian, Thomas Jenkins, a friend of Richard Wilson, as well as a number of the dealers, artists and musicians who thronged Rome hoping to find a patron, sell antiquities, and generally lease out their services. Sir Watkin and the Duke of Devonshire, with whom he shared some of the expenses, were rich targets indeed.

Some young tourists visited the ruins merely because it was expected of them and frequently annoyed their guides by affecting an attitude of bored indifference; probably the same indifference they had shown at Eton or Harrow in their classics lessons. Sir Watkin may have been enthused by Thomas Apperley's enthusiasm, but what either of them made of the duke of Devonshire's studied lack of anything even approaching enthusiasm, except when it came to dogs, is an interesting speculation. Sir Watkin had all too many enthusiasms and his difficulty was in keeping them all in focus and proportionate.

A guide was certainly needed to untangle the multi-layered debris which comprised eighteenth-century Rome. The modern visitor sees a European capital with its wide avenues, its tidied-up archaeological parks and its buzzing commercial life but all of this is a creation of the nineteenth-century kingdom of Italy and after Papal rule had withered and died. In some parts of the city today, especially around the Campo dei Fiori, a hint of what the eighteenth-century visitor encountered may be glimpsed. Here are dwellings carved out of the remains of the Imperial city; narrow streets, which unexpectedly can be lined with a row of Corinthian columns, built into the facade of a medieval house; curved lanes following the outline of an ancient theatre and a settecento palazzo with vaulted roman cellars. The sense of standing upon merely the latest layer of history is quite palpable and an expert was needed to explain, to clarify and to interpret those points of interest which the intelligent visitor would wish to examine. The heat and noise of the city, redolent with unfamiliar fruits, with unwashed roads and piazzas, the overpowering smell of horse dung and the relentless rattle of iron-shod wheels over cobbled streets were the distracting background to intellectual improvement. White silk stockings must have been the most impractical piece of apparel ever devised. One can hardly be surprised that so many young men gave up completely, languished in their hotels during the heat of the day and only emerged when the sun had gone down – and then, only to get drunk again.

Horace Walpole, writing to Horace Man in 1743, noted the following of the Society of Dilettanti, of which Sir Watkin was to become President in 1777:

> ... the Dilettanti, a club, for which the nominal qualification is having been in Italy, and the real one, being drunk: the two chiefs are Lord Middlesex and Sir Francis Dashwood, who were seldom sober the whole time they were in Italy.[25]

Walpole's acid may have been deserved at the time, but it must, in fairness, be recorded that the Society later undertook pioneering work in causing the antiquities of Greece to be measured and published and thus providing invaluable architectural sourcebooks.

Sir Watkin seems to have been taking his tour seriously even though there were other distractions to trouble him. On 5 November, he wrote to Mr Chambre once more and betrayed a worrying degree of preoccupation with things back home, although he seems to be slightly more reconciled to the idea of completing the tour.

Rome, Nov 5th, 1768

Dear Mr Chambre,

Yesterday I received a letter from you dated the 4th of last month which indeed gave me very great satisfaction & pleasure. I am very glad to find everything is so forward & so likely to be completed by the time that I return to Old England

We arrived at this place so famed of old last Wednesday by dinner.

After a very pleasant journey from Florence by Piza, Leghorn, Sienna etc which took up very near a week. In the journey we travelled over a vast deal of very fine Country, but yet the (more) of this Country, I owe, the time I prefer my country. Ours, I sincerely believe take it all in all is the first Country in the world. We have seen very little here yet.

Tomorrow we begin with our Antiquarians, to see everything that this City I believe is so justly famous for. I have seen St Peters which is indeed a very Wonderful Building it Astonished me though I had heard immense praises of it, it very far excelled what I expected though my ideas were indeed immense. Certainly there must be a great many things here that must give me a great deal of pleasure, or satisfaction but for all that I should be very glad if my time to return to England was so much nearer than it is ...

By this time you must know by a letter sent by Sam Sidebotham to my Mother that it is not improbable I should be in Wales next year. The Sooner Pritchard begins to repair & beautify the Chancel of Rhuabon Church the better ...

I am Dear Sir Your (?) and very much Obbg

Servt Wat Wms Wynn

I have not received Mr Adams Plans but if they are not sent out they had better wait for me til I return to Old England again.

We can perhaps detect in this letter some of the cultural confusion which existed in Sir Watkin's estimation of himself. Although English was a generic term for anything British, especially in Italy, he seems to have entertained a romantic notion of Old England which was perhaps implanted during his time at Westminster School. By 'My Country' he certainly means England and not Wales. Mr Chambre was perhaps responsible for the engagement of the Shrewsbury architect, Thomas Farnolls Pritchard, to improve Ruabon church and add a Great Room to Wynnstay for forthcoming celebrations but Sir Watkin obviously had his ambitions set much higher than using a provincial architect to rebuild Wynnstay. Only Robert Adam would do for that, although, even here, a slight ambivalence may be sensed by his decision to commission another set of designs from James Byres. Here we have a young man being assailed by new sensations and experiences and being so overwhelmed by them that he was incapable of making up his mind about anything for the moment.

Modern, that is baroque, Rome must have thoroughly amazed our tourists and a northern protestant youth with any sensibility was utterly defenceless against this city. The Whore of Babylon, Perversion of the Ages, the Scarlet Woman were the long remembered phrases from his youth but all of his prejudices were disarmed the moment he entered through the Porto del' Popolo. Life in Rome was vibrant in spite of clerical injunctures. There were a couple of public theatres but most entertainment was to be had in the private theatres which belonged to the leading families. However, the Spanish Steps were the best theatre in the world; street life, a constant entertainment and Papal ceremonies an endless source of amusement. Rome itself was a theatre. This was modern Rome and it was glorious. The matter of kissing the Pope's toe was gracefully avoided. Clement XIII, an entirely rational man, was much happier shaking hands with his northern visitors. Precautions against too much foreignness were taken at *Signor* Rolland's hotel in an area populated by compatriots. The Spanish Steps, then as now, were the chosen promenade for those who wished to be noticed and cut *'una bella figura'* and assignations were made and carried out among the general bustle of the area. Artists, guides, purveyors of tourist junk, boring pedants prattling on about ancient Rome and their bored charges eyeing the pretty girls, elderly gentlemen re-acquainting themselves with schoolroom classics and Edward Gibbon gathering materials for his *Decline and Fall* and who, incidentally, was worn into the ground by Byres who treated him to an intensive eighteen-week tour of the sites of antiquity. The steps and the piazza were the drawing room of the British tourist.

Habits acquired in Florence were continued in Rome and, two days after arriving, the first bundle of drawings was purchased. The cost was 50 *paoli* but, as usual, Sidebotham does not give us the slightest clue as to what the bundle contained. Were they antique or were they modern? Were they the drawings contained in the portfolio auctioned at Sotheby's in 1947 – we can only speculate? But, ancient Rome awaited and led by the indefatigable Byres, Sir Watkin, and probably the duke of Devonshire, began their trek through those bits of ancient Rome which modern Rome was doing its very best to sell off.

The Forum and the Coliseum were still an uncleared mass of rubble and the latter was known as a gathering place for ladies with an adjustable sense of virtue. It was a very popular stop on the tourist itinerary. Its ruins were rumoured to conceal other, less innocent activities. It was common knowledge, although exclusively Roman, that Thomas Jenkins, unofficial British consul in the city and reputed to be a government spy, had a secret workshop concealed within the vaults and passages of the building where new antiquities were manufactured for the unsuspecting, but rich, visiting aristocrats. Let us hope that the ones which Sir Watkin bought off him, and which he loaned to Josiah Wedgwood to copy in jasperware, had the substance as well as the aura of antiquity about them – '1769. Jan. 7th. Pd Mr Jenkins for 8 Pictures 2 marble statues & an intaglio as of acct.'

Nollekens, the sculptor, and by all accounts an extremely unpleasant man, who later made the monument to Sir Watkin's first wife, was recounted by J.T. Smith to have given the game away somewhat.

> ... he [Jenkins] followed the trade of supplying the foreign visitors with Intaglios and Cameos made up by his own people, that he kept in a part of the ruins of the Coliseum, fitted up for 'em to work in slyly by themselves. I saw 'em at work though, and Jenkins gave a whole handful of 'em to me to say nothing about the matter to any body else but myself. Bless your heart! He sold 'em as fast as they made 'em.[27]

Excursions were made out from the city. On the 15th, again in the company of the Duke of Devonshire, they went to Tivoli, guided by the ever-ready and expensive Byres, and presumably visited the Villa d'Este, the cascades, the Temple of the Sibyl and Hadrian's Villa. Most visitors to Rome made an excursion to Tivoli. Partly, one suspects, to escape the heat and squalor of the city. Here fountains cooled the cleaner mountain air and Devonshire must have been reminded of the not inconsiderable waterworks back home at Chatsworth, although his father had done his best to destroy the baroque cascades and fountains in the gardens. The Villa d'Este had fallen on hard times, but sufficient remained to impress. The Temples of Vesta and of the Sybil – they were given various names and none entirely accurate – clinging to the cliff edge above the tumultuous cascades, were probably one of the most painted views in Lazio and Sir Watkin's cousin, Richard Wilson, positively churned them out. Sir Watkin had probably seen some of them in Wilson's studio in Covent Garden and, curiously, when Wilson went to north Wales to paint some views around Wynnstay in 1770, he converted an unfinished canvas of Tivoli into a view of Castell Dinas Brân above Llangollen.[28] Welsh antiquity bathed in Mediterranean light. Outside the town, the vast remains of Hadrian's Villa had long been a source of antique statuary and at that very moment, Gavin Hamilton and Thomas Jenkins were beginning to systematically despoil the site. There is hardly a country house in Britain which does not possess its forlorn lump of marble claiming to have come from Hadrian's Villa. Exporting sculpture on an almost industrial scale, mostly to England and mostly to enrich the collections of men such as Devonshire, Hamilton and Jenkins were adroit evaders of papal injunctions against the practice. Hamilton eventually obtained a Papal licence to justify his excavations. In 1798, the French occupation of Rome caused Jenkins to flee, abandoning all of his property except his gems and medals. He died, penniless, shortly after his arrival in England. Byres, with greater foresight, abandoned the city earlier and retired to his family estate at Tonley near Aberdeen and enjoyed a comfortable retirement there.

On 19 November, an intriguing entry was made in the ledger – 'Nov 19. I gave the Countess of [...] by Sir Watkins order 102 [Paoli]'. Who was this mysterious, anonymous aristocrat and what had she done for Sir Watkin to earn such a generous imbursement. Sidebotham was particularly careful to name recipients of cash, but here discretion won over and the name remained blank. We may only speculate. The next day, and possibly connected with the last event, Sir Watkin attended a 'Grand Christining' [sic] at Prince Doria Pamphilj's very grand palazzo. Given the social status of the Prince Doria Pamphilj in Rome (the family was under the personal protection of the Pope) and the likelihood that this was the christening of his firstborn, Sir Watkin must have been attending a grand papal ceremony. A stone's throw away from the Palazzo Doria Pamphilj, on the other side of the Corso, the Palazzo Muti-Balestra still housed the remains of the mouldering Stuarts, particularly that member of the family recognised by the disaffected as King Charles III, and it was perhaps a little unwise to fly too close to that particular candle, especially in view of Sir Watkin's father's political leanings. Several days later, and once more with Devonshire, they made a four-day excursion to Frascati and Albano. The towns in the Alban Hills were frequently resorted to because of their delightful situation and the area is dotted with country villas (ancient and modern), small palaces and classical remains. The names of Castel Gandolfo, Ariccia, Lake Nemi, Tusculum and Genzano figure frequently in catalogues of Wilson's paintings and having seen the canvases perhaps Sir Watkin wanted to see the reality. Hopefully, though, not to see the Bishop of Frascati, the Cardinal Duke of York and who, upon the death of his brother, was to be declared by some to be Henry IX of England. The Abbé Grant, Rector of the Scots' College and notorious proselytizer, figures in the accounts doing some minor purchases for Sir Watkin but one may presume that Thomas Jenkins was keeping a watchful eye open. Jenkins may have been thought a secret British spy but, on the other hand, James Byres, a dyed-in-the-wool Jacobite, balanced the situation.

Earlier in the century, Rome had been a hotbed of spies. The Stuarts had still represented a threat to the political stability of Great Britain and the Vatican had recognised the Old Pretender as the legitimate James III. Things had, however, changed. Charles III, (formerly known as Bonnie Prince Charlie but alcohol and dissipation had taken its toll) unrecognised as such by the Papacy, was only received at the Quirinal Palace as the Count of Albany. The Pope, Clement XIII, valued a peaceful existence and stressed as he was by the increasingly intemperate attacks upon the Jesuits by France, Portugal and Spain, certainly did not wish to be drawn into a fight in which he had no interest. Kindly, affable and modest (it was he who had Wincklemann affix bronze fig leaves to the statuary in the Vatican Collections) and by nature pro-British, he was well able to see a lost cause. He could not have been unaware of the fact that his own librarian, Cardinal Alessandro Albani, had acted as a spy for Walpole's administration and was in regular corres-pondence with Sir Horace Mann in Florence. Albani was particularly accommo-dating to British visitors and took care that the modern papacy, exemplified by Clement, should show its civilised, gracious and intelligent face to them. Anti French and anti-Stuart, he smoothed the way for many a tourist. Some suspected that he seduced the innocent visitor by kindness, but had persuaded the Hanoverian Duke of York to visit Rome in 1763, thus recognising the Protestant duke as legitimate and implying that the Catholic one inhabited a doubtful position. The Stuart duke flounced off to Frascati and stayed there, fuming and dripping regal venom until the Hanoverian duke had left.

Henry Stuart, Cardinal Duke of York was a strange creature visited by the tourist as an interesting relic of the past. Brother to Bonny Prince Charlie, son of James (III), grandson to the legitimate and crowned James II and great grandson of Charles I, he had all of his family's pretensions to the 'Divine Right' but was completely blind to political reality. He demanded that the dignity of royalty should be ascribed to his role but was utterly incapable of ascribing any dignity to himself. Created a cardinal by Benedict XIV at the age of twenty-two, with no experience of priestly orders, he proved an extreme embarrassment to the Papacy. Petulant and hot-headed, he exhibited the arrogance of his dynasty with not the slightest concept of how his own behaviour might have tarnished the name of his family. Clement XIII must have been mortified at some of his escapades. The royal dignity needed to be upheld, but did this necessarily involve ignoring the royal pursuit of pretty youths in minor orders? The widely circulated slander that he publicly kept a catamite was, unfortunately, all too credible; Mrs Piozzi certainly believed it. Henry was the last remnant of an entirely dysfunctional family, but at least in later life exhibited the gravitas his role demanded. Granted a pension by George III he had the decency to will the last remnants of the Stuart jewels to the British king and so put at rest the Jacobite cause. The British Crown may have owned their temporal relics, but paid handsomely for the tomb of the errant dynasty in St Peter's, and has continued to pay for its maintenance ever since. George IV seemed especially fascinated by the Stuarts and footed the bill for Canova's cenotaph to failed ambition and foolish practice.

There was a new spirit of enlightened tolerance in Rome. The Pope began to conserve the Vatican collections and put them in order. A city where 'Of the population a quarter are priests, a quarter are statues, a quarter are people who do nothing'[29] (Charles de Brosses) needed the lifeblood, energy and particularly the cash, of the visiting British and the Pope had no intention of damaging the injection. The more intelligent tourist was sure of a welcome at the Villa Albani (now Torlonia) where the Cardinal delighted in showing off both his collection and Wincklemann, its curator. A spectacular collection, unfortunately stolen by the French and, after Waterloo, auctioned off in Munich (in spite of the Treaty of Vienna) it would have been the ideal to which the visiting Milord could have aspired.

When they got back to Rome from Frascati, a spending spree followed. The complete works of Piranesi were purchased from the artist himself and he eventually reciprocated by dedicating a plate in his new collection of prints of vases to Sir Watkin.[30] Prints were bought from a Mr Hamilton, presumably Gavin Hamilton, artist and dealer and co-conspirator with Jenkins in the export of antiquities. Other substantial payments are recorded to Hamilton although the proliferation of people with that name in the accounts can be confusing. The next day, four drawings 'in Oyle Paper after Raphael' were bought and on 3 December 'Pd. Mr Byres a Bill for 2 Cameos. A Ring Prints etc as of Bill. 2197'.

Pages 62 and 63 of Sidebotham's account represent an extraordinary distillation of the experience of Sir Watkin's grand tour; recording, as they do, the extent of his expenditure as a patron of the modern artist and as an antiquarian collector.

1768 (page 62)

Nov	*29*	*Pd Signor Piranezi for His Works Compleat in Vols of Prints*	*1219*	*2*
	30	*Pd a man for four Drawings in Oyle paper after Raphael*	*61*	*5*
Dec	*03*	*Pd Mr Hamilton the Following 3 Prints from Homer 3 Prints at 5 3 Prints at 4 Pd Mr Byres Bill for 2 Cameos, a ring, Prints etc, etc as of Bill*	*2197*	*7*
		Pd Pompeo in Part of Payment of a large full length Picture of Sr Watkin, Mr Hamilton & Mr Apperley 75 Sequins.	*1537*	*5*

1769				
Jan 6		Pd Do in part for a History Picture he is to paint for Sr W 50 Sequins	1025	
	7	Pd Mr Jenkins for 8 Pictures 2 Marble Statues and an Intaglio as of Acct 194	8148	
1769				
	63	Disbursements for Prints Pictures etc brt forward	14246	7
Jan 7		Pd Mr Hamilton for 5 Pictures as of Acct 345	14246	5
		Pd Mr Byres for 9 Pictures as of acct which makes	35275	
		Pd Do for Prints, cutting a Seal etc as of acct	4742	
		Pd Mr Wiseman a bill for Music	1161	5
		Pd Mr Hewson [sic] for a model Bust in clay of Sr Watkin & some casts from it 20 Sequins	41	

Batoni's triple portrait of the three gentlemen was the only such group he painted and, as the most fashionable and expensive painter in Rome, he commanded very high prices and Sidebotham's down payment probably represented the first quarter of his fee. Unlike the 'swagger' portraits of other young British Grand Tourists, where arrogance and stupidity are shown in equal measure, Batoni shows deep psychological perception here. It was generally agreed that Batoni could capture an excellent likeness. In which case the inbred, sullen face with its slavering, drooping lower lip of many of his portraits bore little tribute to the genetic inheritance of the English aristocracy but Batoni drew what he saw. In the case of our trio, there is very little 'swagger' and the poses are unusually restrained for such a very large canvas. There is equal balance given to all three gentlemen. Captain Hamilton, holding a flute, with music on the table behind him, gestures towards Mr Apperley who has a copy of Dante, presumably to indicate his literary interests, and who, in turn, gestures in Sir Watkin's direction. Sir Watkin, dressed in a fur lined cloak which was one of Batoni's studio props (it appears draped over a succession of Grand Tourist shoulders in the 60s and 70s, and in various colours) gazes at the viewer, quietly holding a crayon drawing after Raphael's 'Justice' in the Vatican *loggias*. Most of Batoni's young tourists are shown as either confident or languid, heroic or simply bored, but Sir Watkin seems a little shy, possibly homesick, quite thoughtful but, most of all, a quiet, intelligent nineteen-year-old boy. A shy youth who offers us the best he could offer in his chalk drawing; slightly diffident, but quietly proud of his achievement. Against the sophistication of Apperly, who could speak both Latin and Greek, and against the accomplishments of Captain Hamilton who seems to have been self-assured to say the least, Sir Watkin, in full knowledge of the fact that he was paying for the entire tour, did not seek to dominate. He liked dogs and there are two splendid such creatures included (some of Batoni's sitters complained about the smell of dog in his studio) His drawing lessons had continued in Rome with William Forrester, an engraver of views, and it would not be too fanciful to see in the drawing he holds, perhaps his best effort to date. In a room full of Batoni portraits (National Gallery, 2008) this one stood out simply by not shouting from the rooftops 'Look at me,' but by inviting us in to enjoy this intelligent company and join in with them.

It took four years for the notoriously slow artist to complete the picture and when it arrived in London in 1772, it was hung in pride of place in the new town house at 20 St James's Square.

A further commission was given to Batoni when they returned to Rome from Naples and he was asked to paint a 'History Picture'. This must have been the *Bacchus and Ariadne*, sold at Sotheby's in 1947 and is now in a private collection back in Rome. A further commission was to Raphael Mengs, Batoni's rival. Mengs was in Madrid in 1769 and the contract must have been made through an intermediary and, though no specific mention is in the account, a substantial payment to Mr Hamilton on 6 January of 103 Roman sequins and noted as being 'on account', may be the initial payment. Gavin Hamilton, a painter turned excavator, and colleague of Piranesi and friend of Mengs, was well situated to place the commission. The finished painting of *Perseus and Andromeda* remained in Rome until at least 1779 when Thomas Jones saw it in Mengs' studio. When eventually despatched by sea, it was looted by a French privateer and taken to Paris where Catherine the Great's agent bought it and sent it to St Petersburg. It remains in the Hermitage Museum. As a portraitist, Batoni was largely unrivalled, but Mengs was leading in the new, slightly colder, neo-classical style and was greatly favoured by Cardinal Albani amongst others. They both painted Clement XIII and, interestingly, Mengs' version, now in the Ca' Rezzonico in Venice, the Pope's family home, is much the better of the two. It captures the Pope's essential humanity with deep psychological insight. Contemporary critics thought that Batoni had been merely efficient, but that Mengs had delineated the person himself.

When Wynnstay was sold in 1947, many of the works of art which were housed there were sent off to Sotheby's. In the first sale, on 5 February, amongst the drawings there were works by Guercino (G.P. Barbieri) Magnasco, Zampieri, Palma, Tiepolo, Veronese, Castiglioni and Roman views by Clerisseau. The paintings included works by Ricci, Pannini, Salvatore Rosa, Vernet, Pietro Fabris, and, as well as the triple portrait and the Bacchus and Ariadne, two further portraits of unnamed sitters by Batoni. One cannot be entirely sure how they all came into the collection but it would be a reasonable supposition that a deal of them were bought on the tour. A later sale in 1965 included works by Rubens, Ricci, Apollonio di Giovanni and the ubiquitous 'Venetian School'

Although as we have seen, Sir Watkin had commissioned Robert Adam to design a new mansion at Wynnstay and indeed, was awaiting the drawings in Rome, he now commissioned another from James Byres. An odd choice of architect, Byres largely functioned as a picture dealer, but one can suppose that he must have been very good at selling himself during their tours of the ruins and had promised Sir Watkin something of extraordinary magnificence. Thomas Apperley, who seems to have been something of an enthusiast for architecture judging from his own excursions during the tour, may have had a hand in the commission. Magnificent is possibly a mundane word to describe the Italian Palace which Byres proposed to plonk on a hill overlooking the Dee. Strictly classical, it owes more than a little to Vanvitelli, the architect of Caserta, and with something of that building's enormity about it. It is designed on a princely scale and obviously with entertainment in mind. The central Egyptian Hall is in fact an enormous concert room some one hundred feet by fifty-five, and the rest of the palace seems to have been designed to accommodate large numbers of guests. It has been observed that the designs seem more appropriate for a large hotel with a concert hall attached than for a country seat,[31] but it would seem that Sir Watkin knew exactly what he wanted. The question of paying for it was something else. The mansion was never built, as was the case with any of the new Wynnstay projects, but the designs, originally comprising some fifty-eight sheets, are certainly some of the most beautiful architectural drawings to have survived from the eighteenth century. In 1770, Dr Burney was allowed to see the drawings before their despatch to London.

From hence I went to Mr Byers, who received me very kindly. He had already been appraised of my journey and errand by Mr Lumisden. He had 2 great professors with him, who came to see his designs for Sir W. Wynn's house, which is a noble one indeed. I had the pleasure to see and to hear it explained.[32]

Dr Burney was not an architectural specialist and did not seem to notice that however splendid the proposed building, it was also slightly old-fashioned. Byres disliked the baroque and seems to have harked back to the early stirrings of the neo-classical in Rome of about the 1740s for his inspiration. Had it been built, it would have been a prime target for criticism by the architectural *cognoscenti* in Britain – it would also have been quite unique.

Music was an obsession with Sir Watkin. His cello lessons had continued throughout the tour and he had spent lavishly on concerts in Florence to honour Sir Horace Mann. In Rome, he seems to have continued to promote concerts. In the accounts, a Mr Wiseman figures quite frequently in connection with his musical activities: 'Dec 5. Pd Mr Wiseman a Bill of a Concert, Vocal & Instrumental last night.' Dr Burney explains:

> To the Villa Raphaele I had a monstrous long, hot and dusty walk.
> It is now occupied by a Mr Wiseman, a music-master and copyist, who is an Englishman that has been here 19 years. He now speaks broken English like an Italian.[33]

Wiseman's house, nowadays known as the Casina di Raffaello, is in the gardens of the Villa Borghese and must have been a quite lovely place in which to attend concerts, isolated as it was from the noise of the city. Alas, the Raphael frescos which adorned his favourite house and which were described by Dr Burney later in his diary, no longer exist and the Casina itself has become a children's playground. Though still in a delightful location, it is slightly less tranquil than in Wiseman's day.

In Florence, cello lessons were given by one of the leading instrumentalists living in the city and in Rome no less was required. Accordingly Giovannini, the Maestro di Capella of St Peter's itself, and a noted performer was engaged to continue the instruction. He and some of his colleagues were also engaged to perform in Sir Watkin's concerts although it is uncertain whether they were held in his hotel or in Wiseman's villa. Sidebotham's language master was paid 40 *paoli* for a month's instruction. A concert on the 4th, at Wiseman's, cost 202 *paoli* and *Signor* Giovannini cost 164 *paoli* for playing on 6 December. This was serious indulgence and the warning bells should have been sounding for the future.

Sir Watkin's spending on art was, although excessive, a natural and gentlemanly exercise, but his spending on music does seem more than disproportionate. After all, a picture bought can also be sold again, but a concert given vanishes into the thin air and the memories of those present. Music leaves not a jot behind and musicians can be importunate beasts. This was his worrying extravagance and he was to learn a painful lesson when he became treasurer of the Concert of Antient Music in 1776 and, after the Handel celebrations in Westminster Abbey, was unable to balance the books. Mainly, it must be admitted, because he had helped himself to the treasure chest to discharge pressing debts. Although Sidebotham often tried to act as a restraining influence, his advice was not always heeded and Apperley had amply demonstrated that he was totally inadequate to the task of preaching restraint to anyone; especially his own son, and certainly not to Sir Watkin.

In Paris, Turin and Milan, Sir Watkin seems to have studied courtly behaviour, dancing and general social graces. In Florence, his social milieu expanded and music and art began to predominate. In Rome, they took over completely. His mind seems to have become awakened to the delights of antiquity and Mr Byres' six-week course must have been at times slightly gruelling, but he stuck with it and became genuinely interested in the relics of antiquity.

Winter was drawing in and that of 1768/9 would appear to have been a particularly bad and gloves and an expensive muff were bought on 8 December and on 9 December they decamped to Naples, though not without having the guns and pistols serviced the day before they left. The Campagna was probably why Captain Hamilton had been hired in the first place; a military man being a necessity the closer one approached the lawless metropolis of Naples: 'Dec 9th Pd for cleaning the Guns & Pistols'.

The journey from Rome to Naples took two days, but they had had the foresight to order provisions from *Signor* Benedetto before they left Rome and thus eased some of the inconveniences of the journey. Sidebotham was becoming very familiar with the intricacies of Italian travel and before they left Rome had applied to a *Signor* Baraci, a functionary of the Papal Secretary of State, for a letter to avoid the usual examination by the Papal customs at Velletri on the Neapolitan border.

Naples

If Florence had been a bit of an eye-opener for Sir Watkin, then Naples was certainly not for the faint-hearted. Squalid, violent and lawless; fiercely Catholic and profoundly pagan, it was a distorting lens of a city.

Ferdinando IV had been married to Maria Carolina, daughter of Maria Theresa, sister to Marie Antoinette and the Grand Duke Leopold of Tuscany, the previous May and was generally regarded as a buffoon. Coarse and unappealing, he seemed to prefer the companionship of the hunt to that of his wife although she bore him eighteen children. Sir William Hamilton wrote in correspondence,

> *On the morning after his nuptials, when the weather was very warm, he rose at an early hour and went out as usual to the chase, leaving his young wife in bed. Those courtiers who accompanied him, having enquired of his Majesty how he liked her 'Dorme con un amazzata' replied he, 'e suda un porco.' [She sleeps as if she's been slaughtered and sweats like a pig].[34]*

103

In fairness to the rest of Naples, it must be recorded that even the King's own nobility were embarrassed by him and by their part in his lamentably deficient education. Sir William again:

The Neapolitan nobility, do not conceal their indignation at the neglect of their Sovereign's education and the Foreigners, of which there are many here at present from all parts of Europe, are struck with amazement. The Prince of Nicandro, His Sicilian Majesty's late Governor, hangs his head and those very courtiers who lately encouraged their Master in his youthful behaviour I see are shy of appearing near His Majesty in public lest his familiarity with them should convey (which is but too true) that they have had a share in His Majesty's education.

They probably stayed on the bay front at Chiaia, a popular and safe destination for British tourists, which Goethe pithily observed had been virtually colonised by them. The accounts do not mention the exact hotel, but Casanova gives us a hint about the British in Naples:

I found myself acquainted with all the English visitors. They all lodged at Crocielles, [Corcelle) for the English are like a flock of sheep; they follow each other about, always go to the same place, and never care to shew any originality.[35]

The Corcelle was run by a Frenchman, Luigi d'Arc, who had been butler to the Duke of Gloucester and was very popular with the British. Dr Burney seems to have stayed there as well.

After Paris and London, Naples was the largest city in Europe and although probably, at the time, the most musical city, it was also the most violent. Described in an Italian proverb as a 'paradise inhabited by devils', slums and palaces co-existed with no apparent incongruity. Endlessly fascinating to some, it was equally repellent to others. Dr Burney had his pocket picked three times whilst there! The injunction in the 1925 edition of the Blue Guide to Southern Italy, 'In Naples the persistent attentions of small boys, rarely innocent whatever their age, should be firmly discouraged' has achieved the status of a universal maxim applied to the city. The manner of social regulation was already well on the way to deserving Gladstone's later description of it as 'the negation of God erected into a system of Government.' After all, this is the city whose indigenous saints frequently liquefacted blood over a willing and credulous populace – on set dates.

The usual cast was there. The earls Cowper and Tylney had come to winter in that occasionally milder climate and the notorious Prince Francavilla, whose hospitality was legendary, entertained them. Do not doubt, that southern though it is, Naples can be unpleasantly cold and wet in December, sometimes our expectations of the south are too much. One day hot, the next cold, very much like the ruling passions in that most vibrant of cities.

Naples rivalled Venice in the sexual availability of its populace, but with a much broader understanding of human frailties. Its only recorded shock was when the Prince of San Lorenzo insisted upon riding stark naked in his carriage along the Toledo (officially the Via Roma, but no one calls it that). It was too much, even for Neapolitan taste, although whether the horror was inspired by aesthetic or moralistic considerations must be a matter of speculation.

Casanova recorded one of Prince Francavilla's mildly shocking escapades:

The following day we dined magnificently with the Prince of Francavilla, and in the afternoon he took us to the bath by the seashore, where we saw a wonderful sight. A priest stripped himself naked, leapt into the water, and without making the slightest movement, floated on the surface like a piece of deal. There was no trick in it, and the marvel must be assigned to some special quality in his organs of breathing. After this the prince amused the duchess still more pleasantly. He made all his pages, lads of fifteen to seventeen, go into the water, and their various evolutions afforded us great pleasure. They were all the sweethearts of the prince, who preferred Ganymede to Hebe.

The Englishmen asked him if he would give us the same spectacle, only subsituting nymphs for the amorini, and he promised to do so the next day at his splendid house near Portici, where there was a marble basin in the midst of the garden.

The Prince of Francavilla was a rich Epicurean, whose motto was Fovet et favet. He was in favour in Spain, but the king allowed him to live in Naples, as he was afraid of his initiating the Prince of Asturias, his brothers, and perhaps the whole Court, into his peculiar vices.

The next day, he kept his promise, and we had the pleasure of seeing the marble basin filled with ten or twelve beautiful girls who swam about in the water.[36]

Compared to this, Florence was a model of rectitude and decency.

The Grand Tourists arrived in the city on the 10th and, apart from one entry recording Sidebotham and Morris' visit to the 'Great Opera' (presumably the San Carlo), there is a gap of five days in the records.

Sidebotham's record-keeping was usually meticulous, but he may have been temporarily overwhelmed by the task and his Neapolitan entries are a little bit disjointed. In this section, he not only records expenditure in Naples, but also records money previously spent in Rome and Florence. He was still discharging bills from Piantanida, the Florentine cellist, and was sending money to Rome to pay Mr Wiseman for concerts – perhaps the bills had followed him, or perhaps he had merely forgotten them, but he seems to have managed to put Sir Watkin's financial affairs in order. Things cheered up on the 17th when, not only was a gold snuffbox purchased but they went to Portici to visit Herculaneum.

Herculaneum was only just being explored. It had been deeply buried by the eruption of Vesuvious in AD 79 and the main way of access was through the long tunnels which the Bourbons had excavated through the tufa. Following the line of walls they had begun to rip antiquities and frescos from the soil to enhance the collections in the palace at Portici. It was an unmissable sight and one which was to have a profound influence upon the development of European taste in the decades to come. Sir Watkin may have had a little part in the development and dissemination of this taste.

There was an energy and drive about this lap of the tour and almost every site in the vicinity was visited with an exhausting rapidity. The day after visiting Herculaneum, they went north to Lake Agnano and its volcanic landscape. Interestingly, everyone went, gentlemen and servants, and five calashes were hired for the trip. The next day, they repeated much the same trip but concentrated on Pozzuoli and, hopefully, trampled across the Solfatarra with its stinking volcanic vents and shoe-wrecking debris in the crater.

Two days later, it was north of the city again and Baia was the focus of their interest.

Dec 21st	*Expences to Baia*			
	Pd for the Boat	3	7	0
	Pd for 5 Calashes to Cumae	3	6	0
	I gave the 2 Cicerone	1	5	0
	Pd for Wine	1	0	0
	Pd for seeing several Places	2	7	0
	I gave a Diver	0	6	0
	Pd for 2 Naples Calashes	2	8	0
	I gave the Coachman	0	8	0

A boat was hired to see the underwater ruins and they further extended the trip to include the acropolis at Baia, and that of Cuma although, at that time, the grotto of the Cumaen Sibyl had not been uncovered. Lake Averno was on the way to Cuma and they would have seen the ruins along the circumference of the lake and which were popular subjects with topographical painters, Wilson and Jones included. The volcanic nature of the landscape with its steaming fumaroles, bubbling mud craters and noxious vents fascinated the British visitor and the envoy, William Hamilton, was the acknowledged expert. A popular demonstration of the toxicity of the sulphurous fumes was to be had on the banks of Lake Agnano (drained in 1861) where a dog was thrown into a grotto to be seemingly fatally overcome by the fumes. Upon the poor creature being hauled out, seemingly lifeless, it slowly recovered and was restored to life – usually at least.

On Christmas Eve, they climbed Vesuvius itself. Not a simple undertaking and one which requires a firm resolve, and they all seem to have tipped the resident hermit most handsomely. The volcano is at present 1,277 metres high but in 1768, before the series of eruptions which were studied with such intensity by William Hamilton, it was probably higher and its ascent was not to be undertaken lightly, especially in winter when clouds can descend upon the peak without warning. Perhaps they were comparing the experience with that enjoyed at Chamonix.

On Christmas Day itself, mince pies were bought for all and a day off was had.

The next day Pompeii was visited. A more accessible site than Herculaneum, but one further away. Even today, using the Circumvesuviana railway line and the extension of the Metropolitana towards Pozzuoli, it is not easy to have visited all of these places in the time in which they managed to do it. A certain determination on their part is evidenced by the schedule of their archaeological tourism. The archaeological sites were mostly royal possessions and Sir Watkin was given tickets of admission by Mr Hamilton, who was created a Knight of the Bath and appointed Plenipotentiary Extraordinary in 1772. Tickets were not easy to obtain and needed to be applied for to the prime minister, the Marquis Tannuci, who did not always acquiesce to the request. But our envoy had influence in Naples and could usually be relied upon – 'Dec 23 I gave Mr Hamiltons Servant that brought Sr Watkins Visiting tickets 0. 6. 0.'

William Hamilton was an extraordinary man. Antiquarian and a vulcanologist, his collections of antiquities and his observations of Vesuvius in eruption laid the foundations of study for future generations of scholars. Married to an extremely pleasant and musically-gifted Welshwoman, Catherine Barlow, (the blowsy Emma was as yet to arrive) in Naples he occupied, with much more distinction, the position occupied by Horace Mann in Florence. Lady Hamilton was a distinguished keyboard player and concerts in the Palazzo Sessa were a regular feature of Neapolitan life. The King had authorised the publication of the treasures from Herculaneum in the Royal Collections at Portici although the lavish volumes could only be acquired as a gift from him. Sir William, with limited financial resources, was publishing the contents of his own collection of what were known as 'Etruscan', though in reality Greek, vases. Four volumes were eventually issued and the quality of the plates, coloured by hand, was generally recognised to be of a very superior standard indeed. Sir William was over £6,000 out of pocket when they were published. Sir Watkin purchased the first two volumes, one of which had been sensibly dedicated to King George III. On his return to London, when he collected the volumes from Mr Cordell's shop in Covent Garden, he promptly loaned then to Josiah Wedgwood who, upon the opening of his Etruria works in the same year, based some of his first productions upon the prints. The first vase, thrown by Wedgwood himself, was directly copied from one of the plates. Thus, in small ways, Sir Watkin had an influence upon the taste of his times.

Sir William's other abiding interest was vulcanology and his reports to the Royal Society detailing Vesuvius' many moods and eruptions were well-known, as were his publications, especially *Campi Phlaegri*. The latter is exquisitely illustrated by Pietro Fabris who, in spite of his name, was a British subject. The pair of Neapolitan views by him, signed and dated 1773 and sold in the Sotheby sale in 1947, may represent a commission by Sir Watkin.

Apperley and Captain Hamilton made an excursion to Caserta, that vast riposte to Versailles. Described by some as a 'megalomaniac excrescence', the magnificence of the staircase and the rotunda at its head would allow the honest observers to forgive the rest. If they managed to walk the three kilometres to the end of the main vista, they would have seen the glorious view back over the palace to Capri and the splendid cascade, with Diana and Acteon paying homage to the King's obsession. The adjacent 'English Garden', the joint creation of Maria Carolina and the then 'Sir' William Hamilton, was not begun until 1782 and was obviously the work of someone who had not been to England for some time, planted as it is with palms, ginkos, eucalyptus and other Mediterranean exotica.

It was the custom in Naples to give handsome gratuities to the servants of the houses one visited, and tips are recorded to those of the Countess Mahoni (Lady Anne Clifford), Prince Francavilla, William Hamilton, an unnamed ambassador and the King himself. It seems probable that William Hamilton presented Sir Watkin to the King on 28 December, when he was in residence in the Palazzo Reale in the city and not out at Caserta. Sir Watkin had learned to assume his proper place in society and, however disagreeable he may have found present-ations and the like, he must, by now, have realised that only by bending the knee could that position be validated. Neapolitan society was odd in that, whilst undoubtedly corrupt and licentious, it still observed proper form. Court present-ation was an absolute and one unfortunate British lady, who had been no better than she ought to have been, was refused by Mrs Hamilton on account of her reputation and therefore was equally refused by Queen Maria Carolina. A British lady needed to be presented by the wife of the British ambassador and if the ambassador's wife declined, that was the end of the matter. The doors of Neapolitan society were instantly closed to her, even though her peccadilloes were relatively slight compared with theirs.[37] Form was form and had to be observed. Naples had been part of the Spanish Empire and Spanish etiquette still ruled. Unfortunately, it is not recorded whether the Prince Francavilla, a grandee of Spain, provided further exotic 'entertainment' at his dinner on the 30th. But, had he done so, it would hardly have figured in the account book.

Although printed music and a new cello were bought, there seem to have been no concert promotions in the city; perhaps the musical evenings at the Palazzo Sessa with the envoy and his wife were sufficient. Mr Brown, the servant's hotelier, arranged for the cello to be sent direct to London as, on about the 1 January, they began the journey back home.

The Journey Home Begins

Returning to Rome by about the 3 January (the dates in this part of the account are quite hard to disentangle), they once more lodged at the 'Villa di Londra' (the name had become Italianised by now; a tribute to Sidebotham's Italian teachers) and a six-day frenzy of spending ensued. The banker, Marquis Belloni, was applied to for funds. Mr Jenkins was paid off; Byres received 550 crowns as a fee, though whether for architectural drawings, antiquities, paintings or his services as tour guide is not stated. Mr Forrester was given his fee for teaching Sir Watkin to draw. More concerts were given and music collected under the management of Mr Wiseman and, most touchingly, a set of harp strings were bought. John Parry, the resident, and blind, harpist at Wynnstay, was the most brilliant player of his age and was genuinely treasured by the family and the strings may have been intended as a gift to him. The coach was repaired and provisions collected for the journey to come. Operas and plays were visited by Sidebotham, Morris and Carrara and it is gratifying to note that, for once, Sam Stevens was included in the party, and general thanks and tips were given to the servants who had waited upon them whilst in the city. But Sir Watkin still had sufficient time to sit once more for a portrait, this time by Christopher Hewetson, an Irish sculptor, who belonged to the Piranesi/Gavin Hamilton circle.; 'Jan 7th Pd Mr Hewson for a model Bust in Clay of Sr Watkin & some Casts from it. 20 Sequeens'. The bust is now in the National Gallery of Ireland in Dublin, but the whereabouts of the casts is unknown.

None of them, apart from Antonio Carrara, were ever to see the city again. Sir Watkin planned a later journey with Paul Sandby, the artist, but like most of his later plans, nothing ever came of it. The planned visit, which was first mentioned (by the Father Thorpe in correspondence with Lord Arundel)[38] in 1771, after the Welsh tour, gives us some evidence that Sir Watkin had actually begun to enjoy his time in Italy after the uncertainties of his first arrival in Rome. The purpose of the tour was to impart polish, sophistication and appreciation of fine art and music upon the receptive young mind and in that respect it seems to have been entirely successful.

Venice

They set out on 8 January and, after seven days heaving over the snow bound Apennines, arrived in Venice. The accounts are silent on the matter of the route taken, but it would have been normal to follow the ancient Via Flaminia through Narni, Terni, and Spoleto, emerging from the mountains at Fossombrone and reaching the Adriatic at Fano. The two hundred miles of the route were considered very difficult, but they went further through Rimini and Ravenna before reaching Venice. They must have covered over forty miles a day and perhaps their haste indicated that a decision had already been made to return home as quickly as possible.

The whole party seems to have been put up at Petrillo's establishment near the Rialto Bridge and one most favoured by the visiting British. It was generally found clean and neat and, most conveniently, had a water gate directly upon the Grand Canal itself.

Venice had already become a theme park and the Venetians, hurtling down into unrestrained disease and decadence did not seem to mind. Consul Smith, British agent in the city, printer of fine books and patron and dealer to Canaletto, who had died as they set out on the tour, had been doing his best to preserve the remains of Venetian culture, whilst the Venetians were selling off the family silver. Smith, who was not above shady dealings himself, was responsible for supplying the rich holdings of works by Canaletto now in the British Royal Collections. Sir Watkin acquired some of his fine publications, including a volume of views of Bologna from San Michele in Bosco.

Venice must have been an extraordinary contrast to Rome and Naples. An anti-clerical republic filled with glorious churches whose Doge, Alvise Giovanni Mocenigo, was engaged in a bitter struggle with Clement XIII to restrict the power of the clergy. A virtual police state, controlled by an army of spies, in which political thought may have been unwise, but sexual licence was virtually encouraged. Casanova had only recently escaped from the state prison where his official crime was declared to be wantonness, although his probable crime was thought. But, the Lion of St Mark had lost its teeth and the Council of Ten were mostly incontinent geriatrics, hidden from the light of day and only emerging as darkness fell upon the crumbling city.

The sun was sinking on the republic and, in a little over twenty years from Sir Watkin's visit, it was to end in ignominy when its own senate voted for its dissolution in the face of the Napoleonic occupation (apparently an illegal vote, as there was not a quorum present – Venice should still be an independent republic!) What the Grand Tourist had left behind was pillaged for the embellishment of the Louvre and not everything was returned upon the collapse of Napoleonic despotism.

The standard of San Marco never really flew again, except as part of our modern obsession with an imagined historical past. There surely can never have been as many Venetian flags in Venice in any preceding century, as there are today.

Venice expired under the weight of her own past. A society riddled with government spies, ineffective institutions, corruption and the pox. Painted, garlanded and masked, she danced herself into extinction with one last, endless, ball.

Venice can be an uncomfortably cold city and our party was obviously ill-equipped for the weather and gloves, nightcaps and flannel linings for coats were added to the shopping list.

Jan 18th   *Pd the Gondolire a Bill of sundry Expenses at Venice.*
I lost by Exchange of Belloni's Draft of 239.3
3 Pauls on a banner at Venice
Pd for 6 pair of Woollen Gloves & night Caps for the Servants
Pd for a Barrel of Cypres Wine about 10 Dozen English Bottles
Pd for Lining a Great Coat with flannel

Messrs Sidebotham and Morris developed a strategy to keep warm. They had, by this stage of their Italian tour, so far departed from the principles of the Church of England, in complete emulation of Lady Mary Wortley Montagu, as to have gone to the opera every night. Accompanied, and no doubt encouraged, by Antonio Carrara who, presumably, had no such principles to depart from in the first place. However sophisticated their musical tastes may have become, the outstanding reason for attending the opera was that it was probably the only warm place where an evening could be spent in that bone-chilling city and fortunately for them, the performances were very long. But an evening at the opera could be very expensive, not least in consideration of what to wear and certain standards were expected. In the absence of a court, the theatre was a place to show off.

Jan 18th   *Pd for washing*
                   Pd for sewing ruffles'

In Venice, there was a very thin dividing line between the auditorium and the stage. Everybody acted and most people were in costume most of the time and the theatre was the place for meeting loose women, making assignations and gossiping – generally throughout the performance.

Jan 16th   *To the hire of a Masquarade Dress'*
                   Pd Carriage of a Masquarade Dress from Milan to Bologna & Venice

I wonder what the point was of having a masquerade costume – perhaps Sir Watkin went to the Ridotto where a mask was usual. Easter in 1769 was not until 26 March and the Venice Carnival had probably not yet started and perhaps the original intention had been to stay until it began, but perhaps the weather won out. The winter of 1768/9 was a particularly bad one. The weather had deteriorated badly during September and intense cold and wet lasted through until March, with heavy snow falling at exceptionally low altitudes. The Alps and Dolomites were experiencing one of the worst winters in memory and after five days, the travellers took the boat to the mainland and headed for Padua. Sidebotham had by now become so worldly and sophisticated that in making a purchase in Padua he actually recorded the name of the artist – 'Jan 19th, Pd for 2 small Pictures of Titian's at Padua'!

Sir Watkin must have been in a hurry. The route of the journey back to Paris, was possibly via Innsbruck, Augsburg, Strasburg and Metz, Sidebotham is irritatingly vague on the matter, but, however they went, the journey was accomplished in eighteen days. I presume that it was virtually a non-stop performance and that the absence of the usual purchases in the accounts was simply due to that fact that none were made. Sidebotham records the cost as being 12,818 livres, and that simple statement is virtually all we have. Only on 2 February were any additional purchases recorded. The cold seems to have followed them and in Strasburg fur caps, gloves and a superfine sable muff and a suit of sable were bought; the latter for Sir Watkin and the former for the servants. A dog was also bought there – perhaps to keep his feet warm.

Paris

In Paris they settled back in at the Hotel de Saxe and *Monsieur* Panchaud, the Parisian banker, was urgently contacted. Funds having been made available

(Pauchaud's account, which was honoured by Child's Bank, amounted to £269)
Sir Watkin set off to buy presents for his family, fiancé and future mother in-law.

Sidebotham's accounting must have driven him mad. He was swindled during
exchange transactions in both Venice and Augsberg and several times admitted
defeat in trying to reconcile the various currencies he was working in. He seems
to have felt humiliated on the few occasions when he had to present an
unreconciled account to Sir Watkin. When the account was finally closed in
September 1769 the only imbalance was £1 14s 1d short which, considering the
complexity of his task, was quite amazing. In Paris, for his own convenience and
probably our gratitude, he recorded his transactions in Sterling. Thus,

Feb 8th	*Pd Mons Laufrenage for a Watch Set in Diamonds*
	9000 Livres or £404.10
	& a Vause Clock 780 or £32.2.6
	Pd Do for a pr of Diamond Lady's Shoebuckle 3861 Livres or
	£168.10.4 ½
	& for a Gold Snuff Box 657 or £28.14.10 ½
	Pd Mons Maumett for a set of China Dessert Service Of the
	French Manufacture for the Duchess of Beaufort
	Pd Mr Pernon of Lyon for Sr Watkins best suit 1940 French
	or £84.17.6

This was serious spending. The Sèvres dessert service (still at Badminton) cost
319 *livres* (about £15) and the figure must indicate a deposit and not the full price.
The best suit had arrived from Lyons and the diamond shoe buckles must have
been intended as a wedding present for Lady Henrietta (Sir Watkin's second wife,
Lady Charlotte, was noted for the brilliance and quantity of diamonds she wore).
The purchases were entrusted to a shipping agent and the bills and goods
continued to arrive in London until the following September when Mr Jones of
the Customs House was paid £315 in duty for the last of the consignments - except
for the commissioned works which continued and continued to arrive for several
years afterwards. The various bills, charges for shipping, and duties, which were
paid after their return, amounted in all to £8,643 12s 9d (About £550,513.27 in
today's money) but, in honesty, the hidden costs and the residue of fees yet to be
paid, tend to suggest that that figure was an interim one and that the final cost
was very much higher.

London

Paris was left behind on the 10th. By the 13th they were in Calais and two days later returned to Grosvenor Square. Sir Watkin, Apperley, Hamilton, Sidebotham, Morris, Sam Stephens and Antonio Carrara had returned safely. Christo Bremer and Louis Mark Comte were dispensed with in Paris and likely to be in the market for the next available grand tourist.

Sidebotham was preoccupied with balancing the books. Sir Watkin was preoccupied with his forthcoming marriage. Apperley once again was concerned with his own domestic arrangements and Hamilton and Antonio Carrara were presumably looking for other posts.

The tour was undertaken in an egalitarian spirit which was more Welsh than English. The servants shared their employer's experiences and were now possibly multi-lingual, had seen Versailles, the Alps, the northern Italian cities, the Vatican, Pompeii and Herculaneum, operas and plays. By default, they had received the kind of education which a middle-class boy could only have wondered at. Sidebotham, a competent and educated manager, had done his best in holding together the company. He had profited from the company of Antonio Carrara and had developed tastes which may never have been satisfied again. Morris and Sam Stevens had experienced things which were not theirs to demand and the two other 'servants' had served a most genial employer.

The accounts demonstrate the care and sympathy with which Sir Watkin treated his employees and the fierce loyalty which this jolly, overweight, bumbling but perceptive and shrewd landowner inspired in his employees, friends and acquaintances, seems entirely justified by his behaviour on this his Grand Tour.

NOTES

1. Unpacked, most memorably for a trip across Lake Geneva from Lausanne to Evian. It was so heavy that two men were needed to carry the chest from the hotel to the lake. However, unlike their china, the silverware was unlikely to be easily broken on the tour and therefore it could be seen as an economy of a sort.
2. Apart from the normal observances of his class, Sir Watkin does not seem to have been unduly religious. The squabbles he inherited from his father with the local Methodists seem to have been political rather than doctrinal.
3. James Boswell, *Life of Dr Johnson*, edited by Christopher Hibbert, New York, 1979
4. Dr Burney Journal, 1770, p.1., published as *Music, Men and Manners in France and Italy 1770*, edited by H. Edmund Poole, London, 1969.
5. Wynnstay Papers, Box 115/1–10.
6. Tobias Smollet, Letters, No VI, 1763.
7. It is recorded in the *Almanach du Commerce* for year VIII of the Republic.
8. Joseph Baretti, Secretary of the Royal Academy, was particularly offended by Carrara's flights of fancy and the mischief he caused.

9. Horace Walpole, *Letters to Horace Mann*, published as *Mann and Manners and the Court of Florence 1740–1786*, edited by Dr Doran, London, 1969.

10. Leo Damrosch, *The Restless Genius*, New York, 2005.

11. The suit is possibly the one which is preserved in St Fagans Museum of Welsh Life.

12. The literature concerning the crossing of Mount Cenis is inexhaustible but see Simon Schama, *Landscape & Memory*, Chapter 8, London, 1996.

13. Dr Burney, *Journal*, 1770, p.3.

14. The Music Room is now on display in the Victoria and Albert Museum. Other bits are in the USA. William Farrington described the grand opening of the house and its staterooms. See Desmond Fitz-Gerald, *The Norfolk House Music Room*, London, 1973.

15. *Correspondence of Emily, Duchess of Leinster*, edited by Brian Fitzgerald, Dublin, 1957.

16. Newly restored and opened to the public in 2008 after years of neglect doing service as a military barracks.

17. Edward Gibbon, Journey from Geneva to Rome, edited by Bonnard, London, 1961.

18. James Boswell, *Boswell on the Grand Tour 1765–1766*, New Haven, 1955.

19. PRO, 30/9/40, p.149, quoted in Black, op cit.

20. Flattened during the last war, its site is now occupied by the only modern building in the centre of Bologna which is not a tribute to post-war taste and is still proving controversial.

21. Seymoiur Conway, letter to Horace Walpole of 1773.

22. From Ruspanto – a Florentine penny and rumoured to be what the Medici grand duke paid them for their antics. In spite of public derision, scores of them attended his funeral in 1737 exhibiting obvious signs of distress.

23. *Gazzetta Toscana*, No. 43, 11 October 1768.

24. Sir Horace Mann, Letters to Horace Walpole, edited by Lord Dover, New York, 1833.

25. Thomas Jones, *Journal*, Walpole Society, vol. 32.

26. See Lionel Cust, *The History of the Society of Dilettanti*, London, 1914.

27. J.T. Smith, *Nollekens and His Times*, 1829.

28. Now in the National Museum of Wales, Cardiff.

29. Charles de Brosses, *Lettres historiques et critiques sur l'Italie*, 1799.

30. In the dedicatory inscription, Sir Watkin is described as 'un Cavaliere Inglese' but how could Piranesi be expected to know?

31. Timothy Mowl, *A Roman Palace on the Dee*, National Museum of Wales Catalogue, 1996.

32. Burney, op. cit., p.130.

33. Burney, op. cit. p.133.

34. Sir Nathaniel Wraxall, *Historical and Posthumous Memoirs*, p.173.

35. Casanova de Seingalt, *Giacomo, History of my Life*.

36. Casanova was not of sufficient social status to have attended all of the events he recorded in his memoirs and may not have been present at the Prince's entertainment. However, sometimes, strict truth should not be allowed to spoil an otherwise entertaining story.

37. Lady Maynard had had, whilst plain Mrs Horton, accommodations with the dukes of Grafton and Dorset and a selection of the House of Lords before marrying Lord Cathcart. His lordship was most dismayed by Mrs Hamilton's firm refusal and abused her husband roundly. The Minister was not swayed and allowed his wife's judgment to stand. As a compromise, Mr Hamilton presented the irritated lord to the king.

38. Quoted by Brinsley Ford in 'Sir Watkin Williams-Wynn', *Apollo Magazine*, June 1974, p.439.

Interval

Coming of Age

SIR WATKIN CAME BACK FROM HIS GRAND TOUR a much more assured person than he had been when he embarked upon it and, if the purpose of the journey had been to give him a veneer of sophistication and connoisseurship, to that effect, it had been successful. He had kept his own amongst the princely families of France and Italy, had been presented to the kings of Sardinia and Naples, had patronised some of the most eminent of European artists and had developed tastes which were in advance of their time. He had become 'rounded', but, one also suspects, had developed into a young man who was incapable of restraining his impulses in the pursuit of art. Was it that the examples of good taste and breeding he had witnessed whilst abroad, and which he tried to emulate, contained the seeds of his own financial ruin? Be that as it may, in February, Sir Watkin began characteristic preparations for his marriage to Lady Henrietta Somerset, fifth daughter of Charles Noel Somerset, the fourth Duke of Beaufort (1709–56), by sitting for Sir Joshua Reynolds, in February, for a betrothal portrait. Lady Henrietta sat in March and on 11 April, four days after Sir Watkin's twentieth birthday, they were married at St George's, Hanover Square. Sir Watkin had yet another suit made for the occasion, this time by his own London tailor, Mr Morse. Hinchcliffe & Co. supplied the velvet at a cost of £18 4s and £213 13s 6d was expended on Lady Henrietta's wedding outfit. Lady Henrietta's brother Henry, the fifth duke, had preceded Sir Watkin at Westminster School and Oriel College and they were close neighbours in Grosvenor Square. The Somersets were known to be Jacobite sympathisers and seem to have given the third baronet shelter after the collapse of the '45 and one has the suspicion that the marriage had been 'arranged' a very long time ago. The marriage contract was eased, as was usual with the great landed families, by Sir Watkin agreeing to make a financial settlement upon his new bride and the Act of Parliament allowing the baronet, still a minor, to endow his bride had had an easy passage.[1] The Williams Wynns and the Somersets were not of equal social standing but after all, Lady Henrietta was only the fifth daughter and Sir Watkin was thought to be very rich.

116

Unfortunately, Lady Henrietta died on 24 July leaving, as legacy to her husband, a few unpaid bills – including that for her wedding dress.[2] True to form, Sir Watkin commissioned Joseph Nollekens to create a memorial to her memory. It cost £450.[3] In August, Sir Joshua's services were sought once more and Sir Watkin and his mother were the subjects of a large canvas, which may have been commissioned to celebrate his coming of age the following spring. The portrait had been started before he left for Italy and we may assume that whilst he was away, his mother continued the sittings. Sir Watkin obviously thought a great deal of his mother and, it must be admitted, the pension he settled on her was to cost the Wynnstay estate more than it could afford in later years and he was deaf to any discussion of its reduction. Reynolds had the reputation of being a cold man, with whom it was difficult to do business. Knighted in 1768, he knew his worth and charged accordingly. His usual price for a simple portrait was in the region of 100 guineas and he was relentless in his pursuit of fees owed. Sir Joshua and the young baronet must have had an unusual rapport in that he regularly allowed him to take commissioned works away from his studio before they had been paid for. Patron and painter seemed to have an easy relationship and Sir Watkin became one of his more substantial clients.[4]

His relationships with the leading artists of the day were extensive both as patron and sitter, and as a pupil. On 10 May, he was elected a governor of the Foundling Hospital, traditionally supported by artists, following the example set by Hogarth and Handel, and he must have become acquainted with many of them at the annual dinner but an event of greater significance had occurred the previous year when he had been away in Rome. The foundation of the Royal Academy in December 1768 by, amongst others, Sir Joshua himself, Richard Wilson, Thomas and Paul Sandby, Joseph Nollekens and Francis Cotes and its first student intake, which included William Parry and James Gandon, constituted the group he was to patronise for the rest of his life. Wilson, a distant cousin, and Parry,[5] the son of the celebrated resident harpist of Wynnstay, were in a sense 'family', but the larger circle of the Academy was to embrace him not only as a wealthy patron but as a fellow connoisseur and friend.

In spite of his youth, Sir Watkin was already reckoned a man of taste and his opinion was taken seriously, although it would be reasonable to ask whether or not his enthusiasm for actually buying things, affected the appraisal of his connoisseurship. Wedgwood and Bentley, about to open their works at Barlaston, the famed 'Etruria', openly expressed their gratitude for the loan of Sir William Hamilton's *Antiquities* which Sir Watkin had made available to them immediately upon his return. Although Sir William's cousin, Lord Cathcart, had previously supplied them with separate plates, this was the first complete copy they were able to inspect and it had a profound effect upon the manufactory's output. The 'First Day Vase,' thrown in June 1769, was directly copied from plate 29 of volume 1. Wedgwood himself threw the six copies and acknowledged his debt to Sir Watkin by naming him as a 'legislator of taste.' Sir Watkin responded by spending £98 on creamware for his coming-of-age celebrations the next year and later by having tiles for his new dairy supplied by the firm.[6] The intaglios and cameos he had bought from Jenkins and Byers in Rome were likewise loaned to the pottery works to be remade as jasper-ware medallions.[7] In their 1779 catalogue, Wedgwood and Bentley described Sir Watkin as having a 'truly liberal spirit' but perhaps Bentley's remark of 1770, 'Sir Watkin Williams Wynn must have anything and anyhow so let us know what we must provide,'[8] gives us a clue as to the direction of his liberality. The Wedgwood firm kept volumes of the *British and Irish Peerage* close at hand and knew exactly where their principal market was. A little flattery could make sound commercial sense.

In September 1769, David Garrick organised a Shakespeare Jubilee at Stratford-upon-Avon which promised to be one of events of the year. A special pavilion was erected, Garrick was made a freeman of the town and the Drury Lane Company were in attendance. Sir Watkin had put aside his period of mourning and was often in attendance. The first evening concluded with a masquerade ball and Boswell, fresh from his Italian adventures, attended as a Corsican chieftain – hopefully not with the 'adulterous anticipation' he had suffered in Turin; the burghers of Stratford may not have been as complaisant as the nobility of the Italian city. The next day dawned and the heavens opened. For two days the deluge lasted and the Avon threatened to overflow its banks and sweep all away with it. Marooned in the pavilion in the company of actors, musicians and artists, Sir Watkin must have been in seventh heaven. Here perhaps was the germ of an idea which was to come to fruition the next year when he came of age and held a feast for 15,000 people in the park at Wynnstay.

Preparations for that great event had long been in hand and the new park wall, of which he wrote from Rome, was finished. Also underway was the new Great Room added to the house by Thomas Farnolls Pritchard,[9] a competent Shrewsbury architect who also designed the ballroom at Powis Castle and who was to shortly begin the reconstruction of Ruabon church. A medieval church may have been unsuitable for what Sir Watkin had in mind and it was thoroughly 'modernised'. It has now been restored to its previous form. All of these works must have been instigated at a distance, as there seems to be no reason to think that the new baronet had spent any time at his country seat.

The library at Wynnstay then housed several manuscripts by Handel[10] and the annual fundraising performances of the *Messiah*, to benefit the Foundling

Hospital, must have been very much to Sir Watkin's taste. After his experiences of concert giving in Florence and Rome, he continued the practice in London and engaged some of the best contemporary instrumentalists for his musical breakfasts at Grosvenor Square. The Prince of Wales was known to attend and occasionally participate. His own cello lessons continued and the Queen's harpsichord instructor, Joseph Kelway, had been engaged to teach Lady Henrietta.

Number 2 Grosvenor Square was a rented house – a not uncommon practice for the country gentry in town for the season. Although Sir Watkin had asked Robert Adam to prepare designs for a new house at Wynnstay before he left for Italy and, as we have seen, asked James Byres to undertake a similar exercise whilst in Rome, his mind began to move in other directions. The building projects in Wales (Byres' designs had not yet even arrived and would not until 1770) were gradually shelved and he formed a new and ruinous ambition. In June 1771 he decided to build a new mansion in London which would form a suitable background for his collections and his musical life. Never was a notion more deserving of immediate extinction. The obvious choice of architect was the ruinous Robert Adam – a man who ruined both himself and his clients. When the house was completed in 1776 Sir Watkin was £100,000 in debt. Adam was given a free hand in designing the house down to the last detail. It was a shame that no-one thought to give him a budget as well![11] Sir Watkin was about to enter into his second marriage and his bride, Lady Charlotte Grenville, was sister to the Marquess of Buckingham. The Grenvilles held serious influence and a scion of that family needed to be properly housed. After all, their country seat was Stowe.

On 19 April 1770, Sir Watkin came of age. The house had been extended, the park enclosed and Pritchard had restored (or reconstructed) the village church in preparation for the great event. The later admonition by his solicitor and agent, Francis Chambre, would have been equally timely around this time

> ... *when alterations & additions become a Foible, it cannot be well known where they are to end, or what expense will carry them on, so the less they are undertaken ye better –*
> *Beware of your Architects & Modern Gardineur.*[12]

Advice, which was as wise as it was ignored. Adam was already employed and Capability Brown was to be called in shortly.

Sidebotham recorded the total cost of the feast as being £1,621 17s 11½d of which roughly £1,200 was spent in London on provisions, alcohol and earthenware (Wedgwood naturally). The London purchases were sent by sea to Chester on the *King George* and the Williams Wynn estates of Llanforda, Llangedwyn

(Sir Watkin's childhood home), Llwydiarth and Glan-llyn contributed everything they could. Cooks were brought from London, Chester and Whitchurch and a hundred waiters to serve the food and constables to guard it were engaged. Two post-chaises of musicians came from the King's Theatre in the Haymarket, and in the evening the park was illuminated with Hardwick lamps and a firework display by Domenico Jordan. The grandeur and splendour of the event needs no explanation in consideration of the fact that this was a long-awaited event celebrated by one of the greatest landowners and richest men in Wales. However, Sir Watkin seemed to have developed a taste for junketings on a truly magnificent scale. The restoration of the parish church had a dual purpose as it could also be pressed into service as a concert hall.

There had been a long interregnum at Wynnstay following the death of his father and Sir Watkin may not have been much in evidence on his estates. He had been occupied elsewhere, in London, Westminster and Oxford, and it may be that there was a feeling in the family that changes needed to be made and bridges restored. Being a feudal lord did have its obligations and one of them was certainly the need to be seen by the tenants who were, after all, the source of his wealth. A grand gesture seemed appropriate to announce the return of the baronet to his seat. The locality seems to have descended into a positive frenzy of excitement at the thought of the restoration of the status quo and preparations were put in hand, not only by Wynnstay but also by the neighbourhood, to celebrate the homecoming. Laudatory verses were penned, practised and polished and Mr Carter, the cook at Wynnstay and a talented performer, donned women's clothes and perfected his turn as a ballad singing Welshwoman. He was later paid a supplement to his salary for taking part in the Wynnstay theatricals – as were several other members of the household staff.

One particular effusion was printed and widely distributed and it gives us a clue as to the general tenor of feeling at the event.

A

SONG

SUNG

At Wynnstay on the 19th of April 1770,

WHEN

Sir WATKIN WILLIAMS WYNN *came of Age*

To the tune of, The Bellisle March

I

All hail to the Meeting of this happy Day!
Be chearful, be sprightly, good humour'd, and gay:
Expell from each Bosom all sorrow and Care;
For this joyful Morning gave Wynnstay an Heir:
Then join in the Chorus, and eccho the Lay,
That hails the fair Meeting of this happy Day.

II

Ye Halls, and ye Towers, the Boast of Old Time,
Where Plenty and Bounty long honour'd our Clime,
Your old Hospitality now is restor'd,
For this festal Morning gives Wynstay a Lord:
Then let your Walls eccho with our choral Lay,
And hail the glad Meeting of this happy Day.

It continues in a like vein for eight verses. Verse seven exhorts his father's spirit to approve 'May this Son of thy Hopes prove the Heir of thy Worth' and the final verse hopes for a speedy replacement for the late Lady Henrietta.

April in north Wales is not a time guaranteed to be clement and Wynnstay is inconveniently situated upon an elevated parkland exposed to the prevailing westerly winds, but invitations (8,700) were issued and 'by computation' 15,000 guests arrived and 'Bounty and Plenty once more honoured the Clime'. That figure may seem somewhat excessive until we examine the bill of fare for that single day's entertainment. Apart from the wines, spirits, sugar, tea, mustard, fruit, fowls, asparagus, crockery, the great cask and drinking horns which were imported from London, the family estates of Llanforda, Llangedwyn, Llwydiarth and Glan-llyn were ransacked to supplement the Metropolitan fare.

In total, the provisions were the following:[13]

30	Bullocks
1	do roasted Whole
50	Hogs
50	Calves
80	Sheep
18	Lambs
70	Pies
51	Guinea fowls

37	Turkeys
12	Turkey Poults
30	Brace of Tench
40	Brace of Carp
36	Pike
60	Dozen of Trout
108	Flounders
109	Lobsters
96	Crabs
10	Quarts of Shrimps
200	Crawfish
60	Barrels pickled Oysters
1	Hogshead of rock oysters
20	Quarts of oysters for sauce
166	Hams
100	Tongues
125	Plumb Puddings
108	Apple Pies
104	Pork pies
30	Beef pies
34	Rice puddings
7	Venison pies
60	Raised pies
80	Tarts
30	Pieces of Cut pastry
84	Capons
25	Pea fowls
300	Chickens
360	Fowls
96	Ducklings
48	Rabbits
15	Snipes
1	Leveret
5	Bucks
421	lbs of Salmon
24	Pound cakes
60	Savoy cakes
30	Sweetmeat cakes
12	Backs of Bacon
144	Ice Creams
18,000	Eggs
150	Gallons of milk
60	Quarts of cream
30	Bushels of potatoes
6,000	Asparagus
200	French beans
3	Dishes of green peas
12	Cucumbers
70	Hogsheads of Ale
120	Dozen of wine

There was a great quantity of Brandy, Rum and Shrub.
Salt Butter cost £36 besides French Butter.
Rockwork, Shapes, Landscapes, Jelly Blanc Manges, &c., &c.
A great quantity of Small Pastry.
One Cask of Ale that contained 26 Hogsheads.

The amount consumed tends to give creditability to the 'computed' attendance.

The grand gesture had been made and Sir Watkin satisfactorily exhibited to the lower gentry of Chester, Wrexham, Oswestry and anywhere else within a day's travel of Wynnstay and to the respectable tenantry of his own land holdings. Duty done most agreeably, he began plan his vision of the future at Wynnstay. Subsequent birthdays were marked by a servant's ball in his London house.

Sir Watkin considered himself to be a Welshman and, although one of the few in his family who could not speak the language, he considered it his duty to support Welsh culture and was a regular subscriber to various Welsh charities in London. Therein lies the difficulty. The Welsh in London were familiar to him, but the Welsh in Wales were quite another matter. It is noteworthy that out of the £1,600 spent on his coming-of-age party £1,200 was spent in London and the provisions brought up by sea as though to a foreign land. He could never have afforded any of the schemes for a new Wynnstay, but it is questionable that he really would have ever tried; 20 St James' Square was a much more seductive project. Sir Watkin was quite firmly a member of the London Welsh – singing the praises of his native land, but largely preferring to see it from the perspective of the capital.

Perhaps inspired by the delightful little private theatre in the Palazzo Reale in Naples, which had been completed a matter of months before his visit there as accommodation for the nuptial celebrations of King Ferdinando and Maria Carolina, Sir Watkin decided that he needed one also.[14] Accordingly, a redundant kitchen was fitted up and the first private theatre in the United Kingdom was established.[15] This conversion was adequate but not quite splendid enough and later in the year James Gandon, then a student at the Royal Academy School and architectural instructor to Sir Watkin, was invited to design a proper one.

The reason for the church restoration and the theatre became clear in the summer of that year. It was to become Sir Watkin's habit to retire to Wynnstay for the summer – sometimes extending his residence to include Christmas. But it was not in his nature to seek solitude in his domains; the parties had to continue. In August 1770 the first of his annual festivals was held. Roger Kenyon, a neighbour and later to become Lord Chief Justice, wrote,[16]

Our Jubilee week at Wynnstay is at last over. We had a grand oratorio at the opening of the new organ at Ruabon Church, on the Tuesday, where several solos were performed by Mr Paxton, the first violincello, and Signior Giardagni, the first singer in the Kingdom. The company were all invited to Wynnstay to dinner and a grand entertainment we had. About nine o' clock, we all went to the puppet show, where a handsome theatre and good music were exhibited; but as to Punch, I have seen him much more entertaining for a penny, and [was] never crucified four hours more stupidly in my life. It would have done you good to see how many grave senators were entertaining themselves with old history of Babes in the Wood – Lord Grosvenor, Mr Kynaston, Mr Middleton were amongst them ... the whole must have cost Sir Watkin a couple of thousand at least.

The singer in question was Gaetano Guadagni. Reckoned proud and overbearing by some and charming by others, he was one of the most famous *castrati* in Europe and had created the role of Orfeo in Gluck's opera. He seemed particularly fond of Sir Watkin and dedicated his own version of the Orpheus legend to him in 1772.[17] His fees were stratospherically high although not his voice, as he sang in the contralto range. The London *cognoscenti* would have been well familiar with him but I have often wondered what Sir Watkin's tenants, herded into the church for the occasion, would have made of his voice! He was a truly exotic importation into the Welsh borderlands. Mr Paxton not only performed but gave Sir Watkin cello lessons and other musicians from the Kings Theatre were in attendance to provide music in the house, in which Sir Watkin participated. It seems to have been generally agreed that the music at Wynnstay was on a much more elevated level than the dramatics and both Garrick and Sheridan needed much persuasion to visit. The new organ which was installed in Ruabon church was indeed a Snetzler instrument and its installation excited the parishioners of Wrexham but Sir Watkin, in a rare mood for economy, offered some land for a churchyard instead. The Ruabon organ was played by either the celebrated John Parry, household musician and resident organist or, when he was away on concert tours, by his son, David. Parry was paid £100 per annum for his services and, whenever he was at Wynnstay, he generally delighted the company. In the autumn of 1777, David Garrick wrote to his brother, 'I am writing in ye Dark & Mr Parry ye famous harpist is playing like an Angel.'[18]

Garrick and Sheridan shared the professional's terror of the gentleman amateur and it took a lot of gentle insistence to have them attend a Wynnstay summer. Garrick was not prevailed upon until 1777 and much to his own surprise, enjoyed himself, although his presence terrified the amateur actors. Sheridan had possibly attended in 1773 and it seems that Sir Watkin had had the nerve to act in front of him. It was not for nothing that in 1772 when he was elected as MP for a Shropshire seat, his Parliamentary colleagues promptly nicknamed him 'Bubbles' a name inherited by one of his sons when he entered Parliament.

In general terms, Wynnstay was not a large house and may have been inconvenient for too many jubilee guests to stay in. At the park gates in Ruabon, the Eagles Inn (now the Wynnstay) had been built in 1749 and enlarged over time, so it proved suitable to house the overflow. John Byng wrote in 1784:

> ... we were let out of the park; and then retir'd to our dinner at an ale house with brick floors, and shutter'd casements. Whilst Welsh Squires continue to entertain their visitors horses, the inns at their gate will be shabby. How better would it be for their own fortunes, and their guests and travellers' comforts, to build a good inn at their park gates which charge, a 3 months saving in the stables would defray. (Eagles, Ruabon very civil & cheap.)[19]

In passing, it may be noted that on his next tour, which was to be around north Wales, Sir Watkin adopted the same expedient and frequently stayed in inns.

The company assembled for the first of Sir Watkin's jubilees at Wynnstay was diverse but distinguished. The musical contingent included some of the best in the land and the decision by the young baronet to hold some of the larger concerts in the parish church was almost without parallel at the time. Churches were certainly used for public concerts, but to hold a private concert in a public place and to open it to the public of the vicinity does make one wonder what would have happened if the Byres Palazzo had ever been built; a very small Welsh village as an epicentre of British musical life?

Sir Watkin's devotion to music was his main, and most costly, indulgence but the visual arts were by no means neglected. In addition to the tribe of musicians present at Wynnstay in that summer of 1770, there were also some men who virtually represented the British artistic establishment.

Richard Wilson, generally known as the father of British landscape painting, was part of the company and a tented pavilion studio was erected for him on the hilly edge of the park overlooking the River Dee. His two canvases, *Wynnstay* and *Crow Castle,* were exhibited at the Royal Academy in 1771.[20] He received an advance of £50 and was paid another £430 upon completion. Wilson was not cheap and by June 1770, Sir Watkin had purchased at least five major canvases by him, the receipts for which survive. Wilson's mother was a Wynne and therefore a distant relative but, sad to say, he was already in steep decline through the effects of excessive drink. Even in his portrait by Mengs, painted in Rome in 1752 and which came into Sir Watkin's possession later, his florid complexion could arouse suspicions of over-indulgence rather than over-exposure. His physical decline was to accelerate during the 1770s until, just before his death, his north Wales relatives rescued him. He is buried in Mold – about fifteen miles from Wynnstay. The paintings which Sir Watkin had from him are noteworthy examples of his art but, sad to say, an art which was beginning to be found slightly old-fashioned.

> *Feb 5th 1770. Recd of Sir Watkin Williams Wynn Bar*
> *The sum of fifty pounds on acct of two Large Landsk[ips] now in hand by me.*
> *Richard Wil[son]*

> *Sir Watkin Williams Wynn Bart to Ricd. Wil[son][21]*
> *June 5th 1770*
> *A print of Ceyx Wolle[sic]*
> *Pars Ionian Antiquities bound*
> *Lent at Mr Locke*
> *To a Capital Landskip with Cicero at his Villa*
> *To a landskip taken in the Villa*
> *Ghigi at Lariccia*
> *Its Companion*
> *To the large View near Wynnst*
> *Its Companion 8f by 6*
> *Balance £430*
> *Recd July 3rd 1771 of Sir Watkin Wms Wynn by Saml Sidebotham the above in full*
> *by me Richd. Wilson.*

Another artist made a first appearance at Wynnstay; Paul Sandby was engaged to teach Sir Watkin to draw and to paint some scenery for the theatre. Sandby, who also taught the Royal children, was ideal for this company. Witty, urbane, slightly waspish and at the height of his powers, he seemed to have been a great success. Entrusted with some errands on his return to London on Sir Watkin's behalf, he made an ominous visit to a 'Mr Brown' at Hampton Court. Obviously the landscaping of the newly-enclosed park was yet another ambition of the young baronet. Sandby's bill ...[22]

> *38 lessons at 5.3*   *£ 9 19s 6d*
> *A view of Wenlock Abby in Watercolours*   *£12 12s 0d*
> *Do Bridge North*   *£12 12s 0d*
> *Do a Large Drawing*

Journey to Wynnstay absent from London 40 days	*£84 0s 0d*
Paid for Post Chaise from Woolwich to Hampton Court	
After Mr Brown on Sir Watkin's account	*£1 13s 0d*
Do after Mr Woods to Hoxton Hall	*£1 16s 0d*
Back to Woolwich	*£ 12s 0d*
Loss of time Three days	*£6 6s 0d*
	£150 0s 0d

Recd June 20th 1771 of Sir Watkin Williams Wynn Bart by
Samuel Sidebotham the above in full.
Paul Sandby

... was settled a year later.

Although Sir Watkin owned a sizeable swathe of north Wales he seems not to have seen much of it; a situation which was to be remedied the following year.

The 1770 'Jubilee' having been a signal success, an encore was arranged for 1771 and the delightful Mr Sandby invited back. Sir Watkin's tour of north Wales now loomed and it was to have a significance which went well beyond its intention. Shortly after the tour, Sir Watkin was to marry again. This time to Lady Charlotte Grenville, related to Pitt and sister to a Prime Minister and daughter to another, hers was a powerful family. The wedding was celebrated at St George's, Hanover Square on 21 December 1771. She proved to be more astute and financially capable than her husband. The marriage caused a little stir. Mrs Delany[23] wrote – 'How flexible are the affections of some men. Sir WWW the happiest of men: and so he was not many months ago with Lady Hert.' The prayers of the versifiers at the coming-of-age celebrations had been answered.

NOTES

1. Act of Parliament.
2. Wynnstay MSS. Total £715 13s 6d.
3. The bill also included a bust. The monument, a statue, once occupied the centre of the north chapel. It is now relegated to an indifferent position in the north aisle.
4. Sir Joshua painted Lady Charlotte and three of her children, Master Williams Wynn as St John, Mrs Sheridan as St Cecilia, Sir Watkin and the Dowager Lady Williams Wynn, Sir Watkin and Lady Henrietta, and possibly a portrait of Sir Watkin.
5. In 1770, Sir Watkin funded his studies in Rome on consideration of Parry making some copies of well known old masters. The bargain was fulfilled.
6. The Duchess of Argyll ordered '498 square tiles the same as made for Sir WWW.'
7. The objects loaned to Wedgwood included 172 intaglios and 173 gems or cameos presumably all bought from Byers in Rome.

8. Farrer, Lady Katherine, *Letters of Josiah Wedgwood*, facsimile edition, Wedgwood Museum, 1973.

9. Ionides, Julia, *Thomas Farnolls Pritchard of Shrewsbury*, Shrewsbury, 1999.

10. A list was given by Sir Watkin to Dr Burney of the Handel manuscripts and printed music in the library.

11. *Survey of London*, 29 & 30, part 1.

12. Wynnstay Papers Vol i.

13. A frequently quoted document but one hard to trace. Pritchard states that it was printed in the *Gentleman's Magazine* for May 1770, but I have been unable to find it in that particular issue. Askew quotes if from the Wynnstay Papers and I have used his account.

14. Only just restored and in a working state again.

15. Girouard, op. cit.

16. Historical Manuscripts Commission, 14th Report, appendix, IV, p.502. R. Kenyon to Miss Kenyon at Peel.

17. Guadagni caused an unseemly squabble when he was accused of plagiarising music and Sir Watkin, considering that the work was dedicated to him, felt obliged to intervene on Guadagni's behalf. It did his reputation no good at all. See Howard, Patricia, 'Guadagni in the Dock', *Early Music*, XXVII, February 1999.

18. Little & Kahrl, *The Letters of David Garrick*, iii, p.1194, 1963.

19. John Byng, *The Torrington Diaries*, London, 1938, pp.176–7.

20. Sold by Sotheby's in 1947 and now in New Harvard.

21. Wynnstay MSS, 115/24/11.

22. Wynnstay MSS, 115/21/13. See Appendix 2a.

23. Delany, op. cit.

Sr. W. W. Wynn. 1777

PLATE 17

Fra.ᵉ Cotes Juin.ᵗ   E. Fisher fecit.

Paulus Sandby.

Ruralium Prospectuum Pictor.

publish'd according to Act of Parliam.ᵗ 1763.

PLATE 18

PLATE 19A

XII

VIEWS IN NORTH WALES

BEING

PART OF A TOUR THROUGH THAT

FERTILE AND ROMANTICK COUNTRY

UNDER THE PATRONAGE

OF

THE HONORABLE SIR WATKIN WILLIAMS WYNN BART.

TO WHOM

THEY ARE MOST HUMBLY INSCRIBED

BY HIS MOST OBEDIENT

AND MOST HUMBLE SERVANT

PAUL SANDBY R.A.

MDCCLXXV

N° 2

P. Sandby fecit.

Published according to Act of Parliament by P. Sandby S¹ Georges Row Oxford Turnpike Sep. 20ᵗʰ 1776.

PLATE 21

Overton Bridge
Over the river Dee, on the confines of Denbigh & Flintshire.

Publifhed according to Act of Parliament by P. Sandby S.George Row Sep.r 1.st 1776.

P. Sandby Pinx.t

PLATE 22A

PLATE 22B

Wynnstay, Seat of Sir Watkin Williams Wynn Bar.t from a Cottage above the New Bridge over the River Dee, DENBIGH SHIRE.

Publifhd according to Act of Parliament by P. Sandby S.George Row &c.

Chirk Castle &c. from Wynnstay Park.

Publish'd according to Act of Parliament by P. Sandby S.t George's Row Sep.t 1.st 1776.

PLATE 23A

PLATE 23B

Llangollin in the County of Denbigh, from the Turnpike Road above the River Dee.

Publish'd according to Act of Parliament by P. Sandby S.t George's Row Sep.r 1776.

The Abbey of Llan Egwerst or Vale Crucis, and Castle Dinas Bran.

Publish'd according to Act of Parliament by P. Sandby St. Georges Row Sept.r 1st 1776.

PLATE 24A

PLATE 24B

Conwyd Mill near Corwens in Merioneth Shire, between Llangollen and Bala.

Publish'd according to Act of Parliament by P. Sandby St. Georges Row Sep.r 1st 1776.

IX.

View of the River Dee 3 Miles short of Bala, with Cader-Idris Mountain near Dolgelli 30 Miles distant

Published according to Act of Parliament by P. Sandby St George's Row Sepr 1777

PLATE 25A

PLATE 25B

x

Published according to Act of Parliament by P. Sandby St George's Row Oxford Turnpike Sepr 1777

PIMBLE MEER

The Iron Forge between Dolgelli and Barmouth in Merioneth Shire.

Publish'd according to Act of Parliament by P.Sandby S:George Row Sep.r 1.st 1776.

P.Sandby fecit.

PLATE 26A

PLATE 26B

Harlech Castle in Merioneth Shire with Snowdon at a distance.

Publish'd according to Act of Parliament by P.Sandby S:George Row Sep.r 1.st 1776.

P.Sandby fecit.

Pengwern, Corn & Fulling Mills, with Pont ý Pandy, near Festiniog.

Publish'd according to Act of Parliament by P. Sandby St. Georges Row Sept.r 1st 1776.

PLATE 27A

PLATE 27B

VI

Publish'd according to Act of Parliament by P. Sandby St. Georges Row Oxford Turnpike Sep.t 1777.

Traeth Mawr in the Road to Caernarvon from Festiniog.

Publish'd according to Act of Parliament by P. Sandby St Georges Esqr 1777
PONT-ABER-GLASLLIN

PLATE 28A

PLATE 28B

P. Sandby Fecit.

CAERNARVON CASTLE.

Publish'd according to Act of Parliament by P. Sandby St Georges Row Sepr 1st 1776.

Carnarvon Castle

PLATE 29A

PLATE 29B

View of the EAGLE TOWER at CAERNARVON &c.

Llanberris Lake Castle Dol Badern and the Great Mountain Snowdon.

Publish'd according to Act of Parliament by P.Sandby St. George's Row Sep.r 1.1776.

P. Sandby Fecit.

PLATE 30A

PLATE 30B

Bangor in the County of Caernarvon.

Publish'd according to Act of Parliament by P.Sandby St. George's Row Sep.r 1.1776.

P. Sandby Fecit.

Conway in the County of Caernarvon.

Publish'd according to Act of Parliament by P.Sandby St. George Row Sep.r 1776.

P.Sandby fecit

PLATE 31A

PLATE 31B

THE BRIDGE AT LLANRWST IN DENBIGHSHIRE

Pont y Pair over the River Conway above Llanrwst in the County of Denbigh.

P. Sandby Fecit.

Publish'd according to Act of Parliament by P. Sandby S.t Georges Row Sep.t 1.st 1776.

PS

Rhaidr-y Wennel near Llanrwst in the County of Denbigh

Publish'd according to Act of Parliament by P. Sandby S.t Georges R. Sep.t 1777

THE TOUR OF NORTH WALES, 1771

THE GRAND TOUR HAD BEEN ESTABLISHED since the previous century but another tour was about to become so. The estate at Wynnstay, on the verge of north Shropshire and the Cheshire Plain, is relatively lush. The only hint of what lies further west is the bracken- and heather-clad bulk of Ruabon Mountain which looms behind the estate village of Ruabon itself. Further west was a relatively unknown country and the further west one went the more horrific the eighteenth-century sensibility found it. The memorable, if impertinent, 1720 description by either Edward Bysshe or Bishop Burnett or Edward Ward – there are several candidates[1] – can bear repetition.

The air is the best thing it has to boast of [north Wales] and will sooner procure you an appetite than furnish you with the means to supply it ...

The country here looks like the fag end of Creation, the very rubbish of Noah's Flood, and will (if anything) serve to confirm and Epicurean in his creed that the world was made by chance.

There is not in the whole world a people that live so near to, and yet so very far from, Heaven as the Welsh do.

In Dolgellau he spent a thoroughly entrancing evening.

Misfortunes rarely come single; in the middle of the night (wanting the usual fortifications of lock and bolt to my chamber door) in comes a great sow who, I suppose, had been Tenant in Possession there before, and came to claim re-entry. With this grunting chamber-fellow I was obliged to spend the night.

His attempts to be made decent fared no better ...

I next sent out for a barber ... After some fumbling, he pulls out a thing called a razor, but any man would easily have mistaken it for a chopping knife ... in a short time, he shaved me so clean that not only the hairs on my face, but my very skin, was become invisible.

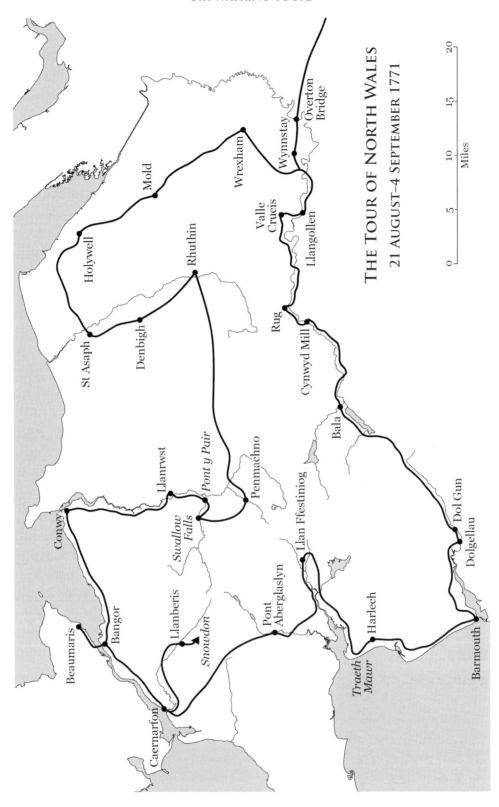

THE TOUR OF NORTH WALES
21 AUGUST–4 SEPTEMBER 1771

Miles

0 5 10 15 20

Overton
Bridge

Wynnstay

Wrexham

Mold

Valle
Crucis

Llangollen

Holywell

Rhuthin

Rug

Denbigh

St Asaph

Cynwyd Mill

Bala

Llanrwst

Pont y Pair

Penmachno

Dol Gun

Dolgellau

Swallow
Falls

Conwy

Llan Ffestiniog

Beaumaris

Bangor

Llanberis

Snowdon

Pont
Aberglaslyn

Harlech

Traeth
Mawr

Caernarfon

Barmouth

Mr E.B. may not have enjoyed his visit but others did and the land slowly started to attract the adventurous visitor of an independent mind.

A great deal of that land was owned by Sir Watkin and he had never seen it. Sensibilities were, however, changing and Sir Watkin himself had demonstrated in Switzerland a willingness to view the mountain scenery for its own sake. The time had come to view his own scenery and to allow himself to be viewed by a grateful tenantry. He had made a little excursion the previous year to Llangollen and Valle Crucis Abbey during his Jubilee celebrations, probably accompanied by Paul Sandby, but his own vast land holdings were largely unknown to him.

The Williams Wynn estates extended throughout Shropshire, Montgomeryshire, Denbighshire, Flintshire, Merionethshire and Caernarfonshire. The third Baronet inherited the estates of his father, Sir William Williams, in 1740 and through his mother inherited Wynnstay; previously named Watstay (Wat's Dyke runs through the park) but henceforward to be known as Wynnstay. Through his marriage to Anne Vaughan, he had added extensively to his holdings and had acquired the Llwydiarth and Glan-llyn estates. Altogether, he possessed over 100,000 acres in Denbighshire, Montgomeryshire and Merionethshire, as well as properties in Shropshire near Oswestry and Much Wenlock. In 1762, during the minority of the fourth baronet, his mother purchased the Mathafarn estate in Merionethshire, which included the manor of Cyfeiliog, and part of the Rhiwgoch estate. The extent of the estates was unrivalled in north Wales. When the fourth baronet inherited in 1749 the rent-roll was £11,921 4s 3d By 1773, it was £19,685 and by 1778 it was £27,111, a figure which remained constant until his death in 1789. The sheer size of the united holdings, which extended from upland farms in Snowdonia to rolling arable pastures in Shropshire, was the cause of some difficulty. They were mostly managed at arms length and the day-to-day administration was left in the hands of a succession of land agents, rent collectors and local overseers. However, as business was transacted in the name of a very specific person and not a faceless company, it was incumbent upon that person to make an appearance to see what he owned and to be seen by his tenants. The verses of the song sung upon his coming of age contain some gentle hints as to what was expected in that direction.

The summer of 1771 had followed the course set in 1770 but without the 15,000 guests; a select few hundred attended instead. Sir Watkin's household at Wynnstay had some curious features. Davis Mackender, the groom, was paid an extra allowance for his abilities on the French horn – presumably he and Mr Morris could play duets together. The cook, Mr Carter, was the highest paid servant at £75 *p.a.*, a reflection perhaps of his local celebrity as an excellent low comedian. The famous John Parry, who was frequently absent on concert tours, was paid

£100 *p.a.* as organist and harper. Salisbury, the steward, had once been a pro-fessional actor and a Mr Roberts and a Mr Meredith were noted as capable performers. Local performers, of any musical ability, were used to supplement the household and in some cases, after Sir Watkin had paid for their training, went on to establish national reputations. Mr Meredith, whom Sir Watkin had heard singing in a cooper's in Wrexham, was one such and became a notable Handelian tenor with the Concert of Ancient Music.

During the summer, the forces were augmented with professional stiffening and William Paxton, cellist and composer, was in attendance as well as three German brothers by the name of Shram, who were violinists. David Parry, son of the harpist, was engaged for the summer as an organist and harpsichord player and when the occasion demanded, the militia bands from Salop and Montgomery were called in. With this in mind, the vast hall at the centre of Byres' proposed *palazzo* would not have seemed redundant.

Gathered at Wynnstay were some familiar characters. Naturally Samuel Sidebotham was there keeping the accounts. Mr Apperley from nearby Plas Grono was also in attendance, as was Mr Morris (hopefully with his French horn), but Captain Hamilton had been replaced by a Captain Gascoin; although the necessity for a military man in north Wales is questionable. Paul Sandby was paying his second visit, fulfilling the roles of Sir Watkin's drawing master and that of practising artist. Architecture was represented in the person of James Gandon, pupil of Sir William Chambers, gold medallist at the Royal Academy, Sir Watkin's architectural tutor and designer of the new Wynnstay theatre whose foundations were laid later that year.

The weather seems to have been benign and there was an outstanding duty incumbent upon the young baronet. That situation was about to be remedied and on 21 August, Sir Watkin, Mr Apperley, Captain Gascoin and Mr Sandby, representing the gentlemen, and Mr Sidebotham, Matthew Rowland, David Mackender, Mr Morris, Thomas Jones and four other servants, two of whom appear to have been stable boys, and fifteen horses set out from Wynnstay for a tour of north Wales. In Italy he had managed with six servants, three gentlemen and four horses but perhaps north Wales, most of which he owned, needed to see him in greater state.

So, what was Wales? A western extension of England but in a ruder state, or another country with its own language and traditions? It was all too easy to play the Welsh gentleman in London, well away from the reality of the country. The Society of Cymmrodorian (literally Aborigines), founded in London in 1751 by the Morris brothers from Anglesey, allowed a decent lip service to be paid to Welshness, but from a safe distance. Without being patronising, they could patronise an imagined country, which they knew but no longer inhabited. Urban society in a country in which Wrexham was the largest centre of population, and its associated gentility and intellectual discourse, was hardly established. A man of talent, curiosity and developed intelligence was usually advised by his own people to seek out a career in London. Then as now, the metropolis swallowed up everything and everybody – usually never to return.

The self-perception of men such as Sir Watkin was intriguing. Their roots and fortunes originated from Wales but their social accolade was bestowed by the society of London and they needed to be aware from where they derived their status. A nod to Wales, as a nod to Norfolk or Northumberland, was all that was required, much more was not. As we have seen, Sir Watkin's thoughts of himself involved 'Old England', English mores and Englishness. Perhaps lazy thinking of the same type which allowed foreigners to lump the British masses together as generically 'English', but should we expect more of a Welsh baronet and in any case, how much did he have in common with his own countrymen?

A Tory member of the Established (Anglican) Church who could not speak the common language was at a disadvantage. Sir Watkin's tenantry were largely Welsh speaking and very many were Nonconformist. Not for them the weary exhortations of a tired and bored ministry exploiting their Welsh benefices for the glory of themselves if not for God. Unable to either communicate with, or exercise pastoral care on behalf of their flock, the Anglican Church in Wales was well beyond a joke. Simony, cupidity and intransigence were its recognisable features. National revival in the hands of those same Methodists, which Sir Watkin's father had most abhorred, was just around the corner.

There had been a handful of adventurous spirits tentatively dipping their toes into the Celtic twilight earlier in the century, but their singularity emphasised their lack of plurality. The Buck brothers, who seemed to have absorbed the whole of the British Isles in their pursuance of views to engrave, and who managed to make every plate they published seem much like the previous, or the next, had done their duty and tramped down the west coast and much else besides. The general point is that no earlier tourist had seen north Wales as a place in itself and for which no excuses needed to be made, no special pleading about its lack of conformity with established academic ways of viewing nature and no ridiculous varnishing of the scenery with vague memories of Tacitus and his druidical maenads cursing and shrieking on the shores of the Menai Strait. Blind harpists were another matter.

The years around 1770 were to see the beginnings of a profound change which was not exclusive to north Wales. The manifestations of that change in the lands which Sir Watkin owned, were to be of a consequence which he was unable to predict. He was not an entrepreneur, his class and education mitigated against it, but had he been, then he may not have suffered the indignities of his later financial embarrassments.

In 1768, the immense copper wealth of Parys Mountain in Anglesey was discovered – the largest copper deposit in Europe. The lead deposits of Minera Mountain which belonged to Sir Watkin's neighbours, the Grosvenors, were described as 'the richest place of such scope in the world.'[2] The annual production of coal in north Wales increased from 80,000 tons in 1750 to 110,000 tons in 1775. Near Wrexham, John Wilkinson had made his ironworks at Bersham into a manufactory of European significance. Wool and flannel manufacture was still an important part of the local economy and the slate industry was beginning its remorseless advance. As we shall see, Sir Watkin probably inspected the iron forge at Dol Gun near Dolgellau, but his fitful interest in industrial expansion –

Have you thought anything abt. the coals in the neighbourhood of Wynnstay whether it will be most advantageous to work them myself or let them – they will certainly be of great value to me either way.[3]

– seemed to be triggered more by his occasional financial embarrassment that by an informed interest in improvement. All too typically, when he proposed installing a flock of sheep on the lawns at Wynnstay he seemed more concerned with their picturesque effect than by their economic value.

In 1770 the first hotel was built in Holyhead for the convenience of travellers to Dublin. Parkgate, on the Wirral, had been previously favoured as the packet station for Ireland, but the silting up of the Dee was beginning to have an effect on the old port and the development of Holyhead was to reduce the time spent at sea, a reduction which most travellers welcomed profoundly. The trouble with Holyhead was that, as yet, there was no convenient road route to the new port. The north Wales coast road with its inconvenient crossing of the River Conwy, the monstrous headland of Penmaenmawr and the occasionally dangerous passage over the Menai Strait placed the traveller firmly between the devil and the deep blue sea. There was no sensible alternative. The route which Sir Watkin took was not chosen for its convenience, but because it was a necessity to see and be seen in precisely those areas which were the rural heartland of his own estates.

As late as 1815, Williams Akers of the Post Office represented to a House of Commons committee ...

Many parts of the road are extremely dangerous for a coach to travel on. At several places between Bangor and Capel Curig there are a number of dangerous precipices without fences, exclusive of various hills that want taking down ... From Corwen to

Llangollen the road is very narrow, long and steep; has no side fence except about
a foot and a half of mould or dirt which is thrown up to prevent carriages falling
down three or four hundred feet into the River Dee. Stage coaches have frequently
been overturned and broken down from the badness of the road, and the mails have
been overturned; but I wonder that more and worse accidents have not happened,
the roads are so bad.[4]

Mr Akers was only giving evidence about the main route from Shrewsbury to
Holyhead. The minor roads experienced by the duke of Rutland in 1797[5] almost
defied description.

From hence we had a most infamous road, as bad as, if not indeed worse than, any
we had before encountered. We still kept winding up the mountains, 'til at length we
found ourselves quite at the top of one ridge, and higher than we had ever yet been
in carriages. Craggy rocks stared at us on all sides, and in wild confusion covered
the mountains summit. For seven miles we could proceed only at a gentle foot's pace,
one moment going down so steep a pitch that the horses were forced to depend solely
on the reins for support, and immediately having an almost perpendicular ascent to
surmount. Add to this the road was so completely covered with large stones and
rocks that it was impossible to proceed above a foot's pace.

It was, of course, the general responsibility of the landowners to maintain the
roads and Sir Watkin was the largest landowner. Perhaps his tour had a beneficial
effect upon the state of the roads after he himself had suffered the indignities of
travelling on them. On the other hand, a work of pure public benevolence which
might enable others to increase their profits but with no hand in the cost may
have been thought unwise. When the road, later to become the A5, was built from
London to Holyhead there were sixteen pre-existing turnpike trusts to be
negotiated with on the section from Shrewsbury to London. On the section from
Chirk to Holyhead, there were only a few and the rest of the road was dire. In
fairness to the Welsh landowner, it must be said that the cost of improvement,
given the terrain, was quite formidable. When Telford began his improvement,
the cost was borne directly by the Government and was, in fact, the first road-
building programme to be carried out by a civilian government. Sometimes it
seemed that Switzerland was more accessible than Snowdonia.

There was an irony about the 1771 tour which should not be lost. As the
perception of the landscape changed and the rudnesses of the Welsh mountains
metamorphosed into sublimities, the accessibility of those sublimities was also
about to be changed. Improving landlords such as Lord Penrhyn were to start

laying down better turnpike roads mainly to benefit their own industries, but with the added effect of encouraging embryonic tourism. The means by which later visitors saw the north Wales landscapes were also bound up with the means by which some of those landscapes were brutalised and over-exploited.

The roads in Italy had been experienced before by most of the party and they would have understood why they were the subject of universal condemnation. They were to experience much worse in their own country. Perhaps forewarned, they sensibly took to horseback and put the luggage into a large cart. Even so, they took two weeks to cover the 220 miles but there were restorative rest days built into the itinerary and a deliberately gentle pace was adopted.

The party managed an average of some eighteen miles a day, although they slowed down considerably on some days which may have been as a consequence of the previous evening's excesses rather than that of the terrain. Word of the cavalcade's progress went ahead of them and when they entered towns or villages where Sir Watkin had important interests the church bells were rung to welcome the young lord; presumably with enthusiastic expectation of the tip which invariably followed. Samuel Sidebotham's meticulous accounts and the associated bills and dockets, which are lost for the Italian journey, are a fascinating means of reconstructing the tour.

The entire cost of the fifteen days was £117 7s. 6d. It is difficult to translate 1771 prices directly as there are a number of factors to be taken into account. But using the method of computation available through the National Archives some modern equivalents are as follows:

Liquor Bill in Caernarfon (Six Gentlemen)	£2,830 3s 0d
Ale Bill in Caernarfon (Servants)	£1,714 0s 5d
Horses Hay & Corn in Caernarfon	£4,870 5s 0d
A Harper in Conwy	£21 9s 7d
Boatman at Hengwrt	£45 7s 0d
Lord Bulkeley's Boatmen	£94 0s 5d

Some totals for the tour:

Gentlemen's drink	£8,587 8s 3d
Gentlemen's food	£11,084 1s 9d
Servants food & drink	£7,752 8s 8d
Horses feed & hay	£20,937 7s 8d
Turnpikes	£1,555 8s 3d
Guides	£2,285 4s 0d
Bell ringers	£3,955 5s 0d
The Poor	£5,397 0s 6d

Truly, Sir Watkin's tenants, local landlords, the poor, bell-ringers, boatmen, harpers and vintners must have looked forward in excited anticipation whenever the young lord made a 'progress' through his lands and possessions. It pleased the 'Lord' to give and it probably pleased the natives of Merionethshire and Caernarfon-shire to receive. It is possible that prices rose as he approached and subsided as he departed – he probably expected no other; he had a position to maintain and largesse was incumbent upon him. He knew where his income was derived from and was acutely conscious of his social obligations.

It is interesting to note that, although Paul Sandby was handsomely paid for his time in north Wales, he was allowed to retain all of the sketches he had made on Sir Watkin's behalf and that, furthermore, for any finished watercolour or painting he executed, he was paid separately. It has been suggested that the inclusion of Sandby on the tour was a deliberate gesture by the baronet to advance an appreciation of the picturesque, but it becomes quite obvious that Sandby was not engaged as the expedition's topographer. His function, and the only one for which he was paid, was to act as drawing master and to teach Sir Watkin how to capture the beauties of his own properties. His own professional needs were indulged whenever possible, but were of secondary importance to the purpose of the tour. That purpose, prosaically, was to view properties and to cement political alliances. Given the circumstances of the tour, Sandby was remarkably productive and he was, in later years, to endlessly recycle sketches he had made on the road. His normal method was to make quick pencil drawings and to work them up later into either aquatints or watercolours. Only one such sketch actually survives. It is of a mill in a mountainous landscape, labelled 'A view between Barmouth and Dolgellau' (National Library of Wales) and a more finished watercolour worked up from the sketch is in the British Museum. Sandby's work was regarded as his own property and when he made a finished study of any of his views which Sir Watkin particularly liked, it was bought in a separate transaction. A watercolour of Bala lake cost the baronet £21 and he seemed pleased with his purchase. Paul Sandby must have appreciated his generous Welsh patron.

The publication, in 1776, of aquatints based on the drawings made on the tour marks a subtle shift in the perception of the north Wales landscape. Its dedication to the baronet indicates a new perception:

XII
VIEWS IN NORTH WALES
BEING
PART OF A TOUR THROUGH THAT
FERTILE AND ROMANTICK COUNTRY
UNDER THE PATRONAGE
OF
THE HONOURABLE SIR WATKIN WILLIAMS WYNN BART

TO WHOM
THEY ARE MOST HUMBLY INSCRIBED
BY HIS MOST OBEDIENT
AND MOST HUMBLE SERVANT
PAUL SANDBY R.A.
MDCCLXXV

The date on the frontispiece would seem to belong to an earlier intention to issue the prints which may have been delayed by technical problems with some of the plates, but the description of north Wales as 'Fertile and Romantick' was ground-breaking indeed. Further publication of north Wales views followed in 1777 and 1786.

Various editions of the prints exist; one of three in the British Library, and the copy owned by the National Library of Wales, have a slightly different sequence of views and are probably a second edition, and Sandby himself suppressed some copies. He particularly asked Thomas Pennant not to mention those of Cynwyd Mill, Caernarfon and Llanberis Lake. His reasons are unclear but may be connected with technical difficulties.[6]

The 1773 and 1776 tours of Thomas Pennant were published between 1778 and 1781 as *A Tour in Wales*, and were generally reckoned to have established the scenery of north Wales in the tourist itinerary. But Pennant was careful to give recognition to Sandby's pioneering work.

Those that wish to anticipate the views in the intended progress may satisfy themselves by the purchase of the late publications of the admirable Mr PAUL SANDBY in whose labours fidelity and elegance are united.[7]

This tour has often been described in terms of its being a sketching tour with the purpose of discovering the romantic scenery of north Wales.[8] That may well have been an unintended result, but a letter from Sandby to Pennant records his frustration at not being able to record all that he wanted to. The baronet's progress took precedence over the artist's labours and the intention was not so much to view wild scenery as to view the wild scenery which was part of the Wynnstay inheritance. The tour was picturesque in a limited sense, although the incidental results conformed to that description absolutely. In a letter of 23 June 1777, Sandby wrote[9] that 'It was to me great mortification not to have time to make sketches of all the fine scenes I saw.' Obviously the picturesque needed to give way to the political and economic interests of the baronet, sensitive as he may have been to the beauties of the landscape.

If one is allowed to ignore the rather complicated history of the sequence of publication of Sandby's aquatints of north Wales views, there seem to be some twenty known prints in all. It has been said[10] that there is a further view of Castell Dinas Bran, above Llangollen and, although there is a watercolour of such a view, a print seems elusive. The surviving plates can be assembled in the sequence of the tour without any difficulty if the numbering of them is disregarded. The common link with them all is that the subject matter invariably has some connection with Sir Watkin's land interests or political affiliations. Romantic they may have been, but there seems a quite hardheaded agenda in selecting the views for publication.

The tour was organised so that Sir Watkin could visit his properties through-out north Wales, visit his political allies and view the scenery – more often than not, his scenery. It was probably the first time he had done so.

The Wynnes, the Vaughans, the Williamses and the Williams Wynns were all related and the overnight stays seem to have been either in hotels or in houses belonging to one of those families. The servants were billeted out in hotels at Sir Watkin's expense, unlike on the Italian tour where they were given an allowance and looked after themselves, but there was probably a limited choice on this journey.

They set off on Wednesday 21 August and returned on Wednesday 4 September. The first part of the journey was from Wynnstay, out through the park gates at Newbridge where they crossed the river and joined the turnpike road through the Dee valley to Llangollen. One shilling and seven pence was the toll charge. A view of the vale is the subject matter of one of Sandby's most accomplished aquatints and when it was published, it must have had a considerable effect in establishing the new medium as one worthy of serious attention. His prints, although reproduced in number, were not cheap and he exercised great care in ensuing that standards were maintained. Less successful fellow artists were known to have made slightly jaundiced remarks about his prices.

Towards Llangollen, the bell ringers of the town rang a festive peal as the party approached and, as became his habit, Mr Sidebotham gave them five shillings for their efforts. Crossing the Dee again, they continued along the north bank, passing close to Valle Crucis Abbey which Sandby and Sir Watkin had visited the year before and on to Corwen through Llantsanfraid (now Carrog), where they partook of the hospitality of the widow, Mary Llwyd, who provided them with bacon and eggs and allowed them to rest awhile in her house. Crossing the river yet again they made Corwen where the servants were quartered in a pub whilst Sir Watkin and the gentlemen re-crossed the river to Rûg [Rhûg] Hall which was then home of some of the Vaughan family of Nannau, relatives to the Williams

Wynns. The young baronet and his party spent their first night there in rather more comfort than the servants – Corwen did not have a good press in the eighteenth century. Their unfamiliarity with the country they were travelling through is evidenced by the frequent payments to 'guides' from the second day onwards. From Rûg, they continued to Cynwyd by the tortuous road which winds by Gwerclas, a house, which is a delightful essay in brick-built Dutch baroque and which is so hard to find that the need for a guide becomes evident. Cynwyd, an extended hamlet, was where Sandby sketched the waterfall behind the mill and Mr Sidebotham paid the 'Millar & boy that held the horses at the waterfall' the tidy sum of 6s 3d. Cynwyd Mill belonged to Rûg and as it was tucked away up a steep-sided valley, the visit must have been a deliberate one. Sandby's aquatint of the mill seems to have caused some technical difficulties (it is very smudgy) and he eventually withdrew it from publication and substituted a view of Valle Crucis Abbey instead. Mills seem to have been on someone's agenda and visits were made to at least five of them during the course of the tour.

After Cynwyd, they rambled through the Vale of Edeirnion, through Llandrillo and Llandderfel, both of which were Williams Wynn possessions, the latter being the birthplace in 1752 of Edward Jones who became known as the King's Bard. His studies were encouraged and subsidised by Sir Watkin and he was to establish himself in London, attracting the approval of Dr Burney and his daughter and being appointed harper to the Prince of Wales in 1788. The position was renewed when the Prince ascended the throne, hence the harpist's grand title. Jones was a quiet and reserved man and may not have adjusted to life in the capital. English was always his second language and, although housed in St James's Palace, he seems to have experienced some social difficulties during his career.

A rest was taken on the banks of the Dee at Bodweni and a drawing session held. The resultant aquatint shows Sandby sketching, perched upon a glacial boulder in a very recognisable part of the valley. The title of the print reveals how Sandby must have become confused with descriptions and place names several years later when he prepared his work for publication. He describes the location as being on the banks of the Dee with Cadair Idris in the distance. Neither Cadair Idris nor the Arans are visible from this part of the river and remain hidden until the river curves to the west almost in Bala. In fact, the mountain is Arenig Fawr, but perhaps no-one in the party actually knew that. His confusion also surfaces later and he gives disparate views the same title.

On the second evening, they reached Bala and Llyn Tegid (Bala Lake and Pimblemeer being the English names) where some of the reasoning for the journey became apparent. Sir Watkin entertained the populace with a bonfire and ample supplies of ale whilst also inviting five of the local gentry to share dinner and a further eleven to supper with him. The Goat, the Eagles and the Bull seem to have been taken over for the evening and whilst Sir Watkin entertained his special guests in one of the hotels, the others were given over to the entertainment of the generality of his tenants. Bala was on the verge of a mass conversion to Methodism, having found the Established church wanting, and it would have been wise to exercise proper care whilst there. George III's refusal to wear anything other than Bala stockings was, I am glad to report, unaffected by the congregational desertion. A peculiar, and perhaps related, fact is that the parish church is a couple of miles along the lake from the town at Llan-y-cil and therefore hardly in the centrality of town life. Perhaps Methodism was more convenient.

A boat was hired for an excursion along the lake (which belonged to Sir Watkin) and generous supplies of alcohol were consumed. The purchase the next morning of 'Tincture of Rhubab' may have had something to do with the previous evening's merriment although, in fairness, it must be also recorded that it was sometimes used as an artist's colour. Sir Watkin was careful to observe the obligations attendant upon his position and a guinea was given to the poor of the place, an act which became invariable practice throughout the journey.

At the end of Llyn Tegid is the estate and house of Glan-llyn which he owned and which had been ransacked to supply the 1770 coming-of-age party with provisions, but rather than stay under his own roof, out of sight, he elected to stay in inns and hotels where he was on conspicuous display. They passed Glan-llyn and Llanuwchllyn where the fifth baronet (Sir Watkin's son) eventually established a proper Church school for the benefit of its youth to free them from the taint of Nonconformity. On the way to Dolgellau, over the bleak and forbidding pass near Drws-y-Nant, where, incidentally, a Welsh 'Lunar Society' (*Y Gymdeithas Loerig*) had been established in the 1760s for the literary improvement of its members, another motivation became apparent.

On the slopes of Cadair Idris, a short distance to the south-east of Dolgellau at Dol Gun were iron forges and smelting works, originally owned by Abraham Derby.[11] The Wynnstay estates were ore rich in several places and the grindings of early industry seem to have been of particular interest. Sandby produced a particularly memorable image of the site, but in his labelling of the print became confused as to its exact geographical location. He labels the view as being between Dolgellau and Barmouth, but there is a sketch in the National Library of Wales and a watercolour in the British Museum with exactly the same title and they bear no relationship to the print. The aquatint of the iron forge is quite well-known as an example of an artist's exploitation of the scenic possibilities of the nascent industrial revolution, but its exact location is not always clear. In the background, a carter drives his horse over a middle-distance horizon and behind that is the unmistakable profile of Cadair Idris itself. Anyone who has stood on that blasted heath by the Cross Foxes Hotel, waiting for the Machynlleth to Dolgellau bus, will have the exact configuration of that forbidding pile of rock lodged forever in their visual memory. Mr Sandby was undoubtedly slightly confused when he labelled the print. Dol Gun is at the head of the steep-sided valley known today for the very scenic Torrent Walk and there are the remains of earlier industry down the length of the valley.

The evening was spent at the Spread Eagles in Dolgellau and John Pugh, the landlord, furnished them with a nice and sophisticated printed bill (of which he must have been quite proud) for the food and alcohol the men consumed and the oats eaten by the horses. The back of the bill has supplementary expenses written on it, stating that the poor of Dolgellau were given a guinea to ease their suffering and the bell ringers given five shillings for celebrating Sir Watkin's visitation. A very generous tip considering that Llangollen church has many more bells and yet they both received the same amount. Perhaps that was the going rate.

On 24 August, they took an entire day to amble the seven miles or so to Barmouth, but on the north side of the Mawddach estuary at Cwm Mynach, there were some mills which may have been owned by the Wynnstay estate. Llanelltyd parish, in which Cwm Mynach is situated, figures largely in the rent rolls. These may have been visited with an eye to increasing their profitability and Sandby seems to have made more drawings of them which he later completely confused with the forges at Dol Gun. These mills are the subject of the two previously mentioned drawings which are labelled, probably correctly this time, with the same description as that of Dol Gun – *The Iron Forge between Dolgellau and Barmouth*. Mr Sandby may well have been temperate, but the bill from the Spread Eagles in Dolgellau shows an immodest proportion of their costs there to have been derived from the consumption of wine, punch, cider, ale and porter; the servants' ale is recorded separately. The seven miles to Barmouth on a hot August day may not have been a totally enticing prospect and the large sum of one whole shilling was spent on ice when they reached the little port but, and not surprisingly considering the indulgences of the previous evening, virtually nothing was spent on alcohol. This part of the tour, along the shores of the immensely beautiful Mawddach estuary, was by a difficult and in places steep and rocky road and the luggage was loaded onto a barge at Hengwrt and floated down the river to Barmouth.

Barmouth was at that time beginning to develop into a quite profitable port. Its earlier brush with celebrity had been when the still standing house on the harbour edge (Tŷ Gwyn) was allegedly used by Jasper Tudor and his nephew, Henry, as a base from which to plot the nephew's ascendance to the English throne. Thereafter, Barmouth sank into obscurity until it began to export locally-made webs (long lengths of white wool, sometimes mixed with cotton) to the southern states of America and the West Indies to clothe the slaves. Slavery was to be effectively abolished in Great Britain by Lord Mansfield's judgement in the year after our party visited Barmouth, but a healthy profit was still to be made from the export of cloth until the American War of Independence ruined Barmouth's trade. Thereafter it dwindled into a resort; a refuge of John Ruskin and the site of the first land holding of the National Trust.

In examining the route of Sir Watkin's journey so far, it seems to conform with that expected of a landlord inspecting his properties. But now some subtleties may lead us to suspect that he was acting upon some very astute advice. When he reached Dolgellau his progress seemed to become less that of a landlord and more that of an aspiring politician. His journey to Barmouth, whilst allowing him to inspect the mills in Cwm Mynach, was hardly of importance. By taking that route he had ignored the substantial holdings at Rhiw Goch, ones which his mother had consolidated for the estate during his minority, but which may have been under populated and therefore unworthy of a visit. Had he simply wanted to go to Harlech, he could have taken the coach road which crossed over the Rhinnogs by the wonderfully abandoned Pont Scethyn and then descended into Harlech itself. There must have been a purpose for going through Barmouth and then up the coastal route. Very little of the west coast actually belonged to him so there seems to have been a pressing reason for taking that particular course. He was not a natural or instinctive politician, unlike his father, and one may suspect that his mother was a guiding influence on his tour. She was a very clever businesswoman who had managed the estates more than capably during his minority. Her political instinct was sharp and it was widely believed that upon the death of her husband, her first act had been to burn incriminating papers and destroy anything which could have been used against the Wynnstay interest. She knew what the status quo was in north Wales and would have equally known that her beloved son was an innocent in that respect. The west coast was an area of influence for families who could be trusted to be sympathetic but who still needed proper acknowledgement of their status. Her husband had done it and now her son needed to.

The tentacles of the Vaughans reached far. A branch of the family was at Rûg, another at Nannau near Dolgellau but their historic seat was at Cors-y-Gedol which was the next place to be reached. Culturally they were about as far away from Sir Watkin as it was possible to get. Although William Vaughan had been a leading light of the Cymmrodorion and *bon viveur* when the society's Chief President, the family culture was not London centric. Virtually hereditary

143

members of parliament, it was only the failure of the direct male line in 1791 which ended their monopoly. They rarely went to London and there is no record of any of them actually standing up in the House of Commons and uttering a word. But contested elections in north Wales were as rare as hen's teeth and when one did happen, as in the notoriously violent Denbighshire election of 1741 when the Williams Wynns of Wynnstay and the Middletons of Chirk locked horns, the results were catastrophic for the family purse; as our Sir Watkin was to discover to his cost in the 1774 election in Montgomeryshire. It was much better and more sensible to parcel out the areas of influence beforehand and avoid unnecessary expenditure. Hence, possibly on the advice of Lady Williams Wynn, the next stage of his tour, which was neither romantic nor proprietorial, seems chiefly concerned with getting the right people on board with the Wynnstay interest. Whether Tory or Whig was almost an irrelevance in the face of self-interest and the gentry of north Wales had given ample demonstration of the fact that in their view, self-interest overrode all other considerations.

The next day they went north up the coast towards Harlech which, although run-down and moribund, was the administrative town for Merionethshire. On the way, they passed by Cors-y-Gedol, the previously mentioned seat of the Vaughans, although there is no mention in the accounts of them having visited the house. It is unthinkable that they did not visit that important family and the gentlemen on horseback were probably quite capable of making side excursions whilst the cart with the baggage trundled slowly ahead.

Sir Watkin's conspicuous generosity was again displayed to the poor of Harlech who were given five shillings; perhaps there were not many of them compared to Dolgellau. A guide to the castle was hired, Sandby sketched and an agreeable day was had. Apart from his published aquatint, Sandby also executed a finished watercolour of much the same scene. The two differ in some respects and the print has a delightful detail in the foreground of a young lad tending his flock, but what is not quite obvious in the monochrome print is that there is a hint in the watercolour that the grasslands immediately below the castle may have still been waterlogged. The castle was built on the cliff edge above the sea and originally had a harbour, but in time the tide had receded and the resultant marshes were drained and put to agricultural use. A date in the 1770s is very late for the castle still to be water-lapped, but we must presume that Sandby drew what he saw.

Sir Watkin had his eye on being appointed lord lieutenant and *custos rotulorum* for Merionethshire and in 1775 his scheming paid off and, although slightly tainted in George III's eyes because of his family's Jacobite leanings, he

144

was appointed to the desired positions. The King's suspicions would have become rampant had he known of the merriment of the next day. Sir Watkin's father had promoted the Cycle of the White Rose, an avowedly Jacobite society, and its leadership had fallen to his son. At Pengwern in Llan Ffestiniog lived a distant cousin, Owen Wynne, a fellow art patron and member of the Cycle. Wynne had property in Denbighshire but had come into possession of Pengwern through his marriage to Anne Lewis, the last remaining child of the original family. He had briefly acted as High Sheriff of Merioneth in 1747–8 but thereafter no longer seemed to find overt politics attractive. Meetings of the Cycle seemed to alternate between Pengwern and Llwyn, his Denbighshire house, and the previous year, John Parry, Sir Watkin's protégée, when he was not painting stage scenery at Wynnstay, had attended the Cycle and made pastel portraits of Wynne and his fellow members.

The Vale of Ffestiniog vied with the Vale of Llangollen for the epithet of the most beautiful in north Wales and Sandby's expressed frustration at his lack of time for sketching probably had its origins here. The party repaired to Wynne's house and Sir Watkin invited anyone of note in the vicinity to join them at the local inn. Then known as Yr Efail (The Smithy) and now christened the Pengwern Arms, it was a substantial establishment where the gentlemen could gather and talk to their hearts content without boring the ladies. Whether politics, art, the Grand Tour, the price of corn, or music were discussed, we shall never know, but a harpist was hired and an entirely convivial evening was spent. Perhaps too convivial; Sandby's rather witty aquatint of the fulling mills at Pengwern, whilst not one of his best in terms of composition, shows the unmistakable figure of Sir Watkin nodding off over his fishing rod and presumably about to slither into the river below whilst a noisy boy proffers another bottle and a scruffy dog enlivens the scene. The bill explains all.

Festiniog, August 26 1771			
Eight gentlemen diend on Monday	£0	16s	0d
Ditto five more diend	£0	2s	6d
Nine servants diend ditto	£0	4s	6d
Five gentlemens coffie on Monday	£0	2s	6d
Five gentlemen swpr on Monday night	£0	5s	0d
Ditto eight servants swpr	£0	4s	0d
Ditto five more on Monday night	£0	2s	6d
Gentlemen and servants for liquor	£1	13s	10d
Twenty one horses to hay and grass	£0	10s	6d
Ditto for corn	£1	7s	0d

Five gentlemen breakfast to day	£0	5s 0d
Ditto five more breakfast	£0	2s 6d
Nine servants breakfast	£0	4s 0d

The next few days are somewhat confused in Sidebotham's accounting and he seems to have become a little mixed up as to the exact sequence of payments and events. He was normally so precise in his bookkeeping but he seems to have forgotten a further payment for ale of £1 5s 0d made at Ffestiniog which he added later. Perhaps the reason for the payment was also the reason for his apparent forgetfulness.

The next day the party was augmented by the inclusion of a Mr Wenman who accompanied them back to Wynnstay. They continued back down the vale passing Plas Tan-y-Bwlch, home of the Griffith family which was about to become extinct and replaced by the enterprising Oakleys. After the sylvan delights of the vale, the road became seriously dreadful and they broke up into two groups, the cart with their luggage going over the Traeth Mawr by ferry and then on to Caernarfon to await them at the King's Head, while the main party went over the road so despaired of by the Duke of Rutland in 1797. It is even now a very high and exposed path snaking over the shoulder of the Moelwyns before dropping down to the edge of the Traeth Mawr at modern day Llanfrothen. The estuary of the Glaslyn was undammed and the high tide must have filled the valley and reflected the high surrounding mountains. Even without the water, it is a place of outstanding beauty with changing colours and extraordinary atmospheric effects. Sandby must have been entranced and took the chance to make some sketches and he later published a view from Llanfrothen across the Traeth to Mynydd Mawr and Moel Hebog. It was one of the first views ever published of the scene and one suspects that J.M.W. Turner knew it very well and was influenced by it when he made his first pilgrimage to Snowdonia twenty years later.

The next part of the road was relatively straightforward, and they reached the bridge at the Aberglaslyn Pass. Even though the main part of the luggage had been sent on separately to Caernarfon, the little that they carried themselves must have proved onerous and several boys were paid to carry that on ahead. At the bridge, they paused for a while. Sir Watkin owned parts of the adjacent Cwm Bychan and a miner who had discovered some samples of copper ore in the Cwm was interviewed and rewarded for his pains – he was given a guinea to have a drink in Beddgelert. In 1771, he could have been blind drunk for a week and still had change from the guinea; sometimes Sir Watkin seemed not to grasp the simple realities of life. The copper ore deposits were hardly commercial and although the valley was later devastated by workings, more people were ruined by the enterprise than ever made a fortune from it.

The way forward must have seemed apparent and Owen Thomas, who had acted as their guide since Bala was paid off and given the same amount as the miner to return home with.

Whilst Sir Watkin was speculating on the value of his holdings, Sandby devoted his time and pencil to capturing Pont Aberglaslyn itself. Within several years, as the tourist circuit of Snowdonia became established, the bridge and the pass were unmissable sights on the journey. John Byng, in 1784 wrote:[13]

We came to Pont Aberglaslyn, a bridge famous for its salmon leap, surprising situation and tremendous rocks. There are so many descriptions of this place that I must retire from weak relation, on my part; and only exclaim that the scene is most truly wonderful. A narrow-winding road looking down upon a foaming stony river and overhung by the steepest mountains, much extravasated by old lead mines; threatening destruction to the astonished traveller.

Byng, and I presume our travellers, found the scene sublime. Nowadays, due to vegetation it is hard to experience that sense of awe which seemed common to early visitors. No north Wales calendar published within the last fifty years has not included a view from, or of, Pont Aberglaslyn. It is indeed the very stuff of commemorative tea towels. The silence of the eighteenth century, broken only by the screech of the falcon and the rumbling of the torrent, may have been preferable to the silence broken today by the roar of the Porthmadog bus and the shriek of the Welsh Highland Railway pushing trekkers off the line and out of the sheltering tunnels. But Sandby can truly claim that his pencil was the first to capture the view. Of all the postcards on sale in Beddgelert, few can match his vision of the scene. Perhaps in several years time, when the intruding rhododendrons have been eradicated and the ospreys have returned, we may share that sense of awe that the early travellers felt.

Sir Watkin's party went through the pass and came to Beddgelert where Sandby gathered materials for a later oil painting of the tiny mining village which he exhibited at the Royal Academy in 1808. Continuing along the southern flanks of Snowdon and passing the Rhyd Ddu and Ranger paths to the summit, both of which seemed to be owned by the Ashton Smith's of Faenol, largely absentee landlords until the nineteenth century, when, as the family rose in social and economic significance, so too did the number and form of the letters in their surname (Assheton Smythe). Only stopping for ale at Betws Garmon, they entered Caernarfon in the late afternoon after what must have been the most tiring leg of the journey so far.

The journey from Ffestiniog to Caernarfon covered twenty-three miles and was one of the longest days in the saddle that the party had endured. They had gone through some of the most sublime scenery in the British Isles and although Sandby had had considerable experience in the Highlands of Scotland during his time as surveyor, even he must have been slightly overwhelmed by the dramatic and ever-changing scenery they passed through.

Caernarfon was their base for three days and to judge from the number of sketches, prints, watercolours and large oils Sandby produced of the town and castle for the rest of his working life, he must have been very industrious whilst there. He was known for his application and the speed with which he worked and it was commented that he often worked from dawn until dusk without a pause; a habit he may have learned when he worked with his brother for the Scottish Ordnance. The architect James Gandon wrote that he was '... indefatigable in cultivating his power as an artist. He commenced painting in water-colour very early in the morning; the pencil and frequently the pen seldom quitted his hand until evening.'[14] Caernarfon was the administrative centre of the county and Sir Watkin had political allies in the town as well as relatives and we can presume that his time was spent visiting them and generally making himself known there. The hotel bill for their time there was £16 13s 4¹/₂d and it is mildly interesting to note in passing that one third of the bill was for alcohol.

Whatever state they may have been in and one might sometimes wonder how, at this stage of their journey, any of them managed to stay upright in the saddle for long, on the 29th they made the excursion to Snowdon. They went boating on Llyn Padarn and dined at the ruins of Dolbadarn Castle and seemed to have the kind of day which Turner complained about in 1799 — 'Much rain but better effects – one clear day and Snowdon appeared green and unpicturesque to the top.' The unpicturesqueness did not appear to distress Sandby and he continued in his clear way to capture a view of the mountain to its top. After their boating expedition, a guide was hired to the mountain itself and men were paid to guard the horses. From the castle, it would have taken a minimum of four hours to ascend to the summit and perhaps a little less to return, but probably longer if it was hot. We cannot know if they went all the way or not, but had they done so, Sir Watkin would have had the pleasure of knowing that he owned most of what he surveyed from the peak. Perhaps in respect of alpine scenery, as in many other things, he had advanced tastes and tried to re-capture some of the frisson of his first alpine climb to the Chamonix glacier.

Joseph Craddock, a Leicestershire landowner, and in the vanguard of artistic taste wrote in 1774:[15]

The two first miles were rather boggy and disagreeable, but when the prospect opened, I soon forgot all difficulties. In the course of the two last I passed by two precipices, which I believe were very formidable, but as I was near the brink, and the wind very high, I did not venture to examine too narowly. On the summit, which is a plain about six yards in circumference, the air was perfectly mild and serene and I could with pleasure contemplate the amazing map that was unfolded to my view. From hence may be distinctly seen the Wicklow Hills in Ireland, the Isle of Man, Cumberland, Lancashire, Cheshire, Shropshire and part of Scotland; all the counties of North Wales, the Isle of Anglesea; rivers, plains, woods, rocks and mountains, six and twenty lakes, and two seas.

One must conclude that Craddock was rarely blessed on the day he chose to ascend the mountain; the views are not generally so all encompassing.

There were festivities of some kind going on in Caernarfon and one of Sandby's more technically accomplished aquatints shows the castle by moonlight, illuminated on one side by the glow of bonfires and with rockets exploding overhead. Nothing is recorded in the account to explain the nature of the occasion. Sir Thomas Wynn, Lord Lieutenant of Caernarfonshire (later Lord Newborough), lived occasionally in the castle and when Dr Johnson and Mrs Piozzi visited him in 1774, General Paoli (whose benefit fund Sir Watkin had subscribed to whilst in Florence) was staying there; distinguished visitors were not uncommon.

The day after the Snowdon trip they crossed to Anglesey and Beaumaris to visit Lord Bulkeley and stay at his mansion at Baron Hill. The Bulkeley family were the most important landowners on the island and ran their fiefdom with a rod of iron. Election results were always a foregone conclusion and yet again we find that the parliamentary seat had become, as so often in north Wales, an hereditary possession. Rabidly Tory, to an extent which alienated a number of their fellow Tory neighbours, the Bulkeleys were also fervent Jacobites. If Sir Watkin's father was thought to be tainted with Jacobitism, the Bulkeley's stank to heaven with it. Mrs Piozzi and Dr Johnson visited Baron's Hill on a similar excursion from Bangor and were shown around the grounds, which had recently been landscaped by William Eames. They were not shown the house but had they beenMrs Piozzi may have been less than amused to find that busts of Charles Edward Stuart and his brother were presiding over one of the salons. The seventh viscount was the last of the line and the busts and a secret docket of letters detailing Jacobite plans in 1715 were discovered well after his death in 1822 when an inventory of the house was being made.

Notwithstanding any ill effects they may have been suffering from, Sir Watkin and his companions were brave enough to cross the notorious Menai Strait. He gave a very large tip (£1 11s 6d and a further shilling for stowing the baggage on board) to Lord Bulkeley's boatmen for getting them safely across which might reflect a degree of gratitude, considering their likely physical condition, in having crossed the rough and temperamental waters without embarrassing inconvenience. The servants escaped the trauma and were lodged at the Eagles in Bangor where the gentlemen who had re-crossed the straits on empty stomachs joined them for breakfast the next morning. After a guided tour of the cathedral, they then left for Conwy, having mislaid Matthew Rowland who had been driving the cart from Caernarfon. Fortunately he had the enterprise to make his own way to Conwy and meet them there.

The continuation of the journey was the stuff of travel legend. The dreaded headland of Penmaenmawr had to be skirted around. Only a couple of years later, Dr Johnson and Mrs Thrale came in the opposite direction and the good lexicographer was quite shaken by the experience despite improvements having been made to the road in 1772. There was certainly no time for sketching on this part of the road and Sandby's hands, as well as everyone else's, were probably gripping the reins tightly as they made their way between a precipitous 200-feet drop to the sea on the left and the towering and loose cliffs on the right. They survived the experience and after passing a pub offering a dram of whisky to steady the nerves, made it into Conwy by nightfall.

The bell ringers of Conwy were paid a guinea to announce their arrival and a bonfire was lit and ale served to amuse the populace. The poor were not forgotten and the usual guinea was given to them and a Mrs Baker was the recipient of ten shillings and sixpence.

The tour now dwindled into something seriously cultural and an unusual abstemiousness set in. Whilst staying at the Bull's Head, they seem to have engaged all available local talent to entertain them. Poets were engaged to recite, bell-ringers engaged to play the jingle bells and, most importantly, a harpist paid for the evening. Five shillings seems to have been the going rate for an evening with a harpist and those at Conwy, Pengwern and Holywell were each paid the same. Harps in Wales were a serious expectation of the English visitor and for once that expectation seems to have been untinged with malice. The blind John Parry of Ruabon, Sir Watkin's household harper, was generally regarded as a prodigy of his art and it would have been foolish to expect playing on his level from a rustic virtuoso, but perhaps the surroundings lessened the expectation.

The poet, Thomas Grey, whom we last encountered struggling over the Mount Cenis Pass, had a serious case of writer's block whilst he was composing his epic narrative *The Bard*. His poem was everything its title suggested, but in 1757 he wrote from Cambridge:

Mr Parry has been here and scratched out such ravishing blind harmony, such tunes of a thousand years old, with names enough to choke you, as have set all this learned body a dancing, and inspired them with due respect to my old bard, his countrymen, whenever he shall appear. Mr Parry, you must know, has set my Ode in motion again, and has brought it at last to a conclusion.

Thus unblocked, Grey completed his work, which was to inspire a generation of painters. Mr Parry fulfilled all expectations in that he was unfortunately blind but he was also a very sophisticated musician whose published compositions became the very bedrock of harp technique. The English visitor expected not only that the harpist should be blind, but also that they should wear a pleasantly druidical costume. They might also have preferred that their style of playing was agreeably rustic. A harpist who was too good might have disconcerted the judgement of the self-appointed amateur connoisseur. John Byng, in 1783, was enthusiastic.

Bala. Our boatman ... added that the harping and dancing were decreasing in Wales by the interdiction of the Methodists who over-run the country. The harper in the town attended (by command) our return, and was very rapid and enlivening; and tho' his harp was not so good as that of yesterday, we thought that he had much more execution; his company was very agreeable until eleven o'clock.

Conway. No sooner had we dismounted and I had gone to the stable ... than Mr P. found out the blind harper of the town (a harper to be compleat shou'd be blind) to whom we gave preference of any we had met with.

Whether or not this was the harper Sir Watkin engaged we cannot know, but he does seem to have been the town harpist and may have been the one sketched by Julius Caesar Ibbetson in about 1792.[17]

Conwy seems to have been a particularly fruitful subject for Sandby. There exist drawings, watercolours and gouaches of the castle and town from several viewpoints and he exhibited paintings of the castle at the Royal Academy in 1779, 1781 and 1809. His aquatint of Conwy is relatively straight forward and shows the castle from Coed Benarth on the side of the Conwy River; now a thickly-wooded hillside. It is a late afternoon view and the sun is silhouetting the castle and casting its shadow across the river. In the far distance we look down the river estuary towards the Great Orme. The walls of the town are stretching up the hill, on the left of the plate, to the south gate, itself the subject of some drawings. Ships and boats are on the river and some men are fishing off the sands in the foreground, a stretch of foreshore with unstable quicksand.

Sir Watkin had family ties in Conwy and some of the early Wynnes are buried in the parish church. His party arrived in Conwy on 31 August and left for Llanwrst on 2 September, thus giving Sandby an entire day in which to sketch. From the number of surviving drawings he must have been remarkably industrious. He imparts to his views a late-summer feel with golden light and, in the Liverpool (Walker Art Gallery) gouache, a wonderfully rich glowing colour. It is interesting to compare the Liverpool and the Manchester (City Art Gallery) views. They are both similar in general outline, but there is significant variation between the two in respect of the figures in the foreground. The Liverpool work shows an artist shaded by a parasol and a gentleman leaning against his horse. The artist is familiar from the drawing of the mill near Dolgellau and the grouping is very similar to that shown in a sketch by William Parry of Sandby drawing which is now in the Royal Collection. The Manchester view has gentlemen riding across the same meadow, which is here peopled with sheep, cows and farm workers. They have obviously both been worked up from the same sketches but with quite different results.

Undoubtedly, Sandby re-cycled his sketches and produced variations of scenes. Towards the end of his career he began to handle watercolour as though it were oil and frequently used body colour. Interestingly he moved over to oils because he could not afford the glass needed to frame sketches and watercolours.[18] It is possible that the Manchester version is that which William Gravatt, a friend and pupil, watched him paint over three days in 1802.[19] These views of Conwy have a glorious Mediterranean warmth about them and one can imagine that after the exertions of Snowdon, the fear of the crossing to Beaumaris and the terrors of Penmaenmawr, Sandby was simply happy to sit in a sunlit field, enjoy the prospect and capture it on paper. Although he taught Sir Watkin to draw and sketching was one of the sub-texts of the tour, there is no indication of what Captain Gascoin, Mr Wenman and Thomas Apperley did whilst the baronet and the artist were indulging their aesthetic inclinations. Perhaps they just dozed in the late summer sunshine enjoying the memories of the last meal and looking forward to the next one. If the artistic evidence can be relied on, Conwy was an idyll!

After Conwy, they followed the river south to Llanrwst and Gwydir Castle from whence the Wynn family had begun its ascendance in Welsh political life and from where the Williams's added the Wynn to their family name. Staying at the Spread Eagles – a Wynn armorial device – where their entertainment was provided by another poet engaged for the evening and possibly yet more jingle bells. Five guineas were given to a Mrs Williams and one guinea to a Mrs

Clarkson, who may have been relations. John Thomas, landlord of the Spread Eagles, was yet another progressive hotelier who had furnished himself with grandly printed bills. Hereafter the documentary evidence, in the form of Sidebotham's accounts, and the artistic evidence in the form of Sandby's prints and drawings, tell a different story. The next day's journey was one of the longest and it would have seemed logical to send the baggage cart directly to their evening destination at St Asaph, either by the route over the Denbigh moors or back down the valley to Llansanffraid Glan Conwy and from there along the coast. The gentleman's party made a detour to the head of the valley before joining their return route, which must have been over the moors from Pentrefoelas, through Denbigh and re-joining the baggage at the White Lion in St Asaph.

Pont-y-Pair is the bridge over the Afon Llugwy (not the Conwy as Sandby thought) and which is today surrounded by Betws-y-Coed. In the 1770s, Betws hardly existed and it is not surprising that Sandby, in his inscription, did not mention it. He would have followed the Afon Conwy from Llanrwst on the same side of the river as Gwydir Castle and probably did not realise that the Llugwy was a tributary of the Conwy.

The view today, as far as the bridge is concerned, is substantially the same. But the bare mountainous valley in which Sandby sets his scene is impossible to verify now. The landscape has become densely wooded and lush.

Although it is generally assumed that Edward I denuded the Snowdon landscape of its forestation, other landowners seemed to have followed and profited by his example until the late eighteenth century. Sir Watkin perhaps needs to plead guilty here as, whenever short of funds, he often resorted to selling timber from his estates. The Victorians began serious replanting around Betws and in a little over 200 years, this countryside has re-established itself completely. Perhaps if sheep were banned from Snowdon's immediate environs, it too would regenerate itself as a mountain forest landscape.

The view of Pont-y-Pair has a mysterious detail under the bridge itself. Under the second arch from the right, dimly seen, is a gentleman fishing, assisted by a youth; a dangerous place to sit when the river is in full spate. Might this be Sir Watkin again? There are several versions of this print executed as gouaches or in watercolour and we, who are so used to the scene, can sometimes forget that to Sandby's audience this was a novel and unusual view, contrasting as it does the works of man with the rude grandeur of primitive nature.

After visiting the 'Pont-y-Pair,' the party continued up the river to the Swallow Falls (Rhaeadr-y-Wennol) which were the subject of another aquatint, again showing Sir Watkin (or at least the same portly gentleman who has appeared in several of the preceding aquatints) plagued by noisy youths and surrounded by tumultuous cascading waters. However, there are other watercolours by Sandby which seem to be derived from sketches made on the tour. From the Swallow Falls it was possible to cross the lower slopes of Moel Siabod to Dolwyddelan and there are watercolours of *Haymaking at Dolwyddelan* and one labelled as being *A Mill at Llanrwst*, but more likely to be of a mill near the Conwy Falls, another version of which is labelled as being *Pen Machno*. Sandby, understandably, became confused over Welsh place names and his notes were made very much 'on the hoof'. There would have been a logical reason for drawing the various scenes as they all belonged to the Williams Wynn estates.

The journey would have likely continued up the Conwy valley until the party reached Pentrefoelas where they could have branched off and crossed the moors. The estate of Voelas belonged to Watkin Wynne, at some point High Sheriff of Denbighshire, who was a relation of not only Sir Watkin but also one of the Mrs Williams (née Thellwell) to whom the latter had given five guineas in Llanrwst.

The White Lion at St Asaph must have been reached fairly late in the evening but they may not have been worn out. The bill includes, apart from music, claret, old hock, madeira, port wine, beer, coffee and beer for the servants. The bells were also rung, although, for the sake of the townspeople, we may hope that it was during their departure the following morning rather than in the evening as they arrived. St Asaph was a necessary post on the tour as it was a major centre of estate influence.

The final stop was to be in Holywell where the horse races had become particular favourites of Sir Watkin and he later presented a gold prize cup to the corporation. Horses were obviously beginning to present a problem and not only was the cart greased, and presumably maintained, but the horses feet were also attended to. There were now only thirteen of them and the bill for one evening's hay was 18s. 6d. The 'Stoping and Greasing of Horses Feet' must have been fairly frequent but here it is itemised separately. Victuals continued in much the same vein as they had been in St Asaph, but here a harper was engaged for the usual five shillings. The next day they returned back to Wynnstay by way of Mold and Wrexham.

After leaving the Conwy valley, Sandby executed no more work. Or, at least, nothing is known to survive of any views of the scenery from Pentrefoelas to St Asaph, Holywell and then back to Wynnstay. The last couple of days involved quite some travelling and perhaps, as he recorded in his letter to Thomas Pennant, there simply was no time to stop and draw. Pennant lived at Downing near Holywell (Treffynon) and although mere speculation, one may hope that he joined the party on their last night, met Paul Sandby, enjoyed the harpist and Sir Watkin's hospitality and perhaps saw and admired some of Sandby's sketches.

The party had spent fifteen days on a sightseeing tour, one of the first of its kind in Wales, possibly the very first, but with very mixed motives as to the particular sights visited. With the outbreak of the Napoleonic Wars and the inevitable closure of the Continent to British sightseers, the Welsh trip was fast emulated. The *XII Views in North Wales* may have played a part in making north Wales newly fashionable.

Paul Sandby certainly made the most of the opportunities Sir Watkin gave him to experience new stimuli and earn the title of 'the Father of English Landscape', a title earned partly in Wales? Towards the slightly sad end of his career, when he was re-cycling views and repainting images to boost his income, he may have thought with nostalgia of his little idyll in north Wales, when he was fashionable and at the height of his powers; when the sun shone each day and the conversation and much else flowed freely each night.

For Sir Watkin, life must have seemed an endless summer. He was the richest man in Wales, a mere twenty-two years old and about to marry for the second time. He relished the company of musicians and artists and was not to know that he had only another eighteen years to live. A kind and generous man he seemed incapable of reigning himself in. Whether it was in alms to the poor, inoculations for the paupers of Ruabon or Robert Adam's exorbitant bills for 20 St James' Square, he seemed to have no concept of relative values. London society, in which he cut a certain figure, was perfectly happy to accept his hospitality whilst, at the same time, they gently mocked him.

Although a patriotic Welshman, he had in reality very little experience of his own country. Educated at Westminster and Oxford, he cannot have returned to his roots very often. His discovery of Wales in 1771 must have been as novel an experience for him as it had been for Sandby. Perhaps, had he spent more time at Wynnstay and less in St James' Square, which was paid for by his Welsh rentals, the financial embarrassments of his latter years could have been avoided. He was rich, but mostly, in the esteem of his friends.

Sandby was an ideal companion for Sir Watkin. The former's wit was well-known and the latter certainly enjoyed a joke. It must be to our eternal regret that a projected tour to Italy did not materialise.[20] Sir Watkin had made his Grand Tour but Sandby never left our shores and we can only speculate as to what the artistic result of such a tour would have been.

Artists and patrons are not always well matched but Paul Sandby and Sir Watkin Williams Wynn should, perhaps, be regarded as joint creators of the *XII Views in North Wales*.

Notes

1. This oft quoted piece is signed 'E.B.' and there are several candidates for its authorship. Edward Bysshe has been suggested, as has Bishop Burnet whose other prose works share similar phrases. It was published under the name of Edward Ward in America. Ward may have plagiarised the work as he had done so before with other travel pieces. Bysshe seems the most likely.
2. W. Linnard, 'A Swedish Visitor to Flintshire in 1760', *Flintshire Hist. Soc Journal*, 30, 1981.
3. Wynnstay, 123, p.35.
4. Quoted in *Snowdonia: A Historical Anthology*, David Kirk (ed.), Llanwrst, 1994.
5. Manners, John Henry, Duke of Rutland, *Journal of a Tour Through North and South Wales*, London, 1805.
6. See David Penn in 'Paul Sandby and aquatint', in *Dolbadarn, Studies on a Theme*, Paul Joyner (ed.), National Library of Wales, 1990.
7. Pennant. Thomas, *A Tour in Wales*, 1778.
8. Schama, Hughes, Andrews and most writers on the picturesque.
9. National Library of Wales, Ms 14005E.
10. Hughes, Peter, 'Paul Sandby and Sir Watkin Williams Wynn,' *Burlington Magazine*, p.459, 1971.
11. Dodd, A. H., *The Industrial Revolution in North Wales*, Cardiff, 1971.
12. William Parry, Sir Watkin's protegee, drew most of the members of the Cycle.
13. Byng, John, *The Torrington Diaries*, London, 1934.
14. See Bonehill and Daniels, 'Paul Sandby,' *Picturing Britain*, London, 2009.
15. Cradock. Joseph, *Letters from Snowdonia*, Dublin, 1770.
16. Byng, John, op. cit.
17. As a matter of interest, the painter loathed his own name.
18. Farrington, Joseph, *The Diary of Joseph Farrington*, New Haven & London, 1978/98.
19. Bonehill and Daniels, op. cit., p.67.
20. A letter from Father Thorpe in Rome to Lord Arundel mentions the planned visit. Quoted in Hughes.

SIR WATKIN

ON 18 MARCH 1773, SAMUEL SIDEBOTHAM WROTE to Francis Chambre,

I am afraid that the above will frighten you as it does me but you may depend that
every shilling I can put a stop to I ever will, I have prevented several pieces from
being bought by reprehending how matters stand.[1]

And this was to be the course of Sir Watkin's existence from then onwards. Here
is not the place to discuss Sir Watkin's later life in detail, but we can pencil in
aspects of it.

By 1776, when Paul Sandby published the first of his views in north Wales, Sir
Watkin's life had settled into its future shape. Married to Lady Charlotte
Grenville, the first of his children had been born and Sandby may have alluded to
that fact by including in his view of Wynnstay from Newbridge a detail, which
seems to show Lady Charlotte and her first two children. The magnificent house
in St James' Square was mostly finished and had been occupied the previous year.
Sir Watkin's musical breakfasts were already becoming a feature of the social life
of London. The final payments on the house were made by 1776 but the burden
was too much for the estates to bear and the debts were discharged with borrowed
money. Over £100,000 needed to be raised, a sum which represented over five
times his annual income.

A very grand house needed to be furnished in a similar vein and Sir Watkin
was well up to the challenge. Works of art had continued to arrive from Italy long
after he had left it. The Batoni portrait was hung in the new house and the tables
made by Gori in Florence were in the drawing room. Paintings, or at least copies
of well-known works, arrived from William Parry, who was fulfilling his bargain
in Rome, but more was needed. The *cognoscenti* were amazed, not to say a little
shocked, when at a sale at Christie's in 1773 he paid the sum of £650 for Poussin's
Landscape with a Snake. Horace Walpole and Fanny Burney both recorded their
extreme surprise at Sir Watkin's behaviour which was likely to inflate future
prices to the detriment of other collectors. His advanced neo-classical taste was

reflected in the furniture, mostly designed by Robert Adam, which slowly filled the house, but it was perhaps sheer extravagance to ask Adam to design a silver dinner service.[2] It was not within Adam's speciality to design silverware but he complied and the service was produced. It was the largest architect-designed service made in the eighteenth century. Now spread through museums and in private collections across the world, the extent of the finished service is uncertain but was certainly vast. Joseph Creswell, who supplied it was paid £2,408 18s in 1775 and like many of Sir Watkin's suppliers, went temporarily bankrupt after-wards. Chambre and Sidebotham were driven to despair by such behaviour. The fact that Sir Watkin's credit amongst tradespersons and craftsmen slowly dried up must be laid completely at his own door. Gentlemen were not renowned for paying their bills promptly, but in Sir Watkin's case, he was often simply unable to discharge his debt and working for him, whilst artistically satisfying, began to be seen as financially foolhardy. Habits he had acquired early in his life were hard to extinguish. The chest of silverware he took on his Grand Tour had contained candlesticks, a stewpan, a saucepan, plates, dishes, sauceboats, a cruet, cutlery, tumblers, decanters and tea wares and had been supplied by Thomas Hemming, goldsmith and jeweller to the king. No wonder that two men were needed to carry it onto the barque at Lake Geneva.

He thought that he was rich. London thought that he was rich. His stewards knew that he was falling headlong into undischargeable debt. Number 20 St James's Square had drained his resources' and Robert Adam had been unchecked in his ambition to design and build the perfect advertisement for his excellence as an architect. Other men such as the Duke of Northumberland at Syon, Robert Childs at Osterley Park or Lord Chandos at Chandos House in Chandos Street, may have had the ready money but Sir Watkin certainly did not and much anguish was to be caused by his inability to acknowledge that simple fact. His Welsh tenants were to be stretched to provide resources which were ultimately inadequate. In 1777, the rents were raised and Francis Chambre had one tenant imprisoned for failing to either pay or leave.

Being a man of contradictions, at a time when he was completely without cash and contemplating rent rises throughout his estates, he established a free dispensary at Wynnstay and inaugurated smallpox inoculations for paupers and tenants. The death of his brother from smallpox had affected him and he took it upon himself to provide advanced medical care for the entire neighbourhood. He was a governor of the Foundling Hospital, supported the Marine Society for the education and training of vagrant boys, subscribed to the Magdalen Hospital, was a governor of St Bartholomew's Hospital and subscribed to the Middlesex and Westminster Hospitals. His charitable credentials were above reproach, but he was being generous in the distribution of alms which he did not have.

Music and the theatre were to prove equally demanding upon his purse. He became deeply involved in the Concert of Ancient Music which promoted the great Handel commemoration in 1784 and of which, perhaps unwisely, he was appointed treasurer. The private subscriptions he diverted to his own use until he absolutely had to apply them to their intended purpose. When the day of reckoning came and the singers and instrumentalists asked for payment, he was in a delicate position. He wrote to his steward that the likely bill would be over £800 and that he was in funds to less than £200 (in fact the final bill was over £1,000). Sir Watkin was continually skating on very thin ice. His involvement with the Ancient Concerts earned him the privilege of being depicted by James Gillray as a fat man with a goat's head and fast asleep as the music played,[4] a caricature which he seemed to be not particularly bothered by. He once rode into the Pantheon on St David's Day, dressed as the saint himself and mounted on a goat. Known amongst his parliamentary colleagues as 'Bubbles', a much sterner judgement was recorded from Elizabeth Freemantle (née Wynne) when she was staying at Stowe. [He was] '… an awkward and rather stupid gentleman,' but Mrs Freemantle's opinion may have been based on unsympathetic hearsay as it was formed long after his death.[5]

At Wynnstay, an old kitchen detached from the main house had been trans-formed into a theatre for the 1770 celebrations. In all likelihood it was the first private theatre in Britain but was found to be inadequate. James Gandon was called upon to replace, or at least re-build, it and the festivities continued. It appears that, in spite of Sir Watkin's increasing financial difficulties, it was again modified in 1782 by John Evans. From 1773 until 1787 it was in regular use and could contain an audience of some 300.[6] Running a theatre is possibly one of the quickest ways to lose money and Wynnstay was no exception. The plays, mostly performed by gentleman amateurs, were lavishly staged. The wardrobe book, although damaged, still survives[7] and suggests a certain prodigality. Equally prodigal was the painting of scenery. Not only were local artists employed, but also Paul Sandby himself had contributed to the decoration during the time of the Welsh tour. Davis Garrick[8] and his wife and Richard Sheridan and his wife were occasional spectators and George Colman, the proprietor of the Haymarket Theatre, drilled the players into an acceptable standard. He also banished the footlights from the edge of the stage and placed a light batten above the stage behind the proscenium arch, possibly for the first time ever. For that innovation, if no other, the Wynnstay theatre must claim its place in theatrical history.

The pit band consisted of 'an harpsichord, violins, clarinets, hautboys, bassoons etc,'[9] although the winter orchestra could not have approached the standards of the summer one, which was stiffened by the inclusion professionals imported from London. Even the admission tickets were properly designed and Charles Bunbury, an old school friend of Sir Watkin, provided the drawings.[10]

All of this, as well as the musical establishment for which the house was well known, were not indications of a 'scale of frugality'. The wise words of Francis Chambre went unheeded and by 1777, the grounds and park at Wynnstay were being transformed. Lancelot (Capability) Brown was called in and besides replanning almost everything, designed a new dairy for which Josiah Wedgwood provided the tile work.[11] Brown was the originator of the sinuous curve in landscape art and it is interesting that whilst he proposed modifying the existing straight canal into something more natural, he nevertheless planted, perhaps at Sir Watkin's insistence, an anachronistic straight avenue of trees from the gateway to Ruabon village. This was never a main entrance to Wynnstay but the old-fashioned avenue may have impressed the locals. The death of Brown in 1783 curtailed the more extravagant of the proposals and one of his assistants, probably John Evans or possibly John Midgley, carried on with a modified version. The brook in the deep Belan valley, between the house and Ruabon was dammed to create a lake and cascade[12] and a neo-classical bathhouse with an open-air swimming pool built at the head of it (possibly designed by John Harrison). The lake was inaugurated with the usual junketings and half the neighbourhood was invited. James Wyatt designed new lodges for some of the most inconsequential entrances to the home park and probably refaced the house, which was added to piecemeal.[13] None of these additions and improvements could be called buildings of distinction. Lack of cash did not prevent Sir Watkin indulging himself in fantasies of what he would achieve when the cash became available. It must have been common knowledge, especially in Robert Adam's circle, that he was having some financial difficulties but if grand projects could not be realised there was no reason to forbear indulgence in small ones. The death of Garrick in 1779 was the cause of universal mourning and Sir Watkin was one of the pallbearers at his funeral.

Extravagant as ever, he commissioned Adam to design a cenotaph to commemorate the actor and to be erected in Wynnstay Park. Surely both Adam and his patron knew that the chances of it being realised were slight but the architect complied, produced the required design and sent in the bill.

It was left to Sir Watkin's son, the fifth baronet, to engage C.R. Cockerell to design the Newbridge Lodge. A miniature masterpiece built ironically when the Williams Wynn's were otherwise tending to avoid high art.

Being a fitful MP who was never once recorded as actually speaking in the House, Sir Watkin had certain privileges. A member could not be pursued for

debt within the precincts of Westminster Palace and he had to avail himself of
that privilege on several occasions. He was genuinely shocked in April 1773 when
he was given a bond at the House of Commons for £4,000 to be paid to Child's
Bank. He wrote disingenuously to Chambre, '... this usage I do not expect nor will
I any longer be kept in the Dark about the situation of my own affairs.' If Chambre
had any sense of humour he must have rolled about laughing when he read that
particular note. In view of his efforts to restrain his employers spending, his later
treatment by the widowed Lady Williams Wynn may strike us as distasteful.

As a politician, Sir Watkin was passive and awkward, like his father before
him, and he opposed rather than facilitated legislation. George III who thought
it imprudent to give office to those in opposition, grudgingly allowed his elevation
to lord lieutenant and *custos rotulorum* of Merionethshire.

*I consent to Sir Watkin Williams being Lieutenant of Merioneth if he means to be
grateful; otherwise, favours granted to persons in opposition is not very political.*[14]

The Vaughans of Cors-y-Gedol had occupied the post before him and it may be
that during the 1771 tour, a gentleman's agreement had been arrived at to allow
Sir Watkin to succeed. This was generally the way in north Wales but when
someone stepped out of line and upset the apple cart, mayhem could ensue. The
Parliamentary election of 1772 saw Sir Watkin returned unopposed as MP for
Shropshire. An intended opposition was dropped on the understanding that he
would stand for Denbighshire at the next election. In 1774, he was unopposed in
Denbighshire, but the Wynnstay candidate was challenged in Merionethshire and
Montgomeryshire. Some families had decided not to play the game. The Vaughans
broke ranks in Merionethshire and the Powis intervention in Montgomeryshire
led to a conflict which, even by the rumbustious standards of the time, was
particularly ill-natured, underhand and generally a dirty contest; bribery and
intimidation were rampant from both camps, and it cost a great deal of money
(£4,804 19s 0^1/$_2$d),[15] a sum which alarmed even Sir Watkin and he became much
more prudent in subsequent political contests, although never conceding any of
his influence.

Although his wife's cousin, William Pitt the Younger, was in power and Sir
Watkin should, by the standards of the time, have capitalised upon that
connection, he seems to have lacked the drive, or interest, to forge a political
career. Dilatory in attendance at the House of Commons, and unrecorded as a
speaker, he seems to have been content to remain an ordinary country member.
Only once did he stir himself out of his torpor and that, characteristically, was
when his own interests were threatened. Shortly after his nomination as Lord

Lieutenant, the government began to find itself short of cash with which to pursue the American War. Under the leadership of Lord North, it was proposed to appoint a new surveyor to the Crown Lands in Wales, to recover arrears of rent and, most alarmingly, to reassert the claims of the Crown to waste lands. In many cases, the waste lands had been encroached upon by enterprising landowners and it was not in their interest to have a searchlight shone on their past activities. Sir Watkin opposed Lord North and became prominent in the general criticism of his ministry for its extravagance and incompetence. The War of Independence mattered far less to the Welsh gentry than the possible curtailment of some of their dubious privileges and rights. Thereafter Sir Watkin consistently opposed both Lord North and Pitt. Politics were not much to his taste except when they could be combined with show. His installation as Mayor of Chester in 1773 was a splendid event and a ball was given and a great feast held in the Exchange. It cost him £500.

A letter from Miss Baldwin (later Mrs Thelwall of Llanbedr) to her sister in Ireland gives us a fair idea of the way in which Sir Watkin preferred to conduct politics.

Monday at seven we went to the Exchange, which was quite full. Lady Williams was a very brilliant. She looked very handsome and the picture of good nature and happiness. Her gown was something of gold but I don't know what. She had a fly cap entirely of Diamonds with the wings bent down close to her forehead. A finer necklace than Lady Grosvenor's, earrings watch and chain all Diamond a stomacher with four bows each of four bows all Diamonds so that she was quite dazzling. Her Bracelets were pearls and she had a row with a large drop falling below her necklace, which was the princess Dowagers and cost five hundred guineas. She was valued at £20,000 pound exclusive of her inestimable self. She is with child so did not dance. The room was hotter than the furnace of Shedrek Mechack and Abednigo, but Sir Watkin's servants broke all the windows and revived us.[16]

If Miss Baldwin's appraisal of Lady Charlotte's jewellery was correct then Sir Watkin's wife was wearing his entire annual income. Keeping up with the Jones's may have been within Sir Watkin's capability, but keeping up with the Grenvilles and the Grosvenors was a different matter.

In fairness to Sir Watkin, we need to consider that for the upper classes in the late eighteenth century, debt was a way of life. Money could easily be raised upon mortgages and the rate of interest at 4% was quite low. Around 1780, Sir Watkin's close neighbours, Lord Grosvenor at Eaton Hall and Richard Myddelton at Chirk Castle, were in debt to the tune of £151,000 and £105,000 respectively, and neither of them had much to show for it. By the time that the Grosvenors had become the Westminsters their star was very much on the ascendant and the Williams Wynns had retrenched into being a 'county' family with some metropolitan interests but with more important regional ones.

By the mid 1780s, reoccurring bouts of erysipelas were seriously debilitating Sir Watkin's health. Trips to Ramsgate to bathe in the sea for the 'Restoration of my health' did not have the desired effect even though the tenants at Machynlleth had been squeezed for £200 to pay the expenses. The money was accompanied by another letter from Mr Chambre.

I wish it may be sufficient to forward the Restoration of your Health, for no one wishes it you more sincerely than myself, but mupon my word I long have, and do still foresee some clouds hanging over you that will certainly burst in a very disagreeable manner if you do not resolve upon a larger scale of frugality than has hitherto been thought on.[17]

Frugality was not a word which Sir Watkin understood and the difficulties continued.

In the end, his infirmity exacted its revenge before his creditors managed to. In 1784, he went to France where he may have recalled the carefree days of his youthful grand tour, but found no cure and in 1789, his last illness began its remorseless course. A slight recovery gave false hope to Lady Williams Wynn but on 29 July 1789, he died at his 'palace' in St James' Square.

John Wynne of Garthewin recalled the last moments.

The late Sir Watkin Williams Wynn made it a particular request that Miss Sheridan should sing to him in his dying moments to which she kindly consented but as she warbled the Hymn 'Sacred to Friendship' the tears of sensibility wetted her pale cheeks.

He died surrounded by friends, the warbling of Miss Sheridan having proven ineffective. Lady Eleanor Butler, one of the 'Ladies of Llangollen', wrote:

The Hearse and Six attended by two Mourning Coaches and eighty mourners, came thro' Oswestry, where it was met by sixty pair of mourners, his agents and tenants. The Body lay in the Dining-room at Wynnstay that night and at twelve next day was interred, Lady Williams having expressly ordered that the burial should be in the Day.

Sir Watkin was the chief actor in his last great pageant. The *Gentleman's*

Magazine, which had paid such fulsome tribute to his father, repeated the compliment to the son.

> *The loss which Wales has sustained by his death will be long felt.*
>
> *At the head of a great and commanding fortune, he did not enter into the vices and follies of his age, but spent it in a rational and noble manner. In his public and private capacity his disinterested integrity was unimpeachable ... As a son, a husband, a parent, a friend and a master he was adored in each walk of life ... In a most peculiar manner it belonged to Sir Watkin to be the more beloved the better he was known – the surest indication of real worth.*

Perhaps it is incumbent upon us to accept the judgement of his contemporaries and not to apply our mores in retrospect to an age which had different priorities. Whatever may be said about the man, it is certain that his patronage of the arts enriched his own and subsequent generations and that our museums, galleries and libraries would be so much the poorer had he not been so gloriously profligate.

He does not have a monument in Ruabon parish church where he and his immediate ancestors are buried, but in the parkland, on the edge of the Belan Lake, his mother had James Wyatt build a Doric column in commemoration. The now vanished inscription once read:

FILIO OPTIMO MATER – EHEU – SUPERSTES
(To the best of sons his mother who – alas – survives him dedicates this)

NOTES

1. Wynnstay MSS 112, Family Papers, I, p.31.
2. See Fairclough, Oliver, 'Sir Watkin Williams Wynn and Robert Adam,' *Burlington Magazine*, 137, June 1995.
3. The house was finally occupied in 1775 and when the final payments were made in 1776, Sir Watkin was over £100,000 in debt; approximately £6.5 million in today's terms. Today, fully restored, it is the corporate headquarters of a software company.
4. British Museum.
5. Wynne Diaries, II, p.198.
6. Price, Cecil, *The English Theatre in Wales*, chapter XI, 'Wynnstay', Cardiff, 1948.
7. Wynnstay Mss 116.
8. Eighteen months after Garrick's visit Sir Watkin was a pallbearer at his funeral in Westminster Abbey.
9. *Chester Chronicle.*
10. As theatre ephemera, the tickets are now counted as highly collectable and are in many national collections.

11. Hinde, Thomas, *Capability Brown*, London, 1986.

12. The topping out ceremony was of the usual extravagance. The gamekeeper, two bagpipers, 80 colliers, 100 carters, 200 labourers, 20 artificers and 150 gentlemen and farmers attended the inauguration and the subsequent entertainments.

13. See Mowl and Earnshaw, *Trumpet at a Distant Gate*, London, 1985.

14. George III to Lord North.

15. Wynnstay, L 1249.

16. Askew Roberts, op. cit., p.90.

17. Wynnstay MSS 112, Family Papers, I.

ACCOUNTS IN FRANCE & ITALY
(WYNNSTAY PAPERS BOX 115/1)

The account book for the tour to France and Italy is a vellum bound, octavo volume with blank pre-ruled pages. There are 32 lines per page and the whole account covers 104 pages. I have transcribed all of the entries as far as page 12 and thereafter omitted all the entries concerning domestic shopping, money exchange rates and minutia, which although interesting at first, are very repetitive.

The earlier sections of the account demonstrate Mr Sidebotham's difficulties in dealing with denominations with which he was unfamiliar. The entries may be headed with the sterling symbols £ and s, but he may be referring to the currency in which he was dealing at the time. Sometimes it can be confusing when he records Louis d'Or and Livres in the same column without stipulating which is which.

Mr Sidebotham's handwriting is not without its difficulties but is generally clear and neat. Occasionally another hand appears, presumably writing out to Mr Sidebotham's dictation and sometimes malfunctioning pens have caused blots and scratches. Otherwise the account is perfectly readable.

Pasted on the inside cover is a small trade 'flyer' for an artist's suppliers close to where they were staying on the left bank. It reads: '*A La Flotte D'Hollande, Rue de Buffy ac Coin de la Rue de Seine, Fauberg Saint Germain 1762*'.

1768 (page 1)		£	s
June 1	Recd at London of Mr Francis Chambre 100 Sterling whch makes 2285 Livres at 22.17 p Pound Sterling	2285	0
10	Recd of Mr Panchaud 200 standby for which he gave at 22.5 sterling	4450	0
27	Recd of Do 100	2225	0
July 4	Recd of Do 500	11125	0
5	Recd of Do 500	11125	0
6	Recd of Do 200	4450	0
7	Recd of Do 100	2225	0
27	Recd of a Merchant at Lausanne 94¹/₂ Louis d'Or for 100 one hundred pounds	2262	0
August 5	Recd of Mr Gaufron at Geneva for 200	4416	4
19	Recd of Mr Torras at Turin 100	2269	4
24	Recd of Mr Torras 400	9066	12
	Carried to Page 33 2500	55899	0
[Pages 2,3,4 and 5 are blank]			
1768 (page 6)			
	Total of each Page		
	7th Page	2747	19
	8	1077	14
	9	878	6

10	612	10
12	556	9
13	158	16
14	9874	18
15	6364	7
16	3923	10
17	2580	15
18	1872	8
29	2386	18
20	269	0
21	312	1
22	89	4
23	606	12
24	398	1
25	1047	17
26	510	8
27	180	16
28	1431	8
29	1300	1
30	691	0
31	1744	16
32	1561	19
Carried to page	44024	5

1768 (page 7)

Expenses & Disbursments in Sr Watkins Expedition into foreign Parts by Saml Sidebotham

	In French Money [added later]	Livres	Sous
June 7	Pd Travelling Expenses from London to Paris per		
	Accompts 113;14;11 English and in French	2599	18
The following is in French Money			
June 8	Pd a Barber for cutting and curling Sr Watkins Hair	12	0
	Pd for Pens, Ink & Paper & Waxe	7	18
9	Pd for a letter	0	2
	Pd for 3 Tickets to the Comedy	10	0
	Pd at the Church the Procession Day	1	7
10	I gave the maids at the Hotel de Saxe		6
	I gave the Porter there		3
	Pd for a map of Paris	0	18
	Pd at the Opera for 3 Tickets	30	
	Pd for 1lb of Tea	12	10
	Pd for [?]	0	6
11	Pd for Powder and Pomatron	4	10
	Pd for a Soap Box	0	10
	Pd at the Comedy for Capt Hamilton	6	0
	Pd Allowance for bags & Silk Stockings for 2 footmen		
	and Coachman	45	0
	Carried to page 6	2747	19

1768 (page 8)

	Travelling Expences Continued	£	s	d
June 10	Pd for a Weeks Lodging at Hotel de Saxe and for			
	a few things broke	194	18	
11	Ps for a Plate for Visiting Tickets	6	0	
12	Pd at the Italian Comedy	18	0	
13	Pd Servants Board Wages from the 3rd to the 12th	113	5	
	Pd the following Weekly Bills			

— APPENDIX 1: ACCOUNTS IN FRANCE & ITALY —

		£	s	d
	Hotel de Saxe Dinner Bill	176	0	
	Pd Sejan Wine Merchant	297		
	Pd the Grocers Bill	37	19	
	Pd Brunet Butter Man etc	11	15	
	Pd the Coffee House Bill	17	2	
	Pd Mr Carrara's Bill with an allowance of 3 Guineas for his Boots & Sadle	129	3	
	Pd Sam Stephens weeks Bill	5	16	
	Pd Duboot, Valet de Place 6 Days Wages due yesterday at 2 Livres p day	12	0	
	Pd for an Umberella	18	0	
	Pd for Mr Morris & self seeing Notre Dame	1	16	
	Pd for the History of Gill Blass	9	0	
	Pd at the French Comedy	18	0	
14	Pd Mr Apperley expenses at seeing Churches etc	9	0	
	I gave a begging Capachine	3	0	
	Carried to Page 6	1077	14	

1768 (page 9)

	Travelling Expenses Continued	£	s	d
June 14	Pd for Mr Carrara, M Morris & self seeing Gobelins Tapestry	4	8	0
	I gave the Comic Singers	3		
	Pd for 2lb of Mustard	6	0	0
	Pd at the Italian Opera WEH	15	0	
15	Pd for 3 Cuttau de Chasse for Mess Carrara, Morris & self & 4 Belt Buckles	114	0	
	Pd for Coffee for Sr Watkin	1	4	
	Pd at the French Comedy EH TA	12	0	
16	Pd first Barber for a Bag 5, Ropes & Dressings 3	9	0	
	Pd Mr Andre for 1 plain Hat French Cap & 3 Livery Hats	159	0	
	Pd for Roses	0	6	
17	I gave Sr Watkin as Receipt	144		
	Pd for a Bottle of very bad Beer	2	0	
	Pd for 6 pr of white Silk Stockings	90	0	
18	Pd for 3 Snuff Boxes	183	0	
	Pd for 2pr of Valencienes Ruffles	120	0	
	Pd Mr Apperley what he gave at seeing Places	15	0	
	Pd for Bread Extraordinary	0	2	
Carried to Page 6		878	0	

1768 (page 10)

	Travelling Expenses Continued	£	s	d
June 16	Pd at the Italian Comedy	18	0	0
	Pd for the Play Book	1	10	0
	Pd for Mr Morris & self at the French Comedy	6	0	0
19 & 20	Pd Expenses to Versailles & Marly & St Germains as of acct	213	0	

21	Pd the following Weekly Bills			£	s
	Board Wages	84			
	Carriage Bill	39			
	Hotel de Saxe for Dinner	145	0		
	Brunet, Butter etc	18	10		
	Wine Merchant	114	0		
	Do Jolly	30	0		
	Grocer	29	9		

Coffee House		56	0	
Dubost Wages		14	529	19
Ps for a Silk Waistcoat			60	
Pd for a Cheese & Bollogna Sausage			8	5
Pd for a pr of black Silk Stockings			15	0
Pd for my self at the Hospital of Invalides			1	4
Pd at the Italian Opera			12	
Carried to Page 6			865	6

1768 (page 11)

		£	s	d
	Travelling Expenses Continued			
June 22	Pd for 2pr more of Valenciene Ruffle	120	0	0
	Pd for 4 Waistct Pieces	147	0	0
	Pd for 4 of us seeing the Benediction in the Gallery			
	of Notre Dame	2	0	
	Pd for 3 of us at the Bulwairs [?]	5	12	
	Pd for 3 of us at the Play	18	0	
23	Pd a Bill for Books	81	14	
	Pd a Messenger to Mr Wodehouse	1	4	
	Pd the little Barber for dressing Sr Watkin twice	2	8	
	Pd for a piece of cambrick 7 ells at 10 pr Ell	70	0	
	Do at 13 pr Ell	91	0	
	Pd Mr Apperley what he paid at several sights	27	0	
	Pd at the Italian Comedy	18	0	
24	Pd for 2pr of Shoes for Sr Watkin	12	0	
	Pd for 4 at the fireworks & coach home	6	0	
	I gave the Postillion	1	4	
	Pd for a White Sword Knot	9	0	
Carried to Page 6		612	10	

[NB. From here onwards the entries have been selected and edited for relevance upon the understanding that the minutia of the tour are of limited interest.]

1768 (page 12)

		£	s
	Travelling Expenses Continued		
June 25	Gave Mr Carrara for 4 Vols of French Songs	36	0
	I gave the Coachman having been twice in the Country	6	
29	Pd the Coachman the expence of of 4 horses to Versailles	6	0

1768 (page 13)

		£	s
	Travelling Expenses Continued		
June 29	Pd at Notre Dame Steeple for Messrs Carrara,		
	Morris & Self	2	8
	at the Palace Royal Gallery	3	0
	I gave the Postilion that went to Versailles	1	4
July 1	Pd seeing the Glass House	6	0
	Pd for Sr Watkin at Notre Dame Steeple	3	12
2	Pd for 3 Horses to see the Queens Funeral	18	0

1768 (page 14)

		£	s
	Disbursements Continued		
July 3	Pd for 4 pr of Silk Stockings	60	0
4	Pd for a Set of Stone Buckles	108	0
	Pd for an Umberella	27	
	Pd for grease for New Coach	1	0
	Pd Mr Carrara's Bill	62	2
	Pd Mrs Eynhorts for pr of Ruffles	486	

1768 (page 15)

	Disbursements Continued	£	s	
July 5	Pd Fencing Master for 21 Lessons @ 8 pr Lesson & for Foils	135	0	
	Pd Mr Hamilton what he Pd at Versailles & other Places	39	0	
	Pd for a cuteau de Chasse	53		
6	Pd Embroiderers Bill **???? Denagne Taylor**	**[?]**		
	I gave Mr Porter for frequent enquiring after the Box at Calais	24		
	Pd a great Rascal for a Travelling Bed which he at first charged 1003	850	0	0

1768 (page 16)

	Disbursements Continued	£	s	
	Pd a Basque for a Coach a month & horse sundry times	456		
	Pd the Coachman 20 days at 1:4 p Day	33	12	
	I paid Mr Hamilton as of Receipts 100 Sterling	228	35	
July 6	Pd Pochereau Bookshop a Bill	360	0	
	Pd the Language Master a Month	96	0	
	Pd him for books	306		
	Pd Hotel de Saxe Bill from June 27 to this day	306	0	

1768 (page 17)

	Disbursements Continued	£	s	
July 6	Pd Pascall for a new Coach 110 Guineas he allowed for Lord Leighs 40 Guineas			
	I paid 20 more the hire of a Chaise for Italy in all 90 guineas	[?]	0	0
	Pd Deuperelles Hatter a Bill	69	0	
	Pd Prince de Condi Coffee House Bill for Ice Cream	125		
7	Pd Mr Dauberville Dancing Master for 20 Lessons at 6 pr lesson	120	0	0
	I gave his apprentice	24	0	0

1768 (page 18)

	Disbursements Continued	£	s	
July 7	Pd for a set of Silver Buckles	24	0	
10	Pd for 4 travelling Capes for the Servants TM, SS, CB, LMG at Dijon	48		
	Pd Mrs Simonetz for a Months Lodging at the Hotel Park Royal	960		
	Pd Saml Stephens a Bill	15	15	

1768 (page 19)

	Disbursements Continued	£	s	
July 7–14	Pd Travelling Expenses from Paris to Lausanne as of acct havingabout 94£	2148	3	
15	Pd for 4 Cups & Caucers instead of those Broke on the Road & a Bason	9	9	
	Pd a fortnights Board Wages for 6 Servts as usual	160		
	Pd Sam Stephens a Bill	15	15	

1768 (page 20)

	Disbursements Continued	£	s	
July 10	Pd for 4 Table Cloths at Lausanne	38	8	
	Pd for a pr of Silver Knee Buckles	6	0	0
21	Pd for a Boat fishing for Serv'ts & Wine etc	9	12	

		£	s
	I gave a Boy for going to MAISAIG with the Horses	0	15
22	Pd for a little Mare for Sr Watkin he bought of Lausanne	192	0

1768 (page 21)

	Disbursements Continued	£	s
July 23	Pd Earnest at Hiring Horses to aride to Maisaig	6	0
24	I gave a boy at Farnese Convent in Savoy	3	
	Pd for a Barque on the lake of Geneva to go there	48	
	Pd for carrying the Plate Box to & from the Lake	1	10
	Pd a Bill for provision for Do	61	4
25	Pd Mr Carrara a Weeks Bill wherein Breakfast is included	94	19

1768 (page 22)

	Disbursements Continued	£	s
Jul-25	I gave an Oxford man returning out of England Italy to England	24	
	Pd for 9 pr of very warm Winter Gloves	40	10
	I pray to be allowed for what I have laid out since I left England & cant account for, having settled my Acc Thursday	15	10

1768 (page 23)

	Disbursements Continued			£	s
July 26	Expenses to Vevay Bea etc				
	Pd a Boy with horses to Vevay		110		
	Pd Dinner Bill there				
27	I gave at the fondemont	7;10			
	Do at the Salne	4;20			
	I gave our guide	6;0			
	I gave a poor Englishwoman at Bea		12		
28	Pd Bill of 2 nights at Bea	26;15			
	Pd Breakfast at Villeneuf	9;6			
	Pd Boatman from Do to Vevay		12		
29	Pd a Voturine for Coach horses & 2 Saddle horses		234		
	His Journey & 4 Postillions			498	3
29	Pd a Language Masr at Lausanne			24	
	Pd two Dancing Masters			40	

1768 (page 24)

	Disbursements Continued	£	s
July 29	Pd for shoeing Sr Watkins Mare	2	8
	Pd hire of Mr Apperleys horse	18	0
	Pd the hire of a Horse 1 day	1	16

1768 (page 25)

	Disbursements Continued	£	s
July 29	Pd Mr Mozarg (?) for Lodging a months Board & riding as of acct	880	10
	Pd Steiner alias Jobson for 2 pr of shoes, a pr of Shelhens [?] & altering boots	24	
	I gave the Serv'ts at the Leon D'or	6	0
30	Pd at a Bridge at a Gate on the Road to Geneva	1	1
	I gave a Custom house officer at a French Town	3	0

1768 (page 26)

		£	s
	Disbursements Continued	£	s
July 30	I gave a Souldier that brt our Pass into Geneva	0	6
	I gave the drivers		
	Pd for 11 horses from Lausanne to Geneva	132	0
	I gave the Drivers	24	
August 1	Pd for the Mare at the Crown	19	10
2	Pd Breakfast at Bonne Velley in Savoy	6	0

1768 (page 27)

		£	s
	Disbursements Continued	£	s
August 2	Ps Dinner Bill at SALANCHE going to the glaciers	18	1
3	I gave a Rev'd Abbe at whose House we lodged last night	24	0
4	Pd Night Bill for 2 Horses to the Glacier at Salenche	36	0
5	Pd for seeing a Church & another Place at Geneva	6	0
	Pd Lewis Comte a Bill of sundry Expenses of the Glaciers		
	& bring 2 mares from Lausanne	36	

1768 (page 28)

		£	s
	Disbursements Continued	£	s
August 5	Pd Mr Fulga for a Gold Stopwatch	360	0
	Pd Mr Lacomb for Coach Sundry times of Geneva		
	& for 13 Horses to the Glaciers as of Bill	333	0
	Pd Mr Apperley what he gave at Sundry Places at		
	Besonson to this Day	33	
6	Pd the Bill at the Golden Balance at Geneva	514	14

1768 (page 29)

		£	s
	Disbursements Continued	£	s
August 8	Pd the Road Bill from Geneva to Lyons Set out on the		
	6th arrived the 7th as of acct	422	14
	I gave a begging Fryer	3	
	Pd Sam Stevens Expenses with Mr Hamiltons Mare		
	from Geneva to Lyons	10	4
9	Pd the Mercer's Bill @ Lyon for a flowered Velvet Suit		
	& waistcoat pieces	552	0
	Pd for a Puppet show for Self & Mr Morris	1	4
10	Pd for seeing some places	9	

1768 (page 30)

		£	s
	Disbursements Continued	£	s
August 11	Pd Mon's Minet for Dinner at Lyons	282	18
	Pd for Wax lights for the Coaches & Chaises	5	10
	Pd for Riding Caps for Mr Carrara & Self	18	
	Pd Mr Blanc for Lodging at Lyons	180	0

1768 (page 31)

		£	s
	Disbursements Continued	£	s
August 11	I gave the Bagnonier at Do	3	
	Pd him for Pomatron	1	10
August 12	Pd Road Expenses from Lyons to Grenoble 13	201	7
13	Pd for an Italian Grammer	3	10
14	Pd the Bill @ the 3 Dolphins for 2 nights at Grenoble	143	9
19	Pd Road Expenses from Grenoble to Turin being 6 days	434	4
	Pd the Voiturine in Part of 50 Guineas that he was to		
	have for bringing us from Grenoble to Turin 30 Guineas		
	we stopt 20 til we had Satisfaction for a mare, Saddle &		

	furniture left in his hands at Geneva	720		
	Pd him for a Sadle Horse from Grenoble to Turin	60		
	I gave the 3 Postilions	37		

1768 (page 32)

		£	s
	Disbursements Continued	£	s
August 19	Pd for Ice Cream at Turin	1	16
August 22	I gave a Begging Fryer	3	12
August 23	I gave another Fryer	1	7
23	Mending the Tea Kettle	1	16

1768 (page 33)

		£	s
	S.S. to Sr www Bart	£	s
August 25	To Cash as of Acct		

[A page of currency calculations]
French to Piedmontese
cant account for 114.0

1768 (page 34)

		£	s
	Here begins Piedmontise	£	s
August 25	Summary		
September 3	Summary		
October 3	To 100 recd of M Giovardi at Bologna for which he gave me 205 Roman Sequins which is as near as I can bring them.		
October 12	ERRORS ACCEPTED		

1768 (page 35)

Here I begin to change my account in Piedmontese
Livres and Sols, 20 Piedmontese Sols makes 26 French Sols.

		£	s	
August 24	Pd Signor Borndino for dinner & Wine from the 19th to this day as of Bills	202	12	6
	Pd an Abbey for a Subscription for a Book	24	0	0
26	Pd for a fan for Sr Watkin	1	10	0
	Pd Carriage of a Sadle & Furniture from Geneva to Turin**??? NO AMOUNT ???**			
27	Pd for Mr Morris & self at the Play	2	0	0
	Pd a Bill for Wine to the Signor Savilliani	18	15	

1768 (page 36)

			£	s
August 29	Pd Signor Borndino a Bill for Breakfast Wine & one Dinner from the 24th to yesterday included		125	
	Pd Board Wages for one Week			
	To Mr Morris	13.7		
	Mr Carrara	13.7		
	Sam Stephens	10		
	Louis Mark Comte	10		
	Christo Bremer	10		
	Myself	13.7		
August 30	I gave a begging Capachine		1	10
	I gave at the Capachine Convent		1	10
	Pd for all the Servants at the Play		4	0

1768 (page 37)

	£	s
	£	s

August 31	Pd for Italian Grammars for Serv'ts	9	0
September 1	I gave at Seperga where Mr Morris & self saw it	2	0
	I gave our guide there	1	10
3	Pf for Bleeding Mr Morris & Louis	3	
	Pd for Physic for Louis	0	18
	Pd Mr Toras Postage & Letters	18	
	Remitted to Pay Mr Gaufoan 16 Louis dor to pay		
	Lacombe the Voiturine of Geneva.		

1768 (page 38)

		£	s
September 3	Pd for 6 Packs of Cards	3	15
September 4	Pd at the Opera	2	10
5	I gave 2 postillions that went to Veneri	3	0
	Pd the Coachmakers bill at Turin	368	
	Pd for a Violincello at Turin	480	
	Pd the Violincello Master	48	0
	Pd an Abbe for teaching the Serv Italian	48	

1768 (page 39)

			£	s
September 5	I gave the Secretary of States Servants having had			
	a Passport		3	0
	Pd Sig Julia for a Coach to Veneri & horses hire 3 times		29	
	Pd Velvet Merchant	286		
	The Taylor at Turin	563	849	0
6	Pd for a Pocket Knife for Sr W		24	0
	Pd Sig Borndino a Bill as for Lodgings etc		837	11

1768 (page 40)

		£	s	
September 8	Pd Road Expenses the 6th, 7th, 8th from Turin to			
	Genoa as of Accompt	875	9	6
	The following is in Genoa Lions & Sols 34			
	to a Piedmont Pistol			
September 9	I gave in a Church	2	0	
	Pf for Music last night		34	
September 10	Pd for seeing places		5	
	Pd for a Messenger to a Violin			
	cello Player.	2;0		
	Pd for 12 Dozen of artificial flowers	64.16		
	Pd for a box to carry 'em	1.4		

1768 (page 41)

			£	s
September 10	Pd for a Felucca Boat	34		
September 13	Pd Road Bill from Genoa to Milan as of Accompt		668	11
15	Pd Mr Hamilton the following that he paid at Turin,			
	Genoa & Pavia			
	Seeing the Palace at Turin	12		
	The Florapeahouse [?] at Do	24		
	Pd for a Box at the Play	18		
	Pd at Sundry Places at Genoa & Pavia	30		

1768 (page 42)

		£	s
September 14 Pd the Banker for Letters	9		
September 15 I Gave [?]	1		

Sr W going to Count Firmans (Firmian)
Pd 5 Serv'ts Board Wages due 12th

TM	29.8
SS	29.8
SS	22.2
NL	22.2
CB	22.2

Pd the Expenses of 2 Postillions & 6 Horses
at Count Firmans   35.1

I gave Sir W as of Receipt 10 Sequins   210

Mr Carrara chooses not to receive his Board Wages Weekly.

1768 (page 43)

		£	s
September 17 Pd a Coachman for repairs at Milan		71	
Pd at the Opera for Mr Morris & Self		6	
September 19 Pd a Weeks Bill at the 3 Kings at Milan	686.8		
20 Pd Do what he gave seeing a Palace at Milan		21	
22 Pd for going to the top of the Dome in Milan		10	
October 1 Pd Road Bill from Milan to Bologna			

1768 (page 44)

		£	s
September 23 Pd for a Chaise for Mr Morris & self to see the			
Chartruse near Pavia & Postillions	26		
September 25 Pd for a weeks Ice Cream	150.5		
I gave Count Firmians Servt	21		
Pd a weeks Bill at the 3 Kings & Lodging Bill			
the 29th following	772		
Pd Coach Hire for 13 Days	102		
26 Pd for Breakfast at Como	15		
I gave at Plini's House	2		
September 27 I gave at another place on the Lake Side	6		

1768 (page 45)

		£	s
September 28 I gave Count Firmians Servts at the Lake			
de Como	105		
I gave the men of 3 Boats	147		
Do Dinner at Como return	60		
I gave 6 Postillions going & returning to Como	126		
I gave the Duke of Modena's Servt at Milan	21		
Pd for Post Horses Sundry times at Milan	414.1		
Pd Sr Watkins Share of Expences to			
Lake Maggiore			
as of Acct & Post Horses	202.5		
I gave Count Fidelis Servt	4.4		
29 Pd another Bill at the 3 Kings at Milan	36		

1768 (page 46)

	P	S

October 1	Pd Road Expenses from Milan to Bologna	1811	0
3	Pd for a letter from Florence	1	1
5	Pd Mr Hamilton what he gave for seeing places at Milan	91	
6	Pd for a small Picture	82	
7	Pd Expenses to Chento with Post Horses as of Account	230	7
8	Pd the Banker for letters at Bologna	23	7
	Pd expenses of Mr Morriss illness as of Acct	127	12

1768 (page 47)

		P	S
October 9	Pd for a Book of fine Prints	210	0
	Pd for Tickets at the Bull Bait	20	0
	Pd the Pilgrim Bill at Bologna in which is included		
	11sq for a Masquarade dress to be sent from Milan	1514	0
	Pd for tacking Ruffles	3	0
	I gave the servants at the Pilgrim	61	
11	Pd Road Expenses to Florence	854	

1768 (page 48)
TOTALS
Oct-12   I pray to be allowed what I cannot account for ... Etc.

1768 (page 49)
Oct-12   This day I settled the Accompt on the opposite page at Florence

[Calculations]

1768 (page 50)

		In *Paoli*
	Here I begin a new Acct [accounting]	
November 3	To 100 recd of the Marquis Belloni in Rome	4200
November 8	To 100 recd of Mr Meighan	
November 21	To 100 recd of Belloni as before	4200

1768 (page 51)

	I allowed 2 footmen for ap' of stockings & Bags	49	
October 19	Pd at St Laurances Church	11	4
	Pd at the Palace Pethi	19	4
October 20	Pd at a Church	2	0
	Pd at a Palace	19	4

1768 (page 52)

October 21	Pd the Carriage of a Box of Clothes from Lyons to Florence		
	Forward to Rome as of acct	483	
	for 10 vol of the Florentine Gallery – Binding as of Bill	867	
	Pd for Letters brt to the Marquess Friscobaldis	3	
	I gave his Clerk for his trouble at the Custom House about the Clothes Box	19	4
	Pd for Essence & Pomatron		
	Books at St Marks Convent	152	0

1768 (page 53)

	Books, Prints, Vauses etc etc at Florence		
October 15	Pd for Views of Florence & sundry country Palaces bound in 2 Volls	117	0

20	Pd for 2 Books of Prints	165	6
22	Pd for 2 small Florentine work figures on marble a Woman & a Turk	195	
	Pd for 10 Vol of the Florentine Gallery & Binding as of Bill	867	
26	Pd for Giustiany's Gallery 16 Roman Sequins	312	
	Pd for a Virgil	19	4
	Pd for a Copy of Tasso	156	
	Pd Mr Harwood of Florence for Vauses & 12 pieces of Marble made like Books as of Bill	1040	
	Pd in part of payment for a chequer Table of all sorts of Marble valued at 205	600	
	Pd Lamberto Gori of Florence in part for 2 Sceoli Tables that he is to make in 7 months	994	4

1768 (page 54)

October 24	Pd for 5 Servt at the Play last night		
25	I gave Lord Fortrose by Sr Watkins order, being his Subscription to Paoli the Corsican General 200 Roman Sequins at 19¹/₂ each	3900	
26	Pd Mr Robinson the Taylor at Florence his Bill	2272	
	Pd Mr Patch for a Painting in Caracature, 4 Figures	312	
	Pd for an Umberella	10	

1768 (page 55)

October 26	Pd Mr Hadfield the Expenses of the Dinner, Concert & Ball given at his Country House by Sr Watkin yesterday as of Accompt wherein is included the Music & Singers	8617	4
	Pd Sr Watkins Bill while at his House from the 11 to the 27th	1544	0
	Pd Paintanida Junr for 12 Lessons on the Violincello	117	0
	Pd him and his Father for playing once in Sr Watkins room	70	
	Pd for Hiring a Violincello	10	
27	Bills appearing on p 53		

1768 (page 56)

November 2	Pd the Road Bill from Florence to Leghorn & from thence to Rome. Set out on the 27th & arrived on the 2nd inst		

1768 (page 57)

		P	B
	In Paoli & Baiocchi 10 to a Paoli		
November 2	Pd with Letters at Rome	3	0
6	Pd for Drawings	50	0
	Pd Carlo the Valet du Place a Bill where is in 20 Paoli for firewood & 21 for a Flambea	109	9
7	Pd for a Hammock cloth & Seat to the Berlin 2nd Hand	42	

1768 (page 58)

		P	B
November 8	Pd Mr Apperley his half Years Salary due the 29th being 309 Roman Sequins	6334	5
9	Pd Benedetto our Landlords bill for last weeks Dinner	297	
	Pd for 3 Artificial Marble Eggs & 3 Apples	12	
	Pd for a Book the description of Rome		
13	I paid 5 Musicians	102	

		P	B
I gave a begging English Black		20	5
I gave Prince [probably Prince Doria-Pamphilji] Servts			
Sr W having been there the night before		20	5

1768 (page 59)

		P	B
November 14	Pd Benedetto a Weeks Bill	272	
	Pd Carlo Achille a Bill wherein is included Wood & Flambaus	121	
15	Pd Sr Watkins share to the expenses to Tivoli with the Duke of Devonshire as of Acct	301	7
16	Pd for a Plan of St Peters an elevation of St Pauls at London	51	2
	Pd for a series of the Heads of Emperors, Grand Turks & Kings of France Spain Portugal & Poland & Popes	117	

1768 (page 60)

		P	B
November 14	I gave the Countess of by Sr Watkins order	102	5
21	I gave the Prince Doria Servts Sr Watkin having been last night there at a Grand Christening	20	
	Pd Carlo Achille a Weeks Bill	122	2
23	Pd for Music for the french Horn for Mr Morris	41	
26	Pd for 12 Flasks of Common Wine for the Servants	9	7

1768 (page 61)

		P	B
November 30			
	(Servants Wages etc)		
	Pd Expenses to Frescati & Albanothe 25th to 28th inst	377	
December 1	Pd Mr Hamilton what he gave 2 Serv where they had been Visiting	41	

1768 (page 62)

		P	B
November 29	Pd Signor Piranezi for His Works Compleat in Vols of Prints	1219	2
30	Pd a man for 4 Drawings in Oyle Paper after Raphael	61	5
December 3	Pd Mr Hamilton the Following 3 Prints from		

					P	B
Homer		30	7			
3 Prints at 5		15				
3 Prints at 4		12				
Pd Mr Byres s Bill for 2 Cameos, a ring, Prints etc as of Bill					2197	7
PD Pompeo in Part of Payment of a large full length Picture of Sr Watkin, Mr Hamilton & Mr Apperley 75 Sequins					1537	5

[The following entries for 1769 were inserted into the account book in their return from Naples and are therefore out of date order]

1769

		P	B
January 6	Pd Do in part for a History Picture he is to paint for Sr W 50 Sequins	1025	
7	Pd Mr Jenkins for 8 Pictures 2 Marble Statues and an Intaglio as of Acct 194	8148	

1769 (page 63)

		P	B
	Disbursments for Prints Picturesetc brt forward	14246	7
January 7	Pd Mr Hamilton for 5 Pictures as of Acct 345	14317	5
	Pd Mr Byres for 9 Pictures as of acct which makes	35275	

Pd Do for Prints, cutting a Seal etc as of acct	4742	
Pd Mr Wiseman a bill for Music	1161	5
Pd Mr Hewson for a Model Bust in Clay of Sr Watkin & some Casts from it 20 Sequeens	410	

Carried to Page 90 · · · · · · 70093 · · 2

[page 64 has been left blank]

1768 (page 65)

	P	B
December 4 I gave a man with Dancing Monkeys	3	0
5 Pd Mr Wiseman a Bill of a Concert, vocal & Instrumental last night	202	7
Pd Mr Torras of Turin in full wherein is included, 3 Trufle [?] Daggs [?] Postage of Letters etc	946	3

1768 (page 66)

	P	B
December 6 Pd Segn Rolland coachmaker for a pr of horses from Nov 6th to Dec 9th	410	
December 7 Pd Jovanini & several other Musicians for Playing last night	164	0
Pd my Language Master a Month	41	0
8 Pd Sr W Music Master a Month	61	5
Pd him for repairing a Violincello	20	5
Pd him the Hire of 2 do		
Pd Mr Byers for a [Entry incomplete]	6	0
Pd for 10 pr of Gloves	21	
Pd for a large Muff	82	

1768 (page 67)

	P	B
December 9 Pd Benedetto for Dinner & provisions on the Road to Naples from the 5th to this Day	213	0

1768 (page 68)

	P	B
December 9 Pd for cleaning the Gun & Pistols	9	0
Pd Mr Byers Sr Watkins half Share of Expenses in seeing Places with the Duke of Devonshire	297	
Pd a Messenger to Mr Baraci for a letter to save visiting by the Popes Officers AT Velletri	2	5
10 Pd Expenses on the Road from Rome to Naples in 2 Days	1624	5

1768 (page 69)

In Duckats, Carlings 10 in a Ducket & Grains 10 in a Carleen
Each Carleen about $4^{1}/_{2}$ English

	D	C	G
December 11 Pd at the Grand Oppera for Mr Morris & Self	0	6	0
17 Pd for a Gold snuff Box	16		0
I gave at Portici seeing the Antiquities of Herculaneum	4	8	0
18 Pd for 5 Calashes to Lago Agnano	4	0	0
I gave at seeing several places	1	0	0

1768 (page 70)

	P	B

December 19 Pd for Calashes to Puzzoli			4	2	
21	Expenses to Baia				
	Pd for the Boat	3.7.0			
	Pd for 5 Calashes to Cuma	3.6.0			
	Gave the 2 Ciceroni	1.5.0			
	Pd for Wine	1.0.0			
	Pd for seeing several places	2.7.0			
	I gave a Diver	0.6.0			
	Pd for 2 Naples Calashes	2.8.0			
	I gave the Coachman & Postillion	0.8.0			
			16	7	
23	I gave Mr Hamiltons Servant that brought				
	Sr Watkin Visiting tickets		0	6	0

1768 (page 71)

Disbursements at Naples

			D	C	G
December 24 Expenses to Vesuvius					
	I gave the Hermit	0.12.0			
	Pd the men & mules	12.6.0			
	Pd for 3 Calashes	3.0.2			
	Pd Mr Hamilton what he gave to the Hermit	2.5.0			
			19	3	4
26	Expenses to Pompeo				
	I gave them that showed it	1.2.5			
	I Gave at Herculaneum	0.6			
27	Pd Mr Hamilton & Mr Apperley				
	Expenses at Casserta	3.4.0			
	Pd for a Boat to the Ship		0	1	0

		P	B	
176 (page 72)				
December 28 Pd Mr Hamilton the Minister for 2 vol of Etruscan				
Designs to be delivered by Cadel at London 32 Ounces	96	0	0	
29	I gave 3 Ambassadors Servts where Sr Watkin had dined	3	6	0
	I gave the Kings Servts	6	0	0
	Pd Piantanida for Music	15	0	0
	Pd for 2 Vol of Prints from Aincient Gems	26	0	0
30	Pd Mr Fitzherbert Sr W share to the Evening Concerts			
	at Rome	11	0	0

		P	B	
1768 (page 73)				
December 30 I gave the Countess Mahonis Servt	0	6	0	
	I gave the Prince Francavilla's	1	2	0
	Pd Mr Browns Bill for Mince Pies, Pickles Gingerbread etc	19	4	0
	I gave Mr Hamiltons servts	18	0	0
	Pd Mr Sullivan for a Picture he is to get coppyed at Florence			
	which he is to bring to England 25 Sequins being	62	5	0
	Pd Stephano's Bill from the 19th wherein is included for			
	the Lodging	153	7	8
	Pd Mr Brown for a Violincello which he is to send to London	53	0	0

1769 (page 74)				
	[General Disbursements]			
	Road Bill to Rome	1620	5	
	Total of Naples Acct	11346	5	

1769 (page 75)
    [Exchange Calculations]

1768 (page 76)

	Cash Carried from Dr Pauls Page 50	50 431
	To 1400 of the Balance of the Turin rec page 50	
December 27	To 250 of Mr Tiernes of Naples to 50 fee by 55 for which he had 1533 Duckets 6 Carleens which make	12 575

1769 January 4

	To 300 ss recd of Marquis Belloni for which I had 1245 crowns 41¹/₂ *Pauls* of Sterling	12 450
6	To 194 ss being the Value of Mr Jenkins Bill at 42 pounds Pound sterling	5148
7	To 650 recd of Belloni for which I had 2697 (Crowns) at 41¹/₂ of £	26 975
	To 550 being the Value of Mr Byers fee at 41¹/₂ p	35 275
18	To 200 I recd of Mr Watson of Venice for which I had neat money of s 512 Venician *Leones* which is 309 *Pauls* as follows	8309

Carried to Page 99   162 163

1769 (page 77)

		P	B
	Disbursements at Rome		
January 5th	Pd Board Wages for 5 servants from Dec 5th to Monday next the 9th January being 5 weeks	626	5
	Pd Mr Carrara 18 weeks Do from September 5th being the lasthe recd to Monday next	531	
	Pd Mr Morris a Bill for Hair Bag Powder etc	28	
	Pd for Harp Strings	100	
	I gave a poor man	2	0
6	Pd Mr Hamilton 103 Roman Sequins being 50 on account at 20 (P) 5 (B) each	2111	5
	Pd for 2lb of Tea	56	0
	Pd for Wine for the Servants	10	4
	Pd for Lemons and Celery	1	0
	Pd for 2lb of Tea more for the Road	56	0
	Pd a man for carrying Wood to Mr Meighan where the Concert was	1	5
	Pd for Pack Thread	0	5
7	Pd Mr Forrester for Teaching Sr Watkin to Draw 20sq	410	0
	Pd him a Bill for Colours, Prints etc		

Carried to Page 90   4065   9

1769 (page 78)

		P	B
	Disbursements Continued		
	Pd Abbey Grant for a Fan Mount	123	
January 7	Pd Mr Wiseman the expenses of the Concert at Meighans last night	303	5
	Pd the Postage of Letters at Rome	785	5
	I gave the Bankers Clark	2	0
	I gave a begging Fryer	5	0
	I gave Mr Wiseman be Sr Watkins Order for collecting music for him and performing 4 times	400	0
	Pd the Coachmakers Bill for Sundry repairs to the Coach & Chariot	200	0

	Pd The Iceman a Bill	225	
	I gave his servant	3	0
	Pd Sam. Stephens a Bill	18	2¹/₂
	Pd Benedetto a Bill for Dinner	415	0
	I gave his Servants	15	0
	Pd for Wax Candles and Torches for the Road	71	1
	Pd at the Play for myself, Mr Morris, S.S. and Mr Carrara	20	5
Carried to Page 90		**2746**	**0¹/₂**

		P	B
1769	Disbursmt Continued		
January 7	Pd Mr Rolland 0 Weeks lodging & for a Coach at the Villa di Londra at Roma	430	0
	Pd for Washing as p. Bill	34	2
	I gave the Servant	2	0
	I gave Mr Meighan, the Concert having been at his House last night	61	5
	I gave his Servant	5	0
	Pd for a pr of Half Bootes	5	0
	Pd for Packing Paper	2	4
	Pd with Letters	2	2
	Pd Carlo Achilli's weeks Bill	103	0
	Pd him 32 Days Wages in Bill to this Day at 4 Pauls p. Day	128	0
	Pd Mr Carrara a Weeks Bill wherein is included the Oppera Boxes	42	1¹/₂
8	Pd Santi for Dressing Hair a Week	20	5
	Pd him for Powdering & Pomatron	12	6
	Pd for Coffee this Morning	6	
Carried to Page 90		**1670**	**5¹/₂**

1769 (page 80)

	Disbursmts Continued			
January "	I gave the Coffee Boy	6	0	0
	I gave the Coachman	20	5	
	I gave Carlo Achilli	61	5	
	I gave Sigr Rollandi's Maid where we had lodged in Rome	20	5	
	Pd for Whipcord for the Servants	1	0	
January 13	Pd Louis for what he pd for a Flag at Naples	3		
15	Pd Expenses from Rome to Naples Venice set out on the 8th & arrived the 15th 8 day v as p Acc	4040	6	
16	Pd for a Book of Prints, St Michilli in Bosco	2	0	
	Pd Carriage of a Masquarade Dress from Milan to Bologna & to Venice	16	0	
	Pd for seeing several Churches Palaces etc at Rome & Naples as of Acct	69	0	
Carried to page 90		**5120**	**1**	

[page 81 has been left blank]
1769 (page 82)

		Fr *Livres*		
	Cash received SS Do			
	French Money			
January 20	To Cash Sr Watkin drew upon Mr Childs in favour of Gulman & Son at Augsberg for 110 Sterling for which he had 110 Louis D'or	2400	0	0
February 8	I settled a Acct with Mr Panchaud wherein he			

	accompted for 800 which makes	17800	
9	To Cash recd of Messr Panchaud 300	6675	0
	To Cash recd for the Travel-ing Bed 15 Louis D'or	360	
10	To Cash recd for the Coach 35 Louis D'or	840	
	To Draft on Mr Panchaud in Favour of Basin the		
	Printseller for see Page 89	1058	0
		29133	
	To Cash recd of Mr Panchaud 50	1112	10
		39245	10

Carried to page 91		30245	10

1769 (page 83)

		Lires	Soldi
	Disbursements at Venice		
	In Lires & Soldi, 21 Lire To a Roman Seqeen		
	8.22 To a Venecian Seguine		
January 16	To the hire of a Masquarade Dress	44	0
	Pd for a Masquarade Hat	22	0
17	Pd for a pair of Lace Ruffles	176	0
	Pd for a quire of Dutch & 6 Quires of Packing Paper	6	0
	I gave the Boatmen at Venice to get their Dinners	3	0
	Pd for Mr Morris, Mr Carrara & self at the Oppera	10	0
18	Pd the Gondolire a Bill of sundry Expenses at Venice	75	0
	I lost by Exchange of Belloni's Draft of 239.3 Pauls		
	on a Banner at Venice	56	0
	Pd for 6 pair of Woolen Gloves & night-caps for the		
	Servants	51	0
	I gave the Bankers Servant	6	0
	Pd for a Barrel of Cypres Wine about 10 Dozen English		
	Bottles	248	0
	Pd for Lining a Great Coat with flannel	55	

Carried over		760	

1769 (page 84)

		Lires	Soldi
	Disbursments' Venice		
	brought forward	760	
January 18	Pd for washing	17	10
	Pd at 2 Operas	12	0
	Pd for seeing Sundry Places	53	5
	Pd 4 Gondoliers for 3 days	88	0
	Pd for Sewing Ruffles	2	0
	Pd Petrillo for Lodging, Dinners, Wine etc etc etc	779	0
	Pd for 4 Drawings in Imitation of Deal Boards	174	0
	Pd Sam. Stephens a Bill	12	0
19	I gave Petrillo's Servts	29	0
	Pd Mr Carrara a Bill at Venice	279	0
	I gave the boatman	21	0
	Pd Mr Watson Postage of Letters at Venice	70	0
	Pd for 2 small Pictures of Titian's at Padua	63	
February 7	The Road Expenses from Venice to Paris comes to		
	12,818.0 Venise Lires Part I charge here, the remainder		
	was paid with the Strassburg money	11,006	8
		14246	13

1769 (page 85)

					Pauls	Baiocchi
	Brought forward from					
	Lires	*Soldi*				
Last Page	14246	13	which make		13907	0
	Pd Mr Hamilton in part of £50 31 Roman Sequeens					
	See Page 93				635	5
Carried to Page 90					14542	5

Venise *Lires*   *Soldi*

14246   13   make 13907 *Paoli* as follows

```
        VL   P    Z
if      21  20.5:                    14246
                                      20.5
                                     71230
                                    204920
     21 292643,0         13906
                 2
              190
              143
               17
```

I add 1 more Paoli as there is a remainder of 17 & the 13 Soldi not brought in to save the Decimals which makes 13907 Paoli

[page 86 has been left blank]

1769 (page 87)

Disbursments Continued

French Money		L	s
February 2	Pd for a Fur Bag for Mr Carrara bought at Strasburg	10	
	Pd for a Fur Cap for Mr Morris	12	
	Pd Do for Stephens	5	4
	Pd Do for John Davies	3	10
	Pd for a pr of fur Gloves for Sr Watkin	1	10
	Pd for a Book of Prints of Strasburg	84	0
	Pd for 2 fine fur caps	120	0
	Pd for a Superfine Sable Muff & a suit of Sable 22 Louis	520	0
	Pd for a dog at Strasburg	12	0
7	Pd the remainder of the Road Bill from Venice to Paris	461	0
	See Page 84		
	Pd for a Coach to and from Mr Panchaud	1	16
	Pd the hire of a Masquarade dress	21	
8	Pd 5weeks Board Wages to 6 Servants as usual. From		
	Jan 9th to the 13th ensuing	420	0
9	Pd the Hatter at Paris a Bill	87	0
	Pd Mr Eynhonts for 3 pr of fine Lace Ruffles	442	0
Carried to Page 91		2709	8

1769 (page 88)

Disbursmt Continued

February 8	I settled with Mr Panchaud the following Bills		
	Pd Mon s Lafrenage for a Watch Set in		
	Diamonds 9000 Livres or £404 10s	97	0
	& a Vause Clock 780 or £34 2s 6d		

Pd Do for a pr of Diamond Lady's Shoebuckle 3861 Livres or £168 10s 4$^{1}/_{2}$d		451	8
& for a Gold Snuff Box 657 or £28.14.10$^{1}/_{2}$			
Pd Mon s Maumett for a set of China Dessert Service of the French Manufacture for the Duchess of Beaufort		319	2
Pd Mr Panchaud the Postage of Letters 541.5 or £23;13;6		541	5
Pd Mr Pernon of Lyon for Sr Watkins best suit 1940 French or £84; 17;6.		1940	10

Carried to Page 91   19995;15

1769 (page 89)

		L	s
	Disbursments Continued		
February 9	I gave to Mr Panchaud's Servt	12	0
	Pd Mr Pascal the Coachmaker for Sundry repairs to the Coach 3 Louis, the hire of another to Calais 5 & to restore his Chaise to its former state 6 Louis	336	0
	I gave his man	12	0
	Pd for mending the Hangers	11	16
	Pd for a Coach to Mr Panchauds	1	16
	Pd for Packing Paper	0	18
	Pd the Wine Merchant	40	0
	I gave his servant	3	0
	Pd for mending Sr Watkin's Watch	4	0
	Pd for Fire Wood	22	0
	Pd for tacking Ruffles	3	0
	Pd for a Coach for 3 Days	36	0
	I gave the Coachman	9	0
	Pd Mr Basan for Prints & Books as the Bill	1058	0
	Pd the Valet de Place a Bill	87	4
	Pd Mr Brunet for Butter & Milk	6	6

Carried to Page 91   1643   0

1769 (page 90)

		L	s
	Disbursments Continued		
February 9	Pd Mrs Simoneh for Lodging	240	0
	Pd her for Candles etc	8	12
	I gave the Servants	12	0
	Pd Mr Henry the Taylor a Bill	1863	0
	Pd the Hotel de Saxe Bill for Dinners	76	0
	I gave the Taylors servant	6	0
	Pd a Bill for Coffee, Biscuits etc	22	12
	Pd for washing Pocket Hand ks	1	4
	Pd the Valet de Place for Sundry things he brought this morning	16	16
	Pd him his Wages and gave him 12	20	
	Pd for a Coach to the Banker	1	16
	Pd the Savoyard for Sundry Messages that he did	12	
13	Pd for 2 pr Stockings at Calais	28	0
	Pd for 3 pr of Gloves at Do	3	0
15	Pd expenses from Paris to London as of acct	2502	

Carried to Page 91   4815   0

1769 (page 91)

Disbursments in french money continued   £

186

February 20 Pd Mr Hamilton in Part of fifty Pounds as of Accompt
see Page 93   577

French Livre

Page 87	2709	8
88	19995	15
89	1643	0
90	4815	0
91	577	0
	29740	3

Cash recd see Page 82	30245	
Disbursed as above	29740	
Balance due Sr Watkin	505.7	

Livres	Sols		£	s	d	
505	7	make	22	14	0	English Money

Carried to Page 100

[page 92 has been left blank]

		£	s	d
1769	Disbursments in English Money			
February 20	Pd Mr Hamilton £50 on accompt I paid part in 31 Roman Sequeens. See Page 85, another Sum in French Money 577 Livressee Page 91 & the remainder in English	9	12	6
22	Pd Mr Carrara his Wages and all Demands for their Journey	50	0	0
	I gave him by Sr Watkins orders	20	0	0
	I pray to be allowed £1.14.1 which I have laid out since I left Naples & can't Account for. About 30 of which was lost in Exchange of Venecian Sequeens into Louis D'or at Augsberg	1	14	1
	Pd James Rowland for taking an Empty Post Coach from London to Dover	4	4	0
		85	10	7

1769 (page 940				
	Disbursments in English money brt forward	5	10	7
March 22	Pd Mr Jones of the Customs house a Bill of Sundry Expenses Duty & freight of Sundry things from Paris, Turin. Leghorn etc 17; 14;00 wherein is included the Duty, Freight etc of 3 Hhdds of Burgundy 53; 4; 4 which I charge in Page 144 in new acct book, the remainder I charge here	64	10	4
April 11	Pd Mr Woodfall for newspapers and Postage to France, Italy etc as the Bill	18	15	0
12	Pd Mr Graff for Lord Leighs travelling Coach	40	0	0
May 10	Pd Mr Hamilton on acct	200	0	0
26	Pd Carriage and the French Duty on 4 Boxes of Crayons from Lausanne	0	16	6
Carried on		417	11	11

1769 (page 95)

	Disbursments brt forwd		£	s	d
June 27	By a letter from messrs Panchaud of Paris Dated April 24th 1769 Sr Watkin is informed that they have drawn upon him at Mr Childs for 269 Sterling being the Value of the following Articles at 22.5 French at Pound Sterling.				

Pd to Dolermo for packing up the China	44.16	
Pd Vernon Le Crat of Lyons a Bill for Silks etc	3791	
Pd for Packing the Clock & Charges	13.1	
Pd Postage of Letters after we left Paris	62.10	
	3911.7	

		£	s	d
		175	15	5

		£	s	d
In that Acct is the two following Articles		593	7	5

P Bafans Sr Watkins	1058
Draft see Page 82	
In Peyrons Bill is belonging to	
Mr Hamilton	452.2
Likewise Do Taylors Bill at Lyons	

1769 (page 96)

	Disbursments brought foreward		£	s	d
			593	7	5
June 27	Pd Mr Watson of Venise a Bill of Sundry Disbursmts for Music & Wine etc as of Acct		193	4	11
July 18	Pd Mr Byres a Bill for sundry Disbursments he laid out since Sr Watkin left Rome Viz. Packing up his Pictures & expenses there on, 40 toMarrow for a coppy from Raphael, 40 to Mr Dean for a Landskip etc etc etc as of Bill		175	2	7
	Pd Mr Francis Jeremy of Leghorn for disbursments to Sr Watkins use by draft which Mr Child paid this Day seepage 102		12	18	10
	Pd Mr Hamilton £300 which with £700 paid at Sundry times made 1000 in all [written with a heavy hand which might suggest disapproval on the part of Sidebotham]		300	0	0

		£	s	d
Carried to next Page		1274	13	9

1769 (page 97)

	Disbursment brt forward		£	s	d
			1274	13	9

September 24	Pd Mr Jones of the Custom House a Bill of the following articles

Expense on the Dutchess of Beauforts China	4.17.4	
Charges of Violincello from Naples	2;13;10	
Charges on Cases of Crayons	0;6;0	
Charges on Florence Wine	9;12;6	
Charges on Books, Cordials	21;5;4	
artificial flowers from Venise		

Mr Nef Draft for 30 hds of Burgundy, Swiss Wine & Crayons	97;00		
Charges on Cyprus Wine from Venise	28;00		
Mr Audibert Draft for export of Swiss wine & Crayons	17;7;7		
Charges on Do at London	9;10;11		
Charges on Pictures & Books from Rome	123;17;9		
Charges on the Vauses & Table from Florence	10; 1;6		
		315	12	9
		1590	6	6

APPENDIX 2

ACCOUNTS & RECEIPTS FOR THE TOUR OF NORTH WALES

(WYNNSTAY MSS BOX 115, BUNDLE 22)

Wynnstay Box 115. Bundle 22/17

1771   Travelling Bill, the Tour through North Wales, Sir Watkin,
Mr Apperly, Capn Gascoin, Mr Sandby and at Festiniog joined
by Mr Wenman 9 servants and 15 horses

		£	s	d
Aug 21	Pd Turnpike to Llangolen	0	1	7
	Pd for Ale atLlandisilllio	0	1	0
	Pd at Widdow Llwyd at Llansantfraid, dining	1	7	0
22	Pd at Corwen for 5 horses & two serv	0	15	10
	Gave a guide to Gwerclas from Rug	0	2	6
	Gave the Millar & boy that held the horses at the Waterfall	0	6	3
23	Pd the Bill at Bala	15	13	10
	Pd 2 messengers with Grouse from Hugh Sands	1	2	0
	Gave the servts at Glan-y-Llyn	0	5	0
	Gave the poor at Do	1	1	0
	Gave the Fisherman at Do	0	10	6
	Paid for carrying part of the baggage to Dolgelle	0	15	0
24	Pd Bill at Dolgelle	6	2	10
	Pd Boatman for bringing carriage of Baggage from Hengwrt to Barmouth	0	10	6
	Pd Help to embark and disembark it	0	3	6
25	Pd for 3 serv & 4 Horses a night at Do	0	19	10
26	Pd for carrying part of the baggage toFestiniog & Pont Aberglasllin	0	24	6
	Gave the poor at Harlech	0	5	0
	Gave at the Castle 2 Pd a guide 2.6	0	4	6
	Pd Festiniog Bill	10	14	9
	Gave the woman at Pont Aberglasllin	0	10	6
	Pd for carrying Baggage to Do	0	5	0
	Pd for 2 measures of oates at Do	0	4	0
	Gave the miner at Do to drink at Borthcelet	1	1	0
	Gave Owen Thomas our Guide from Bala	1	1	0
	Gave Do to give Mrs. Mary Holland	1	1	0
	Lent Sr Watkin at Do 5. of Llansaintfraid 2.6	0	7	6
	Pd for ale at Bettus near Carnarvon	0	5	3
	Pd Mathew's Expenses at Penmorva	0	10	0
1771	Travelling Bill brought forward	46	2	106
	Pd for ale sent to the Bonfire last night	1	5	0

190

Aug 28	Gave an Old Sailor	0	5	3
	Gave 3 boys that brt baggage from Pont aber Glasllin to Carnarvon	0	3	0
	Gave at the Town Hall 1, Castle 2.6	0	3	6
29	Gave to the Poor at Llanverres Castle where Sr Watkin dined	0	5	0
	Gave several men that held the horses	0	5	0
	Gave them to Drink	0	5	3
	Gave the Boatman on Llanverres Pool	0	10	6
	Gave the Guide to the Mountain	0	2	6
	Gave the Carnarvon Guide	0	10	6
	Gave the Music at Carnarfon	1	1	0
30	Gave the Poor there	0	10	6
	Gave the Bell Ringer there	0	5	0
	Paid the Kings Head Bill at Do	16	13	4
	Gave Mr Williams and Servants where Sr Watkin lodged	0	7	6
	Gave a Boatman that helped on Board	0	2	6
31	Gave the Ringers at Beaumarris	1	1	0
	Gave Lord Bulkeley's Boatmen	1	11	6
	Pd for carrying the Baggage on Board	0	1	0
	Pd Do from on Board to Bangor	0	1	0
	Pd for seeing the Cathedral at Do	0	2	6
	Pd the Eagles Bill at Do	3	9	0
	Pd Turnpikes from Bangor to Conway	0	4	7
Sept 1	Pd for Ale at the Bonfire at Conway	1	10	0
	Pd the Ferryman	0	10	6
	Pa Matthew Rowlands Dinner at Carnarvon & Turnpikes to Bangor, being left behind	0	1	6
2	Pd the Bulls Head Bill at Conway	7	9	3
	Gave the Ringers at Do	1	1	0
	Gave the Poor at Do 1;1;0. Mrs Baker 10.6	1	11	6
	Travelling Bill brt forward	0	0	6
Sept 2	Gave the Ringers of 3 Jingle Bells as Llanwrst	0	7	6
	Gave Ellis y Cooper, a poet at Do	0	5	0
	Gave a poor woman at Do	0	2	6
	Gave the Clark at Do	0	1	0
3	Pd the Bill at Llanwrst	3	13	4
	Gave Mrs Williams a Grand Daughter of Col Thellwell of Plas y Ward	5	5	0
	Gave Mrs Clarkson, Daughter to the late Mr Owens of Boditha	1	1	0
	Gave a guide that went with the Chase Marine to Belhes	0	2	6
	Pd Turnpike to St Asaph	0	2	1
	Pd White Lyon Dinner Bill	3	10	8
	Pd Turnpike to Holy Well	0	2	0
4	Pd Night Bill at Holywell	5	6	6
	Pd [? damaged] for Mr Morris [? damaged] out from Holywell	[?]	0	10
	Pd Mr Tho Jones what he had paid at Bala for a Boild Ham & b 6 Roasted Chickens went to Glan y Llin the 23rd	0	15	0
	Laid out this journey acct for	0	4	6
	Pd Matthew Rowland what he paid at Ferries Turnpike etc	0	16	5
	Pd David Makenden sundry payments he made this journey as of Bell	1	5	2
		117	7	6

[This summary, on a folded sheet, is of the total costs of the two-week tour. Most of the entries are supported by separate bills contained within the bundle and are as follows. The numbering of the documents is random but I have put them in the order of the itinerary. Each paper is folded with a label indicating its contents, inscribed on the outside. The original spelling is preserved throughout.]

Wynnstay Mss Box 115. Bundle 22/7

1771 August 21, Pd Llansaintfraid Bill, £1 7s 0d

1771 Llansaint Fraid, Tŷ Ucha [?], Mary Llwyd Widdow

	£	s	d
To Eggs & Bacon, the hire of the house etc	0	10	6
To Ale & Tobacco		0	4
To Hay for 12 Horses	0	2	0
To Corn	0	3	0
To the Ringers	0	5	0
To the Servants	0	2	0
	1	7	0

Wynnstay Mss Box 115. Bundle 22.8.

1771 August 22, Pd Corwen Bill, £0 15s 10d

Corwen 22nd August 1771

	£	s	d
Eating	0	2	0
Ale	0	1	0
Horses Hay	0	3	4
Do Corn	0	4	4
	0	11	4
Servts	0	2	0
	0	13	4
Black Smith	0	2	6
	0	15	10

Wynnstay Mss Box 115. Bundle 22.4.

1771 August 23rd, Pd Bala Bill   £15 13s. 10d.

Bala, August 23d 1771

	£	s	d
5 Gents at Dinner		12	6
11 Do Supper		16	6
4 Do Breakft		2	8
Wine		6	0
Punch	1	0	6
Cyder		2	8
Porter & Ale		9	0
Ale to the Boat		3	0
20 Servts at Dinr		10	0
14 Do at Supr		7	0
11 Do at Breakft		5	6
Do Ale & Punch		11	2
Ale for the Boat in the morng		3	0
	5	15	6
Waiters & Maids	1	5	0
Pd for ale for the Bonfire at the Goat, Eagles & Bull	3	3	0
Pd for Supper & ale for Boatman	0	11	0
Pd for Music	1	1	0
Gave the Poor	1	1	0
Pd for Tincture of Rhubab	0	0	9
Gave the boatmen	1	1	0
Pd for Gun Powder	0	2	4

	£	s	d
	13	0	7
15 Horses Hay		10	0
Do Corn & Beans	1	6	3
Sadlers Bill		5	6
Pd Smith		2	6
Dogs		3	0
	4	7	3

115.22.4 Cont...

	£	s	d
[Cleaning] of Boots	0	5	0
Greasing the Carriage	0	1	0
	2	13	3
brought from above	13	0	7
	15	13	10

Wynnstay Mss Box 115. Bundle 22.14.

August 27th 1771, Alban Parry, £6 15s 0d   ~~Cash £20 0 0~~

	£	s	d

Bala August 24th 1771

	£	s	d
To a boild Ham 22d		12	0
To 6 Roasted Chickens		3	0
		15	0

fowd Augst 27 [?] this Contents   £0 15s 0d [received]
By Alban Parry [signature]

Wynnstay Mss Box 115. Bundle 22.9

1771 August 24th. Pd Dolgelle Bill, £6 2s 10d

	£	s	d

[Printed Hotel Bill] JOHN PUGH at the Spread Eagles
in DOLGELLEY

	£	s	d
To Breakfast		2	8
Wine		2	0
Punch		5	6
Cyder		1	8
Ale		0	4
Porter		0	6
Supper		6	0
Servants Eating		12	0
Do Ale		9	8
Hay		8	8
Corn	1	5	8
[added in manuscript] Soft Soap & Basket		1	0
	3	15	8

[on back of Bill]

	£	s	d
Ostler	0	3	0
Servts	0	4	0
Bill	3	15	0
2 Lodgings	0	5	0
Smith	0	6	8
Sadler	0	2	0
Ringer	0	5	0
Poor	1	1	0

6	2	4
Cleaning Boots	0	0	6
6	2	10

Wynnstay Mss Box 115. Bundle 22.5.
1771 August 25th, Pd Barmouth Bill, £0 19s 10d

	£	s	d
August 24th 1771			
For ale		4	4
Do Punch		0	6
Do Diners		2	0
Do Breakfast		1	6
Do Beans & Corn		7	0
Do for Hay		2	0
	0	17	4
Ostler 1, Maid 6d	0	1	6
	0	10	0
Ice last night	0	1	0
	0	19	0

Wynnstay Mss Box 115. Bundle 22.3
1771, Pd at Penmorva, £0 10s 0d

	£	s	d
Penmorva 27 August 1771			
To Richrd Griffith			
To Eating		1	6
To Ale		1	0
To horses hay and Corn		5	1
To Guide		1	6
To hostler		0	10
	0	10	2
pd at trath (sic) Bach	0	0	6
	0	10	6

Wynnstay Mss Box 115. Bundle 22.16
1771 August 27th, Pd Festiniog Bill, £10 13s 9d

	£	s	d
Festiniog August 26 1771			
Eight gentlemen diend on Monday	0	16	0
Ditto five more diend	0	2	6
Nine Servants diend ditto	0	4	6
Five gentlemens coffie on monday	0	2	6
Five gentlemen swpr on Monday night	0	5	0
Ditto Eight Servants supr	0	4	0
Ditto five more supr on Monday night	0	2	6
Gentlemen and servants for liquor	1	13	10
Twenty one horses to hay & grass	0	10	6
Ditto for corn	1	7	0
Five gentlemen breakfast to day	0	5	0
Ditto five more breakfast	0	2	6
Nine servants breakfast	0	4	0

	£	s	d
bearar from cors y gedol of meat & drink	0	1	0
Meat and ale to Pont aberglaselun	1	1	0
	7	3	0
Monday nights Bill	1	7	9
	0	10	9
Pd for ale to the Bonfire	1	1	0
Gave the Poor 5, a Harper 5, the Bellringer 2.6	0	12	6
Gave the Ostler & Maids 10.6	0	10	6
	10	14	0

Wynnstay Mss Box 115. Bundle 22.6.

1771, Carnarvon, Pd ~~Festiniog~~ Bill, £16 13s 4½d

	£	s	d
Kings Head, Caernarvon, August 30th 1771			
To Eating	1	19	0
To Servts Eating	2	5	0
To Wine and Punch	2	12	6
To Cyder	0	2	0
To Ale	1	19	0
Paid for Cards	0	2	0
To the [?] Ham	0	9	0
To Do loyn and Legg of Mutton	0	4	0
To Do Meat	0	2	0
To Do Chickins	0	1	6
To Do Bread	0	1	6
To Do 2 Bottles of Brandy	0	7	0
To Do 1 Do of Rum	0	3	0
paid for lemon jues	0	1	6
Do for Concumbers	0	0	6
Do for Gilt Paper	0	0	2
Do for Tobacco for the hills	0	0	4
Do Horse Heiring	0	1	6
Horses Hay and Corn	4	12	11
Paid for White Brown paper	0	0	2½
	15	3	1½
The Smiths Bill	0	3	3
The Sadlers Bill	0	0	0 [?]
Ostler 10.6 Maids 10.6. cleaning Boots	1	3	0
Gave two men that went to the Hills yesterday	0	4	0
	16	13	4½

Wynnstay Mss Box 115. Bundle 22.10

1771 August 31, Bangor Dinner Bill, £3 9s 0d

	£	s	d
Eagles Bangor			
5 Dinners		3	4
5 Suppers		3	6
5 Breakfasts		2	6
9 Dinners		6	0
Punch		2	0
Porter & Ale		8	10

	£	s	d
Horses Bill	1	14	2
	3	0	2
Gentlemen Eating		1	4
Punch		1	0
	3	2	6
Waiters	0	2	6
Ostler	0	4	0
	3	9	0

Wynnstay Mss Box 115. Bundle 22.11
1771 September 2nd, Pd Conway Bill, £7 9s 3d

	£	s	d
Bulls Head Conway	1	12	6
Eating	1	12	6
Wine	0	2	0
Mulled Wine	0	2	0
Punch	0	14	6
Ale	0	16	6
Brandy	0	0	6
Horses Hay	0	17	4
Corn	2	2	3
[illegible line]			
Horses feed	0	2	2
	6	10	9
Pd the Smith	0	1	0
Gave the Maids 5, Ostler 6.6	0	11	6
Gave the Bootcleaner	0	1	0
Gave a Harper	0	5	0
	7	9	3

Wynnstay Mss Box 115. Bundle 22.12
1771 September 3rd, Pd Llanwrst Bill, £3 13s 4d

	£	s	d
[printed Bill] John Thomas at the Sign of the SPREAD EAGLES in LLANWRST			
Eating	0	14	0
Wine and Negus	0	4	0
Punch, Rum & Brandy	0	6	0
Porter	0	2	6
Ale	0	1	0
Cyder and Perry	0	0	8
Tobacco	0	0	2
Servants Eating and Ale	0	13	8
Horses Hay and Corn	1	2	8
	3	4	8
[manuscript addition]			
Waiters	0	4	0

	£	s	d
Ostler	0	4	0
	3	12	0
Mt Jones's Breakfast	0	0	0
	3	13	4

Wynnstay Mss Box 115. Bundle 22.15
1771 September 3, White Lyon Bill St Asaph

	£	s	d
Thompsons Wt Lion near St Asaph			
Eating	0	10	8
Claret	0	11	0
Old Hock	0	5	0
Madeira	0	4	0
Port Wines	0	2	0
Beer	0	1	6
Coffee	0	3	4
Pd for letters	0	0	3
Servts Eating & Beer	0	6	4
13 Horses Hay & corn	0	12	3
	2	17	0
Music	0	5	0
Waiters	0	3	0
Ostler	0	2	6
Bells at St Asaph	0	10	6
	3	10	0

Wynnstay Mss Box 115. Bundle 22.13
1771 September 4th, Pd Night Bill at Holy Well, £5 6s 6d

	£	s	d
Supper	0	12	0
Port wine	0	2	0
Claret	0	5	6
Madeira	0	4	6
Rum lemmon & sugar	0	4	0
Tea	0	6	8
Chards	0	3	0
Candles	0	3	6
3 [?]	0	1	6
Servants Eating & ale	0	14	6
Porter & ale	0	3	6
	3	0	8
Horses	1	10	4
Harper	0	5	0
Ostler	0	3	6
Boots	0	1	0
Waiters & Maids	0	5	0
Smith	0	1	0
	5	6	6

197

[separate bill inserted] Holywell

	£	s	d
13 Horses Hay	0	8	8
Do Corn	0	18	6
Greasing of Carriage	0	1	0
Stoping and Greasing of Horses Feet	0	2	2
	1	10	4

Wynnstay Mss Box 115. Bundle 22.(un-numbered)
1771 September 3rd, Pd White Lyon at St Asaph

	£	s	d
[printed bill]			
Servants Eating and Hay		5	4
Horses Hay and Corn		4	8
Ostler		1	0
		11	0
Waiter			6
		11	6

Wynnstay Mss Box 115. Bundle 22.2
1771 September 4th, P Matthew Rowland

	£	s	d
Septmbr 2 Turnpikes		0	6
pd at the ferry		10	0
the 3 Turnpikes		1	6
pd for setting a shoe on		0	2
the 4th Turnpikes		2	1
Beating [?]		1	0
Ostler		0	4
Wating and Boeer [beer]		0	10
		16	

Recd the above   Matthew Rowland [signature]

BIOGRAPHICAL DETAILS OF PEOPLE MENTIONED IN THE ACCOUNTS

THE NUMBER FOLLOWING THE ENTRY is the page number in the account book in which mention is made. Persons known by title e.g. 'The Secretary of State', 'the King' etc are not included but are likely discussed in the main text. Mr Sidebotham's system of orthography is highly original, wholly inconsistent and can cause some difficulties in identifying people. In justice it must be remembered that he was dealing with languages with which he was initially unfamiliar and that he compiled his records in the evening after the days transactions had taken place and his memory may have been stretched. During the Italian leg of the tour he becomes much more confident in the handling of personal and place names (Mr gradually becomes replaced by *Sig*) presumably because of his continuing language lessons, but when they returned to Paris his spelling of French names had acquired a distinctly Italian flavour. His was a remarkable achievement in that not only did the languages change but also so did the currencies and that he managed to keep abreast of any of it is a credit to his perspicacity, thoroughness and his devotion to his employer.

Achille, Carlo (59, 60, 79, 80)
Carlo Achille seems to have been a valet du place whose services were engaged in Rome when they first arrived. He obviously proved satisfactory and was engaged again when they returned from Naples. He was paid by the week for his services and, when the party finally left Rome for Venice, Mr Sidebotham gave him a handsome gratuity.

Andre, M (9)
A Parisian hat maker. It is impossible to say whether Andre is a surname or a forename adopted as one, as in the manner of a hairdresser or suchlike.

Apperley, Mr (8 and thereafter)
Thomas Apperley (1739–1819) son of a Wrexham doctor (also Thomas) who had been made a Freeman of Chester 1736 under the auspices of the then Mayor, Sir Watkin Williams Wynn –

3rd Baronet (the 'Great' Sir Watkin). The family seems to have originated from Grafton near Leominster in Herefordshire and was of solid 'gentry' stock. Thomas was the eldest son and received a good Grammar School education. The third Baronet died in 1749 several months after the birth of the fourth Baronet but one must presume that the two families remained on familiar terms. In 1765 Thomas became a Gentleman Commoner of Oriel College, Oxford and accompanied Sir Watkin to that place although he was ten years his senior; he matriculated one month later than Sir Watkin and presumably left at the same time. On the grand tour he seems to have acted as an informal guardian to Sir Watkin. A role for which he was singularly ill fitted when one considers the disastrous and indulgent upbringing he gave to his own son Charles - best known as the sportswriter Nimrod; a man who proved incapable of managing either himself, his debts or his matrimonial affairs. Upon his marriage in 1778 to Ann Wynn, daughter of an antiquarian and poetic clergyman, he took up permanent residence at Plas Gronw, on the Erddig estate, although he had signed the lease in 1774. The house was former home of Elihu Yale, part founder of the eponymous university which seems to be the repository of a goodly portion of the contemporary materials relating to the European Grand Tour.

C. L. Shadwell, *Registrum Orielense*, II. London & New York, 1902.

Audibert, Mr (97)

The mention of M. Audibert occurs upon a page of the account book concerned with customs duties. A letter from Edward Bancroft to William Temple Franklin dated to 1779 mentions a M. Audibert who was Captain of the Port of Calais. However a letter from Thomas Jefferson dated 1787 to the Count de Moustier (French Ambassador to the USA) praises the wine of a M. Audibert from Frontignan near Montpellier. The sum recorded £17: 7: 7d seems far too high to represent an import duty and must therefore represent the cost of wine. Therefore it is probable that this particular M. Audibert was a wine merchant. The Audibert family Chateau at Lambesc still produces a celebrated Chateauneuf du Pape. M. Audibert may not have supplied the crayons included in the assignment.

Baraci, Mr (68)

Mr Baraci seems to have been a customs functionary in service with the Papal States and under the authority of Cardinal Torregiani, the Papal Secretary of State.

Basan, [Basin] Mr (82, 89, 95)

Pierre-Francois Basin (sometimes Bazin) (1723–1797) was one of the leading printsellers and engravers of Paris. Specialising in very high quality work he was known as an engraver himself but is better known for the lavishly collections of prints which were published under his aegis. He published an important Dictionaire des Graveurs in 1767. His business was still operative from 14 Rue Serpente, towards the end of the century although he was in London in 1797 complaining that he had been owed several thousands by persons who had been caused an involuntary default by means of the guillotine.

Beaufort, Duchess of (88, 97)

Elizabeth Somerset, Dowager Duchess of Beaufort (1713–99) was Sir Watkin's future mother-in-law. The expensive Sevres Dinner Service which he bought for her from the Manufactory in Paris was a tactful gesture. She lived at 10 Grosvenor Square and was therefore a near neighbour. Henrietta Somerset died after several months of marriage. At the time of Sir Watkin's second marriage, in 1771, to Charlotte Greville, cousin of William Pitt, the Dowager Duchess took herself off on her own Grand Tour and spent a decent three years doing it. She met with James Byers in Rome and ordered a marble chimneypiece from him for Badminton House, which Byres had originally designed as one of the fixtures of the 'new' Wynnstay. She must have inspected the designs for the proposed house and been taken with them. The chimneypiece, ironically, seems to have been the only part of Byres' comprehensive portfolio which was ever realised. It was unusual, at that time, for a woman to undertake the tour under her own steam but the Duchess seemed to know her own mind.

Belloni, Marquis (50, 76, 83)

The Belloni's were an important and extensive family of Bolognese origin who lived in great splendour in the Palazzo Belloni-Battaglia, designed by Longhena, on the Grand Canal in Venice. Girolamo Belloni was an economic theorist whose published works were highly valued, 'Dissertazione sopra il Commercio' 1751 was influential throughout Europe. Ennobled by Clement XII for sorting out the Vatican's parlous finances he founded what in effect was to become a banking dynasty. When the indigent Stuarts landed upon Italian soil, Gian Angelo Belloni placed the Casa Belloni and his country villa in Bologna at their disposal. Mary of Modena had previously trusted the management of her investments to their bank. Thereafter the Belloni's were to become not only the Stuart bankers, but also the bankers of anyone allied to their cause. They were looked on with extreme suspicion by Westminster. Gian Angelo Belloni was a general agent in Italy with branches in Venice, Bologna, Rome and Naples and agents in Portugal, Parma and England and Mr Sidebotham drew funds upon him quite frequently. The wisdom of that particular connection was not questioned. In 1766, Francesco Belloni (d. 1806) had become sole heir to the bank but was not much interested in managing it and preferred to spend his time gracing the salons of the sociable classes. Towards the end of the century, their bank failed and was closed in 1793 and thus demonstrated that the first marquis' theories of economic management, upon which the bank was founded, may have been slightly flawed.

Benedetto, Sig (58, 59, 67, 78)

An hotelier in Rome possibly running the establishment in which the servants stayed in the vicinity of the Piazza di Spagna and near Sir Watkin's establishment which was undoubtedly better.

Blanc, Mr (30)

M. Le Blanc kept one of the better hotels in Lyon-apparently with an attached bathhouse. James Boswell described him as a Baigneur and stayed there in January 1766 and recorded that there was an adjacent restaurant, which furnished him with meals and wine. This may be the establishment kept by Mons. Minet, which rendered a similar service to Sir Watkin and party. The hotel may also be identified as L'Hotel de la Croix de Malthe which Mrs Piozzi stayed at and which had a bathing establishment.

Brady and Pottle (eds), *James Boswell on the Grand Tour to Italy, Corsica and France 1765–1766*, McGraw-Hill.

Piozzi, Hesther Thrale, *Observations & Reflections made in the Journey through France, Italy and Germany*, London, 1789.

Borndino, Sig (35, 36)

A traiteur in Turin who supplied the party with meals and wine.

Brown, Mr (73)

An English hotelier in Naples and at whose establishment the servants stayed.

Brunet, M (8, 89)

A supplier of dairy provisions in Paris resident at the Rue du Vieux Colombier 315.

Byres, James (62, 63, 66, 68, 76, 96)

Architect, antiquarian and general guide, James Byers (1734–1817) and his younger partner Christopher Norton (1740–99) the engraver, were an institution in Rome. Byres and his family left Britain for France after the '45 and Byres was educated there. He was in Rome by 1758 where he intended to study painting. He later took up architecture but was best known as a dealer in the antique and as a guide to the city. Byres wore out Edward Gibbon during an intensive sixteen-week tour of the ruins although that tour was also responsible for implanting the germ of an idea regarding Rome's decline and fall in Gibbon's mind. Gibbon had been virulent and very public in his condemnation of certain aspects of human sexuality and Byres, who was necessarily discreet over the nature of his relationship with Norton, may have taken a justifiable but vicarious delight in exhausting the historian. Expensive and relentless he was also one of the chief players in the British artistic mafia, which tried to control business in Rome to their own ends. His greatest coups were when he managed to buy and sell the Barberini (Portland) Vase to Sir William Hamilton and the first version of Poussin's *Seven Sacraments* to the Duke of Rutland. Slightly graceless, he was nevertheless to be endured as one of the most informed guides to the glories of ancient Rome and secure in that knowledge he charged accordingly. He had first come to Rome as an painter, later as architect and it was in that capacity that he was elected to the Accademia di S. Lucca in 1768 – in 1762 he had won

3rd prize for architecture. Why Sir Watkin commissioned him to design a new mansion at Wynnstay must remain a mystery, but Byres was obviously proud of the collaborative results and was happy to exhibit them to any interested party before he sent the drawings off to London. They are probably one of the most impressive products of an architect's drawing office ever seen in the eighteenth century and perhaps better as drawings than as a realised project. All in all, Mr Byres made quite a lot of money out of Sir Watkin.

Byres lived on the Via del Babuino (then the Strada Paolina) with Norton, his mother and father, sister and later his nephew. A family group by Franciszek Smuglevicz (1775) has Byres standing at the side of a shadowy sculpture of Jupiter and Ganymede and Norton under an equally shadowy portrait of perhaps Charles Edward Stuart. In 1790, sensing which way the wind was blowing, they all returned to Tonley, the family estate in Aberdeenshire, and Byres enjoyed a long and happy retirement. In 1792 Norton, at the age of fifty-two, married Byres' niece and enjoyed seven years of married life before his own death in 1799. Byres lasted, alone, until 1817. It has recently been discovered that the splendid portrait of Byres by Hugh Douglas Hamilton had a companion piece in a matching portrait of Norton both of which were hung in the apartment in Rome and later at Tonley, although its present whereabouts is unknown. See *DNB*

Cararra, Mr (8 and thereafter)

Antonio Cararra had an ambivalent position on the tour. Hired as Sir Watkin's valet, his duties extended to translator, guide, factotum and anything else required. He spoke several languages and, most importantly to Sir Watkin, was an accomplished singer. Recommended by David Garrick after accompanying him and his wife on their tour in 1760 he was in much demand and seems to have been one of the most reliable cicerones available. He may have joined the party in Paris as that is the first time he figures in the accounts. Dr Burney met him in Rome in 1770 when he was accompanying a Mr and Mrs Earle and he was able to deliver to him a letter from David Garrick and recorded how well he was spoken of by other clients. The highly respectable Joseph Baretti, Secretary to the Royal Academy, who suspected him of telling wild stories about Italian sexual licence to gullible, but fascinated, tourists, took a slightly less charitable view of him. He wrote, 'This Antonio, who, by what I have heard of him, piques himself much upon his good education, upon his extensive knowledge of men and manners, and upon his having written comedies, as he says, full as good as Goldoni's ...' He also records Cararra's first visit to England as being in 1767 but in this he may have been mistaken. Baretti seems not to have shared Cararra's sense of humour. In fact the waspish Mr Baretti seems to have no sense of humour whatsoever.

Burney, Dr, *Tour Journal 1770*, published as *Music Men and Manners in France and Italy*, Ed H. Edmund Poole, 1969.

Baretti, Joseph, *An Account of the Manners and Customs of Italy*, London, 1769.

Chambre, Francis (1)

Francis Chambre (d. 1793) was a solicitor, resident in Oswestry and of a Shropshire family from Petton who acted, in effect, as financial controller for the Wynnstay estates. He was distinguished in his own circle and was mayor of Oswestry in 1776. However, his was a thankless task and correspondence between himself and Samuel Sidebotham, especially after Sidebotham had moved to Wynnstay in 1780, record a deepening sense of despair at Sir Watkin's extravagance and utter refusal to understand the meaning of economy. In spite of his admonitions by 1776 there was a debt of about £100,000 to be managed. Although Lady Williams Wynn was convinced of his mismanagement, Sir Watkin could not bring himself to dismiss him. In 1791, after Sir Watkin's death and over a misunderstanding about a missing sum of money, Lady Williams Wynn, with the support of her brother, dismissed him for incompetence, which must have come as a blessed relief although in a small rural society it was an embarrassing circumstance. He died shortly afterwards and may not have been fairly treated. His list of clients also included the monumentally difficult Ladies of Llangollen – Lady Eleanor Butler and Miss Sarah Ponsonby – and the equally tedious grandmother to the Duke of Wellington, Lady Dungannon.

Child, Mr (82, 95, 96)

Robert Child (1700–82) Sir Watkin's London Banker and Director of Child's Bank and cousin to the notorious Henry, Earl Tylney. He had a network of agents throughout Europe who could be relied upon to cash money orders for his numerable clients. Although uninvolved in the daily business of the bank, he made spectacular use of its profits in the work of reconstructing Osterley Park House. He had inherited the house from his brother in 1763 when Robert Adam had already been engaged to re-model the mansion. Child continued the work in advanced neo-classical taste. Sir Watkin could not have been unaware of the work and commissioned designs for two houses from Adam although only one was ever built. In 1773, as 20 St James' Square was being built, Sir Watkin had a special viewing of Osterley Park and Syon House examples which cannot have helped him to practice economy.

Cordel, Thomas (72)

Thomas Cordell (1742–1819) was one of the most important publishers and booksellers in London. Alderman, sheriff (1800) and treasurer of the Foundling Hospital, he briefly became bankrupt when his warehouse burned down in 1776 but he recovered and his son, also Thomas, united the firms of Cordell and Davies in 1793. First based in Covent Garden, the firm later moved to the Strand. Publishers of Edward Gibbon, Adam Smith, Mrs Piozzi and many others, Cordell, in association with Longmans, opposed the liberalisation of copyright law. Cordell seems to have been Sir William Hamilton's publisher and handled distribution of his *Antiquities*. He must have supplied Sir Watkin with the copy which he loaned to Josiah Wedgwood in 1769. Cordell & Davies was dissolved in 1840.

Daubervalle, Mr (17)

Jean d'Auberville (1742–1806) was one of the great dancing teachers and choreographers of the age. Appointed *Premier Danseur* to the Academie Royale de Musique in 1763 he was to choreograph the original *La Fille mal garde* (1789) whilst ballet master at Bordeaux. Expensive and in great demand, Sir Watkin certainly nailed his colours to the mast when he chose him as instructor in dance.

Davies, John (87)

An extra servant who seems to have joined the party for the return journey, probably in Strasbourg.

Dean, [Deane] Mr (96)

Possibly Hugh Primrose Deane (1745–84), an Irish painter from County Down who was in London in 1768. He went to Rome under the patronage of Viscount Palmerston by 1771 and had some moderate success there. Primarily a landscape painter he also acted as a copyist. He was elected to the Florentine Academy in 1777 when he was described as 'Claude, l'Irlandais'. The Earl Cowper was one of his patrons. Unfortunately he never achieved greatness nor did he have it thrust upon him and being of an unsettled nature turned from painting to preaching and, that proving unsatisfactory, laboured in a dockyard when he returned to England.

Denagna (15)

A Parisian embroiderer and tailor who appears to have been outrageously expensive.

Devonshire, the Fifth Duke of (59)

William Cavendish (1748–1811) became the fifth duke of Devonshire in 1764 at the age of sixteen. Heir to an immense fortune, he was brought up by his three bachelor uncles who thought it unwise to allow him to attend university in case he should be paid 'dirty court' to by opportunists. Thus, in need of an education he went on his grand tour in 1768. He was an odd cold fish of a man who rarely exhibited enthusiasm for anything other than his dogs; he seems a strange travelling companion for Sir Watkin who exhibited all too many enthusiasms. Their travelling companionship seems to have lasted from Florence to Rome, Tivoli and Frascati and after Sir Watkin went to Naples their paths seem to have diverged. Batoni painted his portrait at the same time as he embarked upon the triple portrait for Sir Watkin. Staggeringly rich, he may have given bad example to Sir Watkin. His sister Dorothy Cavendish became very friendly with Jean Jacques Rousseau when the latter stayed at Wooton Hall, close to Chatsworth. Cavendish was best known for marrying Georgiana Spencer and prosecuting a very public affair with Lady Elizabeth Foster, daughter of the earl bishop of Bristol, an inveterate 'Grand Tourist'

Dolermo (95)

A Parisian export facilitator who packed up the Duchess of Beaufort's china.

Doria, Prince (60)

Giovanni Andrea IV, Prince Doria-Pamphilj, Prince of Landi (1747–1820) was the proprietor of a large *palazzo* (Palazzo dei Principe) overlooking the sea in Genoa and a vast one on the Corso in Rome (Palazzo Doria Pamphilj). He visited London in 1767, shortly before his wedding and stayed as a guest of the government in Somerset House. He married a princess of the Savoie-Carignano family from Turin, whose sister was the ill-fated Princess de Lamballe, friend of Queen Marie Antoinette and who was torn apart during an unfortunate incident at the La Force prison in 1792. The 'Grand Christening' may have been that of his first-born son, Giovanni Andrea Doria Pamphilj, Marchese di San Stefano. Born in July 1768, he did not survive infancy. Two of the Prince's brothers were cardinals and Clement XIII seemed to have taken a particular interest in the family. Sir Watkin's acquaintance with the Prince may have begun during his London visit. Just after Sir Watkin's visit he created a sensation in Rome during the visit of the Austrian Emperor and his brother the Grand Duke of Tuscany, in 1769, when he had an internal courtyard in the Palazzo Doria Pamphilj floored over at first floor level and the windows of the surrounding, and very splendid, galleries torn out to allow access to his new ballroom. The damage was, fortunately, rectified when the princely pair returned home.

Duboot [Dubost] (8, 10)

Valet du Place at the Hotel de Saxe in Paris.

Duprey, Mr (79)

A wine merchant in Rome with premises close to the Piazza di Spagna.

Eynhorts (87)

Mr Sidebotham's spelling may not be entirely reliable but from the gentleman and his wife several sets of fine Valencienes lace ruffles were purchased.

Firmian, Count (42)

Carl Joseph Count von Firmian. (1716–82) Count Firmian was the unusually enlightened minister plenipotentiary to Lombardy. Appointed by the Empress Maria Teresa he had previously been ambassador to Naples (1753) where he distinguished himself and undertook several successful, although secret, missions. Appointed to Milan in 1756, he was nominally under the jurisdiction of Duke Francisco d'Este III of Modena, imperial governor of Lombardy, but in fact he was charged with the government of the duchy. Strongly anglophile, he read widely and encouraged the establishment of a newspaper *Il Caffe* modelled after Addison's *Spectator*. A serious patron of the arts and sciences, he reformed agriculture and established libraries and counted Angelica Kaufmann and Johann Winckleman amongst his protégées. Responsible for commissioning the young Mozart's first major opera (*Mithridate, Re di Ponto*, 1770) he also oversaw the building of the Teatro alla Scala in 1778 after the Reggio Ducale theatre burnt down in 1776. In his will he left most of his library, which contained an unusual number of English books, to enrich the collections of the Brera. He was assiduous in encouraging the development of emerging talent and freely gave of his time to assist the aspiring artist. His attention towards the young Sir Watkin was part of his benevolent interest in the visiting British. His passing was much regretted by the Milanese and a suitably splendid cenotaph, by Giuseppe Franchi (1731–1806) was erected in the church of S. Bartolomeo (rebuilt on the Corso Magenta in the 1860's)

Fitzhherbert, Mr (72)
Seems to have been a kind of 'fixer' for the evening concerts in Rome.

Forester, Mr (77)
James Forrester (1730–75) An Irish artist who trained at the Dublin schools. After winning the first prize for painting in 1752 he went to Rome to continue study. At first sharing a house in the Strada della Croce with two compatriots, he came to the notice of several important patrons. The Duke of Gloucester and the Earl Fitzwilliam purchased works from him. He eventually shared a house with Father Thorpe, Jesuit confessor to Lord Arundel, who wrote extensively about him in his letters to England. Noted for his moonlight scenes and also for painting 'plein air' his promising career was cut short by his premature death at the age of 45. He may have studied with Richard Wilson and, like many aspiring artists in Rome, supplemented his income by teaching drawing to well-heeled clients. He seems to have fluctuated between Rome and Naples. It may have been under his tutelage that Sir Watkin drew the chalk version of Raphael's *Justice*, which he holds in the Batoni portrait.

Fortrose, Lord (54)
Kenneth Mackenzie (1744–81) was created Viscount Fortrose in 1766. Of a Scottish Jacobite family he managed to buy back his attainted grandfather's estates and became MP for Buteshire and Caithness in 1768. The representation of his constituents did not much overly concern him and he promptly made for Italy, although the death of his first wife in 1767 may have prompted his wanderings. In Naples he cut a sociable figure and was valued for the sensibility of his conversation, his kind hospitality and his musicality. Created first Earl Seaforth in 1771 he made a sensational second marriage when he legalised an attachment he had formed with Harriet Powell; a lady described as a 'fashionable beauty' and as 'frail and famous'. In 1778 he formed the Seaforth Highlanders and in 1781 was drowned at sea on the way to the West Indies. His second wife, in common with his first, pre-deceased him.

Francavilla, Prince (73)

Dissolute and hospitable in equal measure, the Prince was an endless source of gossip in Naples. Residing in the vast Palazzo Cellamare, off the Via Chiaia and within a stone's throw of William Hamilton's Palazzo Sessa, his household seemed to comprise mostly attractive and compliant young men. The Palace was epicentre of gay and carefree hospitality and its musical evenings were famous. His princess, Eleanor Borghese, was equally hospitable to visiting British gentlemen, many of whom took away an unexpected souvenir of their Grand Tour which necessitated a stop in Paris to have it cured before they returned home. Lord Rockingham, future British Prime-Minister, had good reason to regret his brief acquaintance with the Princess. Francavilla was the subject of much malicious (and probably true) gossip by Casanova. His personal peccadilloes did not prevent him from being major-domo to the king of Naples, nor his being invested with the Order of the Golden Fleece. A grandee of Spain, his sojourn in Naples was much appreciated by Charles III of Spain, father of King Ferdinand of Naples, who feared the effect his presence might have had upon the young princes and their morals were he to become resident in Madrid instead of Naples. Prince Francavilla exemplified that which British parents were most afraid of their sons meeting whilst in Italy; his wife no less so.

Letter from Charles Hotham 1754. Quoted in Black, *The Grand Tour*, Sutton, 2003.

Casanova de Seingalt, Giacomo Girolamo, *Story of My Life*.

Frescobaldi, Marquess (52)

The Frescobaldi family were eminent as Florentine bankers and winemakers with a long connection to England. They funded the wars of Edward I and Edward II and were bankrupted when the latter became disinclined to repay his debts in 1270. Henry VIII made some amends by writing to them in 1519 (the autograph letter is still in the Family Archive) and appointing them vintners to the Royal establishment. Gradually their banking ventures declined and their vineyards became more important in the late eighteenth century.

Fulga, M (28)

A watchmaker in Geneva who supplied a gold stopwatch to Sir Watkin which had a very advanced and costly mechanism.

Gaufoan, M (1)

A banker or a merchant who could honour a note, resident in Geneva.

Giovardi, M (34)

Although the Belloni bank was based in Rome the family had originated from Bologna. In 1717, Giovanni Belloni had loaned the Casa Belloni in that city to the exiled James III and had been banker to Mary of Modena. An important branch of the bank was maintained in Bologna and we may presume that M. Giovardi was a representative there and was able to pay upon a draft to Mr Sidebotham.

Gori, Lamberto (53)

Lamberto Cristiano Gori (1730–1801) was one of the most accomplished workers in scagliola in Florence. Using pulverised marble and various other coloured elements, floated in a paste of various components, he produced elaborate decorative pieces of inlaid work which, when polished, resembled smooth marble much valued as tops for side-tables and the like. He certainly represented the luxury end of the market in collectable furniture and his work was in much demand by the grand tourist. The two tables which Sir Watkin ordered from him, and which were to take seven months to complete, represent Sir Watkin's first foray into the serious work of being a connoisseur and patron. Interestingly, Gori's father was English although the family had been long resident in Florence. His brother, a monk, had initiated him into the mysteries of the craft. Two side tables with scagliola tops were recorded as being in the drawing room of 20 St James' Square.

Graff, Mr (94)

Daniel Graff (also spelled Graaff or Graeff) seems to have been Lord Leigh's Brentford steward (Lord Leigh had a house at Old Brentford). He appears in the Stoneleigh archive where he writes about Lord Leigh's physicians, in 1769, and the difficulty in replacing one with another. In 1806 his widow appears with entertaining effect when she refuses to relinquish the management of Stoneleigh Abbey to a Mrs Smart, even though she was 72. Her battles with proposed successors is diverting to us but was obviously a trial to her contemporaries. The matter was eventually resolved and her retirement effected. At about the same time the Brentford residence, New Grove House, Boston Lane (now Ealing) was closed up and most of the servants dismissed.

NB. If one finds the worst aspect of human behaviour entertaining, the Stoneleigh Archive is an endless source of amusement.

National Archives. Shakespeare Archive (Warwickshire) DR 18/17/27/205; DR 18/17/32/120.

Grant, Abbe (78)

A notorious proselytizer and Jacobite sympathiser, Abbe Grant was one of the 'fixers' of Rome and could effect introductions throughout the city. Much rumoured to be a spy, although for which side no one quite knew, his services could be very valuable. Grant made himself agreeable to most visitors although his spiritual director was worried that his social life was interfering with his religious mission. His provision of mounts for a fan to Sir Watkin is an illustration of his scurrying agreeability. His brother was the secular rector of the Scots' College in Rome.

Gulmani [Gulmann] **& Son** (82)
A banker resident in Augsberg upon whom Child's Bank had given Mr Sidebotham a draft for £110. Where the draft was presented is not entirely clear.

Hadfield, Mr (55)
From Manchester and from an affluent family background, Charles Hadfield (1717?–76) kept a very comfortable hotel in Florence. He had been dismayed by the standard of accommodation on offer when he made a tour of Italy and decided to rectify the situation. His first venture was in Leghorn (Livorno) and he later moved his operations to Florence when he bought an hotel there (the Locanda di Carlo on the Lungarno Capponi mentioned by Boswell). He eventually bought another (Angelo's on the Lungarno Guicciardini) near the Palazzo Manin, Sir Horace Mann's residence, and a country villa (Palazzo Bruciato) just north of the city outside the San Gallo Gate. This latter he hired out to visitors who wished to entertain as local social conventions would not allow a lady of rank to visit an hotel. His was a very English establishment and his guests included Angelika Kaufmann and Sir Joshua Reynolds, although not Charles Edward Stuart who was refused admission on the grounds that it might upset the other English guests – much to the delight and satisfaction of Sir Horace Mann, his chief patron. Married to Isabella, née Pocock, (1730–1809) a close friend and correspondent of General Paoli, his children were to find fame elsewhere although the first four were suffocated by a lunatic nursemaid who thought to speed their journey to Heaven. Fortunately she was overheard commending her actions to the Lord and was thereafter incarcerated. Maria, the eldest surviving child, (b. 1760) became better known as Maria Cosway, the artist, her brother George (b. 1763) was one of the first professional architects in the United States of America and a Greek revivalist of note and her younger sister, Charlotte, a miniaturist, married William Coombe of Dr Syntax fame.

Hamilton, Capt (7 and thereafter)
Captain Edward Hamilton a cavalry officer and amateur musician of whom not much is known. Not overstretched by military duties, his main claim to fame appears to consist in having been one of the trio in Pompeo Batoni's triple portrait. He is recorded in the printed British *Army List* for 1765 as being Lieutenant Captain Edward Hamilton in the 15th Regiment of (Light) Dragoons. He seems to have been commissioned on 12 July that year. Mr Sidebotham may not have been impressed with him. For some reason Wedgwood seems to have intended to make a commemorative medallion of him but, although the model survives, it is unclear whether the medallion was cast or not.
Army List, 1765, National Archives, Kew (WO65).

Hamilton, Mr (62, 63, 77)
Gavin Hamilton (1723–98) was a Scottish painter and antiquarian. He was resident in Rome

by the mid 1740s, studying under Agostino Masucci. In 1751 he returned to London but five years later was back in Rome where he remained. A highly secretive man, very little is really known about him except that he was probably the most productive excavator and dealer of the century. Virtually every major collection acquired sculpture from him (usually much restored or re-invented) He flits through the pages of most accounts of the Grand Tour without leaving much of a certain mark. Perhaps the shady dealings he entered into, in common with Thomas Jenkins, were a reason for his personal reticence.

Hamilton, Mr [the Minister] (70, 72, 73)

William Hamilton (knighted in 1772) was the British minister in Naples. Later raised to the post of envoy extraordinary, he ornamented his position to a degree which made him a celebrity throughout Europe. Born in 1731, his mother was most likely the mistress of the Prince of Wales. He was raised in the Royal Nursery with the future George III who later called him 'foster brother'. After attending Westminster School and service in the army he became MP for Midhurst in 1761 and resigned in 1764 to take up a diplomatic post in Naples where he remained for the rest of his career. Married to Catherine Barlow of Pembroke, together they set up a salon of the highest refinement and celebrity in the Palazzo Sessa. His interest in archaeology and vulcanology made him one of the most celebrated connoisseurs and scientists in Europe. Highly accomplished, he and his wife established the Palazzo as a centre of musical life in the city. Eventually he took upon himself the role of guide and lecturer to visiting celebrities curious about the volcanic sites in the region. Friendly with, but undeceived by, King Ferdinand, he enjoyed a secure position in that rather dubious court. His collection of 'Etruscan Vases' – in reality Greek, was as famous as the lavish and expensive publication illustrating the collection; a copy of which Sir Watkin bought. His publication of his geological observations *Campi Phlaegri* of 1766 was the cause of his election as a member of the Royal Society. The death of Catherine affected him deeply and his reason appears to have been totally deficient when he allowed his nephew Charles Greville to dump his discarded mistress upon him in 1786. The blowsy Emma brought little distinction, but a great deal of merriment, to his embassy. He was sufficiently detached from mundane matters as to be able to ignore the resultant gossip entirely. The later liaison of his wife and Admiral Lord Nelson is outside of our scope.

Harwood, Mr (53)

Francis Harwood (1726/7–83) was a British sculptor resident in Florence. Virtually nothing is known about his early years but by the time that he was twenty-five he was living in Rome at the Palazzo Zuccari. In Rome he briefly shared lodgings with Sir Joshua Reynolds but by 1753 he was in Florence studying with Joseph Wilton. Although a sculptor of considerable merit, he was mainly occupied in providing copies 'after the antique' to tourists. He supplied various items to Charles Townley, the earl of Shelburne, Grand Duke Leopold II, Catherine the Great as well as Sir Watkin. Much afflicted by drink, he converted to Catholicism shortly before his death in 1783.

Henry, Mr (90)

As with M. Andre, Mr Henry may be utilising a forename as a surname. He was a tailor in Paris who, to judge from the size of his bill, may have made up some of the velvet pieces Sir Watkin bought both there and in Lyons.

Hewson, [Hewetson] Mr (63)

Christopher Hewetson (1739–98) A neoclassical sculptor born in Dublin, he went to Rome for further study in 1765 and stayed there for the rest of his life. Much in demand for his fine portrait busts his clients numbered, apart from Sir Watkin, Clement XIV, the Duke of Gloucester, Gavin Hamilton, Anton Rafael Mengs and the Grand Duchess Paul (later empress of Russia). He was a member of the British artistic 'establishment' in Rome and frequented the notorious Cafe dell'Inglese where he met Thomas Jones. His prices were not modest.

Jenkins, Mr (62, 76)

Thomas Jenkins (1722–98) seems to have had the trade in antiquities in Rome in his back pocket. Apparently born in Rome although educated in England. No more honest than he should have been, his Devonian grace and courtesy managed to sideline James Byres, who had a very thick Scottish accent, into a subsidiary position and there was a constant rivalry between the two. He was undoubtedly 'smooth' and had managed to acquire connections in the city which extended to the Pope himself. Seemingly working with the shadowy Gavin Hamilton he absolutely cornered the business of dealing. It was rumoured that he had a secret workshop in the vaults of the Coliseum where he manufactured new antiquities for the gullible tourist, but those which had the substance, as well as the aura of antiquity, which he dealt in, were considerable. Britain had no ambassador or even consul in Rome although the Pope had formally acknowledged George III as British sovereign in 1766, and Jenkins effectively filled both the posts and was acknowledged to be doing so. He exercised an extraordinary control over the business of the British in Rome.

Jeremy, Mr Francis (96)

Francis Jeremy (1708?–81) was Factor at the English settlement in Leghorn (Livorno). Regarded as the principal merchant and banker he amassed considerable wealth. Unmarried, on his death he left substantial sums to Earl Tylney, Sir Horace Mann and Earl Cowper, £5,000 to John Udney, British Consul, and £500 to his naval son. He further left the rent rolls of a vineyard he owned to subsidise the English Church in Livorno and his two theatre boxes to the visiting English or the poor – he did not stipulate which was to receive precedence.

Jolly [Joli] (10)

M. Joli was a *marchand de vins* residing at Quai de Union 14, close to Sir Watkin's Hotel. His firm survived the Revolution and was recorded in the 1799 *Almanack du Commerce de Paris*.

Jones, Mr (94, 97)

Customs House official in London who took charge of levying import duties on Sir Watkins purchases abroad. He must have been a constant visitor to Grosvenor Square.

Jovannini [Giovannini] (66)

Giovannini, a Roman cellist and composer, not to be confused with the Giovannini who adopted the pseudonym of the Count de Saint Germain, and who was in Berlin at the time. Dr Burney attended vespers at St Peter's, which was celebrated by the Cardinal Duke of York, and wrote 'The fat Giovannini, famous for playing the cello, as well as for being one of the Maestri di Capella of St Peter's, beat time'
Dr Burney, *The Present State of Music in France and Italy*, 2nd edition, 1773.

Julia, Sig (39)

A gentleman of Turin who hired out coaches to take Sir Watkin to Venaria Reale to be presented to King Carlo Emanuelle.

Lacomb, M (28)

A Geneva coachmaker and hirer. He was also responsible for the provision of the thirteen horses with which the party ascended to the Chamonix Glacier.

Lafrenage, [Lafresnaye] Mons (88)

Sir Watkin spent a great deal of money with M. Lafresnaye. A watch set with diamonds, a travelling clock, diamond shoe-buckles for a lady and gold snuffbox were amongst the purchases. Lafresnaye seems to have been one of the partners in Simmons, Bouchot & Lafresnaye, goldsmiths, on the Quai Pelletier 16 (later the Quai Gesvres and now the Hotel de Ville). In modern terms, something in the region of £38,000 was spent in his establishment – £548 in 1769.

Leigh, Lord (17, 94)

Edward, 5th Baron Leigh (1742–86) was brought up by his sister at Coombe Abbey. He attended Westminster School and Oriel College, Oxford. Buying furniture, books and art works he had plans to re-build Stoneleigh Abbey, the family seat. In 1766, payments were made on his behalf to Bethlehem Hospital and to Dr Munro (George III's attendant physician) and in 1774 he was declared not only insane but that he had been for five years previous. He died in 1786 and his sister, with the help of John Dodson, a fellow of Oriel College to which he had bequeathed his library, burnt all of his personal papers. It seems that 'certain of the late Lord Leigh's papers' were embarrassing. The squabbles over his will lasted for several decades

Mahoni, Countess (73)

Lady Anne Clifford, Countess Mahoni (1715–93) was the daughter of the Hon Thomas Clifford and Charlotte Maria Livingstone, countess of Newburgh in her own right. In 1739, she married Count John Joseph Mahoni a lieutenant-general in the Neapolitan army and son of Daniel O'Mahony, *comte de Castille*. Lady Clifford's family were tainted with Jacobitism and made their lives away from the United Kingdom. In 1773, she married Don Carlo Severino and in 1793 died whilst visiting Ischia. Her daughter, Cecilia, married the 5th Prince Giustianini and became a stalwart of Roman society. Her descendants were eventually able to re-claim the earldom of Newburgh back for themselves, the House of Lords, in 1858, setting aside objections that they were Italian nationals although the then Princess Giustianini had become naturalised British by Act of Parliament in 1857. In spite of long residence in Italy, Lady Anne remembered how to speak English; her daughter the Princess Giustianini, born in Italy, did not.

Marron (96)

Anton von Maron (1733–1808) was one of the pre-eminent neo-classical painters working in Rome. Born in Vienna he came to Rome whilst relatively young. Studying under Rafael Mengs, and eventually marrying his sister, he became part of the close-knit circle and artistically advanced circle which revolved around Mengs and Wincklemann. He was an accomplished portraitist and his studio became an alternative to that of Batoni for the grand tourist. When Mengs went to Madrid, in 1761, Maron took over the business. In 1768, he painted James Byres in an advanced 'romantic' style and in 1771 was called to Vienna to paint the imperial family. On return, he lived in Rome for the rest of his life. The implication in the accounts that Maron acted as a copyist must be wrong, he was far to distinguished to undertake such work, and the suspicion must be that he acted as agent in having a painting by Raphael copied for Sir Watkin. Considering that Mengs was not in Rome during Sir Watkin's visit, it may well be that the commission for the *Perseus and Andromeda*, which Sir Watkin gave to Mengs, was funnelled through Maron to the artist. Another equal possibility would be that John Parry, son of the Wynnstay harpist, whom Sir Watkin had funded to study painting in Rome in 1771 handled the commission.

Maumett, Mons (88)

A dealer at the Royal Manufactory (Sèvres) in Paris and from whom the Duchess of Beaufort's dessert service was purchased.

Meighan, Mr (50, 77, 78, 79)

A banker in Rome and possibly an agent of Belloni's bank.

214

Minet, Mons (30)

See Mr Blanc.

Modena, The Duke of (45)

Francisco Ercole III d'Este, duke of Modena, was nominally imperial governor of Lombardy but Count Firmian carried out the actual work of government. Sir Watkin was mistaken in presuming that he was to be presented to the Duke and his Duchess due to that lady's unfortunate demise several years earlier. Dr Burney described the Duke as painted and in high colour and his daughter, who fulfilled her late mother's ceremonial role, as being pale and insipid. She was to marry into the Austrian imperial family whilst her highly-coloured father mouldered on in Lombardy until 1780.

Morris, Mr (9 and thereafter)

Upper servant and horn player. He also accompanied the 1771 tour of North Wales.

Mozarg, M (25)

Landlord at Leon d'Or in Lausanne, although the spelling of his name may be unorthodox.

Paintanida, [Piantanida] Sig (55, 72)

The Piantanidas were a distinguished family of musicians mostly resident in Florence. Giovanni (1705–82) was a virtuoso violinist who played for Handel in London from 1739–42 before returning to Bologna. Francesco, either his son or brother, was active as a cello teacher in Florence from 1766 until 1782 where he was styled 'Professor of Cello'. He was elected as a member of the Philharmonic Academy in Bologna in the same session which admitted the fourteen year old Mozart to membership in 1770. He seems to have died in 1789. It is likely that it was his son who gave lessons to Sir Watkin who could not have been unaware of the Handel connection of the family. Both father and son played for Sir Watkin in his rooms. Interestingly, the work which Lord Cowper presented in a concert to celebrate Sir Horatio Mann's investiture was Handel's *Alexander's Feast*. Handel revised the score in 1742 and it was presented at Covent Garden whilst Giovanni Piantanida was still in London playing for him.

Panchaud, M (1, 82, 87, 88, 89, 95, 100)

An Isaac Panchaud was naturalised by Act of Parliament in 1728 and it seems that the same person was declared bankrupt in 1732. Interestingly, in 1729 a Paul Torras was also naturalised. It seems a complicated family and his son, another Isaac, was an Anglo-Swiss banker in Paris, born in London, but with residence in Geneva and a man of the utmost integrity although a brilliant speculator. An associate for Child's Bank and much favoured by British visitors, he reciprocated by being an outspoken admirer of English fiscal policy. He acted for Lawrence Sterne amongst many others. The severe losses he incurred whilst investing in the British East

India Company proved a temporary setback but he recovered and survived to speculate, in company with Mirabeau, in the early years of the Revolution. He was somewhat elusive and his history is hard to disentangle – perhaps, on his part, intentionally.

Paoli, General (54)

Pasquale di Paoli (1725–1807) was a Corsican patriot much lauded by liberal British society. Following his father, after an abortive revolution, into self-exile in Naples, he was educated there and entered the Neapolitan king's service. Corsican frustration at the bad government exercised by the Genoese resulted in a movement for independence from them and Paoli who, by then, had become a considerable political figure was elected president of the Corsican Diet. A secret agreement made in 1764, under which the Genoese Republic had sold the island to France was made public in 1768 and Paoli sought refuge in London where Boswell espoused his cause. He became a hero of the Whigs and was granted a pension by George III. On the outset of the French Revolution he returned to Corsica but broke with the revolutionaries over the matter of regicide. The constitution he drafted for an independent Corsica was a model of enlightenment principles and was the envy of many an older-established society. From 1794 until 1796 he established an Anglo-Sardinian kingdom in Corsica; George III being titular head. Eventually, the venture failed and he took refuge once again in London, dying there in 1807. He is buried in St Pancras' Churchyard. Somehow the romantic figure he presented united both Whigs and Tories. Sir Watkin's subscription to his cause (£100, but greatly exaggerated by the British press) may have been an indication as to his slightly confused political principles. He was in north Wales in 1774 when he stayed at Caernarfon Castle with Sir George Wynn and met Dr Johnson and Mrs Piozzi.

James Boswell, *On the Present State of Corsica*, London, 1768.

Pascall, M (17, 19, 89)

A coachmaker in Paris who provided the coaches for Italy and part exchanged Lord Leigh's coach for them. Evidently satisfactory, he was again employed when they returned to England

Patch, Mr (54)

Thomas Patch (c.1725–82) was best known as a caricaturist painter. Exiled from Rome by the Holy Inquisition for making too free with Roman youth, he moved to Florence and became an institution. His misdemeanours in Rome must have been either spectacularly indiscrete or wilfully blatant for the Holy Office to have taken such a severe attitude to what was hardly a rare occurrence in the city. Intimate with Sir Horace Mann, who delicately described the reason for his expulsion as 'some indiscretion about Religion' and recorder of the foibles of the British in Florence, his works were much valued for their humour. His landscape paintings are very attractive and competent, but it is for his caricatures that he is best known. Sir Watkin purchased one of them which featured himself, Mr Apperley, Captain Hamilton and Antonio

Carrara. That was probably lost in the Wynnstay fire, but a slightly cruel etching of Sir Watkin does survive (B.M.). Most Grand Tourists had a caricature by Patch as a souvenir of their time in Florence and many of them survive in country houses (e.g. Dunham Massey) throughout Britain. He was, however, a trustworthy expositor on the complexities of Italian art and was painted as such by Zoffany in his view of the *Tribuna* in the Uffizi Gallery. Much to his credit, the very fastidious Horace Mann nursed Patch throughout his final illness.

Pernon, Mr (88)

Camille Pernon (1753–1808) was a leading manufacturer of silks etc. in Lyons. Due to the association of luxury silk, his business and the ancient regime he wisely fled to Italy on the outbreak of the Revolution, eventually settling in Spain where he established a manufactory under the patronage of the king. Sir Watkin spent rather a lot of money on silk, velvet and brocade, in Lyons and seems to have had some of his purchases made up into suits before he returned to England. His 'best suit' must have been made up in Lyons and delivered in Paris where the bill was paid – an astonishing £84 17s 6d (Slightly over £5,500 in modern terms)

Petrillo (84)

Signor Petrillo was landlord of one of the best, or to the British most acceptable, hotels in Venice. Situated on the Grand Canal it also overlooked the Rialto Bridge. Many visiting British stayed there, as it was known both for its cleanliness and its excellent table. From descriptions by other tourists the hotel seems to have been the Scudo di Francia which was situated in the Ca' Dandolo, now the Ca' Farsetti and, in effect, the present Municipio of Venice. Arthur Young was particularly taken with the establishment: 'I was conducted to an apartment that looked on to the grand canal, so neat, and everything in it so clean and good, that I almost thought myself in England' – otherwise Mr Young seems not to have been particularly xenophobic. Arthur Young, *Travels in France 1787, 1788, 1789*.

Piranezi, [Piranesi] Sig (62)

Cavaliere Gian Battista Piranesi (1720–78) was, together with Pompeo Batoni, probably the most celebrated modern artist working in Rome. Irascible and brilliant in equal measure he was, together with Batoni, one of the human sights of Rome. Through the medium of his engravings he could almost be credited with having invented ancient Rome. Many a visitor recorded their slight disappointment when faced with the actuality of the city and finding that it was not as grand, awesome, magnificent, sublime or simply monumental as the artist had depicted it to be. Originally from Venice, he established himself in Rome permanently in about 1747. A stout defender of the primacy of Roman art against the opposing claims of the adherents of the Greek or Gothic, his publication of the *Vedute di Roma* not only established his own reputation but also established an archaeological approach to the interpretation of the existing remains. Patronised by Pope Clement XIII (another Venetian) his position became unassailable. Always with an eye to business he was assiduous in promoting the sale of his prints. Sir Watkin bought a complete set and was rewarded, in 1778, by the dedication of plate 29 in *Vasi, candelabri, cippi*, although in the dedication he is described as '*un Cavaliere Inglese*'. His only completed work, as an architect, was the neo-classical Priory Church of the Knights of Malta on the Aventine Hill, but other slightly more dubious works by him, flooded the market. In collaboration with the likes of Byres, Jenkins and Hamilton, he was not above cobbling together new antiques out of fragments of the old and many a collector was taken in by the deception.

Pochereau, M (16)
Bookseller in Paris

Pompeo [Batoni] (62)
Cavaliere Pompeo Batoni (Lucca 1708 – Rome 1787), the most famous Roman painter of his time who's extensive output can sometimes obscure the fact that he was supremely gifted. An extraordinary draughtsman, his early work could diverge into roccoco sweetness but his brilliant technique and intense sense of colour marked him out as someone who had inherited all of the traditions of a great past. He became the preferred portraitist of the grand tourist and his fees reflected his celebrity. He never, however, gave up history painting and would, without commission, produce a canvas of an historical or mythological subject, which he carefully tucked away, but within sight, in his much-visited studio. Pretending that the canvas was too important to himself to consider selling, he, of course, pushed up the eventual purchase price. The triple portrait he made of Sir Watkin, Mr Apperley and Captain Hamilton was the only one of its sort he ever attempted and although he took several years to finish it, it is an outstanding achievement. Sir Watkin further commissioned from him a painting of Bacchus and Ariadne, sold at Sotheby's in 1947 and now in a private collection in Rome, it is an especial piece from an artist at the height of his powers. Brilliant at capturing the sheen of silk, the richness of embroidery, the intricacy of lace and with rare insight into the psychology of his sitters, Batoni excelled himself in painting Sir Watkin and his companions. Perhaps he found them sympathetic. In 1768, apart from Sir Watkin, he also painted the Duke of Devonshire and Sir Gregory Turner (later Page-Turner) both of whom had been at Sir Horace Mann's investiture in Florence and at Sir Watkin's subsequent musical soirée. In 1769, the double portrait of Joseph II and Leopold II won an Austrian nobility for Batoni. He also portrayed Pope Pius VI. According to a rumor, he bequeathed his palette and brushes to Jacques-Louis David. He was married twice, to Caterina Setti (d. 1742) in 1729, and then to Lucia Fattori in 1747, and had twelve children; three of his sons assisted in his studio. From 1759 Batoni lived in a large house on the Via Bocca di Leone in Rome, which included a studio as well as exhibition rooms and a drawing academy. He died in Rome. His facility and the extent of his output inevitably caused a dip in his reputation after his death. For almost a century he was

regarded simply as a portraitist or as a decorative artist. Recently re-evaluated, the extent and brilliance of his achievement has become more widely recognised and the portrait of Sir Watkin and his companions can be seen as central to his work.

Bowron, Kerber, *Pompeo Batoni*, Yale, 2007 (National Gallery Exhibition Catalogue).

Robinson, Mr (54)

A tailor in Florence who was British and who could therefore be regarded as being dependable.

Rolland, Mr (79, 80)

A gentleman from Avignon and proprietor of the Ville des Londres; a hotel in the Piazza di Spagna and one which was most popular with the visiting British. At the bottom of the Spanish Steps and opposite the Cafe degli Inglese and next to the modern Babbington's Tea Rooms, the hotel was in the centre of the 'English Quarter'– '*Ghetto dei Inglesi*'. Generally reckoned one of the best in Rome, it underwent several name changes, most of which retained the name London in the title. Eventually Rolland gave it to his daughter, the delightful Teresa, who, in 1762 had married Jean Casanova, the philanderer's brother. Unfortunately she died of consumption in 1772. The hotel survived for another hundred years and was recommended in the 1869 edition of *Baedeker*. It no longer exists.

Rowland, James (93)

The Rowlands were a Ruabon family in service at Wynnstay.

Sejan, M [Sege?] (8)

Wine merchant Paris

Simoneh, [Simonet] Mrs (90)

Mrs Simonet was the landlady of the 'Hotel Park Royal', where the servants stayed in Paris. Evidently a pleasing establishment, they stayed there both on the outward and homeward journeys.

Stevens, Sam (8, 78, 84, 87)

Stevens was a servant who seems to have been a general factotum. Probably a groom, he took charge of horses, the coaches and their equipment when required. Obviously trusted, he was frequently away from the main party carrying out errands as needed.

Tiernes, [Tierney] Mr (76)

George Tierney (d. 1787) a banker and merchant of Irish descent; born in Limerick and resident in Naples. His brother Thomas was prize agent in Gibraltar where he represented the firm of Tierney, Lilly & Robarts, Spanish merchants of Lawrence Poutney Lane. George Tierney was close to Sir William Hamilton and James Byres and counted several members of the Neapolitan nobility as intimates. He lived in Naples for long enough to find the manners of some of the visiting British distinctly embarrassing when compared with the native grace of the Italians (Moore. Letter LXIII) His detailed will, proved in 1788, gives a fascinating insight into the lavishness of the establishment he ran in Naples and into his personal wealth which included paintings (Rubens and Maratti), antiquities, coaches, plate and a very large sum of money deposited in the S. Gerolamini Bank (although, in common with Isaac Panchaud, he lost a great deal of money when the English East India Company stock devalued in 1769). His nephew, another George, was the Whig politician who famously fought a duel with William Pitt on Putney Heath in 1798.

Torras, Mr (1)
Paul Torras was a banker, possibly naturalised British, in Turin. Boswell wrote (8 January 1765) 'and went to Torraz, [sic] my banker, a good, brisk, civil fellow'". Mr Sidebotham drew over £500 from him. Dr John Morgan, a doctor from Philadelphia, wrote 'Call'd this afternoon on Mess'rs Torrass who are very consid'ble Men here. & Gen'l Bankers of the English'. The Torras and Panchaud families seem to have worked in tandem and, apart from Belloni in Rome, were the chief financial agents to the visiting British.
Morgan. Dr John, *Journal for 1764*, Philadelphia, 1908.

Veron (95)
See entry under Pernon

Watkin, Sir (7 and thereafter)
The object of the exercise.

Watson, Mr (76)
John Watson was a Venetian banker used by Boswell. Succeeding Sir John Udney, who had previously been in Livorno, he was appointed British Consul in 1790 by the British Resident Sir Francis Vincent, whom it seems was at death's door. After Sir Francis' demise he continued in post until 12 May 1797 when he wisely left. Four days later, Napoleon entered the lagoon unopposed and thus ending over one thousand years of Venetian autonomy.

Woodfall, Mr (94)
A postal agent in London who forwarded letters and newspapers to Mr Sidebotham whilst he was abroad.

Wyseman, [Wiseman] Mr (63, 65, 78)
Carlo (Charles) Wiseman was a music-master, composer and copyist who had lived in Rome

for eighteen years and spoke English with a very pronounced Italian accent. He lived in the Casino of Raphael in the gardens of the Villa Borghese where he often gave concerts – once a week in the winter months – or allowed others to do so – to visiting tourists. His services were especially valuable in tracing old music, an accomplishment which was exploited to the full by Dr Burney. His own compositions included trios for flute and cello and six sonatas for the same combination. Given the particular instrumental interests of Sir Watkin and Captain Hamilton, the printed music which Mr Sidebotham bought from Wiseman may well have included some of the above. The Casino survives although much reduced by bombardment during the siege of Rome in 1849. Mr Wiseman, although not a composer of the first rank, seems to belong to that band of curious individuals whose works are mostly known by their inclusion in the modern examination syllabus of instrumental scholars who may slave over their attempting mastery of the *Sonata in D* but have no idea whatsoever of who exactly wrote it.

REFERENCES & SELECT BIBLIOGRAPHY

The following should be taken as only referring to Sir Watkin's Grand Tour and tour of North Wales. The Grand Tour generally has been the subject of so much literature that I have been careful to cite only those works which are directly relevant to the subject of this study and have not attempted to give a comprehensive bibliography of mid to late-eighteenth century British tourists abroad.

Manuscript Sources

National Library of Wales/Llyfrgell Genedlaethol Cymru

    Wynnstay Papers

    Box 115/1 Grand Tour Account.

    Box 115/21 /13 & 14, Autograph Receipts from Paul Sandby

    Box 115, Bundle 22, Accounts and Receipts for the North Wales Tour

    Box 115/24/11 Autograph Receipts from Richard Wilson

    Misc MSS, 122, Sir Watkin's Letters from Italy

    Misc MSS, Vol. 16, Inventory of 1790 of Wynnstay Pictures and Furniture

    Ms. 14005, Letter from Paul Sandby to Thomas Pennant

Original Printed Sources or Modern Reprints.

Anon, *The Gentleman's Guide in his Tour through France*, 1770.

Baretti, Joseph, *An Account of the Manners and Customs of Italy*, 1769.

Boswell, James, Ed Frank Brady as *Boswell on the Grand Tour, Italy, Corsica and France, 1765-1766*, Yale, 1955.

Byng, John, Ed C. Bruyn Andrews as *The Torrington Diaries,* New York, 1938.

Burney, Dr Charles, *General History of Music* 1776.

Journal 1770 Published as *Music, Men and Manners in France and Italy 1770*, Ed H. Edmund Poole, London, 1969.

Casanova, Giacomo de Seingalt, *History of My Life* (posthumous pub).

Cradock, Joseph, *Letters from Snowdonia* 1770.

An Account of Some of the most Romantic Parts of North Wales, 1774.

Gazzette Toscane, Vol 3, 1768.

Garrick, David, Ed G. W. Stone, *The Journal of David Garrick describing his Visit to France and Italy in 1763*, New York, 1939.

Hughes, Charles, Ed. *Mrs Piozzi's Thraliana*, London, 1913.

Jones, Thomas, *Memoirs Walpole Society* Vol XXXII London, 1951.

Kelly, Michael, *Reminiscences* London, 1826.

Lyttleton, George, *Account of a Journey into Wales*, 1756.

Mann, Sir Horace, Ed. Dr. Doran, Letters published as 'Mann and Manners and the Court of Florence 1740-1786, London, 1876.

Montagu, Lady Mary Wortley, *Letters*, London, 1906.

Moore, Dr John, *A View of Society and Manners in Italy*, 5th ed, 1790.

Pennant, Thomas (Ed David Kirk) *A Tour in Wales*, Llanwrst, 1998.

Piozzi, Mrs Hesther Lynch, *Observations and Reflections made in the Journey through France, Italy and Germany*, 1789.

Smollet, Tobias, *Travels through France and Italy*, 1766.

Thicknesse, Philip, *A Years Journey through France*, 1777.

Ward, Edward [?] *A Trip to North Wales, 1701*, (commonly attributed to Edward Ward and published as his work but possibly by Edward Bysshe. The foreword is signed B.E. although Bishop Burnett has also been advanced as a candidate.)

Wyndham, Henry Penruddocke, *A Tour through Monmouthshire and Wales made in 1774 and 1777*, 1781.

Young, Arthur, *Travels in France 1787–1789*.

Select Bibliography

General

Acton, Harold, *The Bourbons of Naples*, London, 1957.

　　　　　　　　The Last Medici, London, 1932.

Andrieux, Maurice. *Daily Life in Papal Rome in the Eighteenth Century*, London, 1969.

Brewer, John, *The Pleasures of the Imagination*, London, 1997.

Fothergill, Brian, *Sir William Hamilton, Envoy Extraordinary*, London, 1969.

Lees-Milne, James, *The Last Stuarts*, London, 1983.

Porter, Roy, *Enlightenment*, London, 2000.

Vaussard, Maurice, *Daily Life in Eighteenth Century Italy*, London, 1962.

The Grand Tour

Black, Jeremy. (1) *The British Abroad, The Grand Tour*, Stroud, 1992.

　　　　　　　　(2) *Italy and the Grand Tour*, Yale, 2003.

Burgess, Anthony, *The Age of the Grand Tour*, London, 1967.

Ciricone, Gloria, (Ed.) *Memorie Inglese del Grand Tour*, Rome 2007 (exhibition catalogue).

Dolores Sánchez-Jauregui and Scott Wilcox (eds.) *The English Prize; An Episode of the Grand Tour*, Yale, 2012.

Hibbert, Christopher, *The Grand Tour*, London, 1969.

Ingamells, John, *A Dictionary of British and Irish Travellers in Italy 1701-1800*, Yale, 1997.

Redford, Bruce, *Venice and the Grand Tour*, Yale, 1996.

Trease, Geoffrey, *The Grand Tour*, London, 1967.

Wilton, Andrew & Bignamini, Ilaria, *Grand Tour, The Lure of Italy in the Eighteenth Century*, London, 1996 (exhibition catalogue).

Art, Architecture and Music in Italy and Wales.

Baur-Heinhold, Margarete, *Baroque Theatre*, London, 1967.

Bonehill, John & Daniels, Stephen, *Paul Sandby*, London, 2009. (Exhibition Catalogue)

Bowron, Edgar Peters & Kerber, Peter Bjorn, *Pompeo Batoni*, Yale, 2007 (exhibition catalogue).

Bramham, Alan, *Architecture of the French Enlightenment*, London, 1980.

Council of Europe, *The Age of Neoclassicism*, London, 1972 (exhibition catalogue).

Cust, Lionel, *History of the Dilettanti*, London, 1898.

Fleming, John, *Robert Adam and his Circle*, London, 1962.

Haskell, Francis, *Patron and Painters, Art and Society in Baroque Italy*, Yale, 1980.

Hawcroft, Francis, *Travels in Italy 1776-1783*, Manchester, 1988 (exhibition catalogue).

Herrmann, Luke, *Paul and Thomas Sandby*, London, 1986.

Hunt, John Dixon, *The Picturesque Garden in Europe*, London, 2002.

Irwin, David, *Neoclassicism*, London 1997.

Kluckert, Ehrenfried, *European Garden Design*, Cologne, 2000.

Lablaude, Pierre-Andre, *The Gardens of Versailles*, Paris, 2005.

Martineau, Jane & Robinson, Andrew, *The Glory of Venice, Art in the Eighteenth Century*, London, 1994. (Exhibition Catalogue)

Mosser, Monique & Teyssot, Georges, Eds, *The History of Garden Design*, London, 1991.

Parissien, Steven, *Adam Style*, London, 1992.

Price, Curtis; Milhous, Judith, Hume, Robert D, *Italian Opera in Late Eighteenth Century London*, Vol I, The King's Theatre, Oxford, 1995.

Robertson, Bruce, *The Art of Paul Sandby*, New Haven, 1985 (exhibition catalogue).

Rosselli, John, *The Opera Industry from Cimarosa to Verdi*, Cambridge, 1984.

Schutze, Sebastian, *The Complete Collection of Antiquities from the Cabinet of Sir William Hamilton*, Taschen, 2004.

Solkin, David H, *Richard Wilson*, London, 1982 (exhibition catalogue).

Southey, Roz; Maddison, Margaret; Hughes, David, *The Ingenious Mr Avison, Making Money and Music in Eighteenth Century Newcastle*, Newcastle, 2009.

Spinosa, Nicola & Di Mauro, Leonardo, *Vedute napoletane del Settecento*, Electa Napoli, 1993

Stillman, Damie, *English Neoclassical Architecture*, London, 1988.

Sumner, Ann & Smith Gregg, Thomas Jones, *An Artist Rediscovered*, London, 2003. (Exhibition Catalogue)

Wilton-Ely, John, *Piranesi; The Complete Etchings*, California, 1992.

Wittowker, Rudolph, *Art and Architecture in Italy 1600-1730*, London, 1985.

Worsley, Giles, *Classical Architecture in Britain: The Heroic Age*, New Haven, 1995.

Young, Hilary (Ed.) *The Genius of Wedgwood*, London, 1995 (exhibition catalogue).

The Tour in North Wales

Andrews, Malcolm, *The Search for the Picturesque Landscape; Aesthetics and Tourism in Britain 1760-1800*, Stanford, 1989.

Bristow, Adrian, Ed, *Dr Johnson & Mrs Thrale's Tour in North Wales 1774*, Wrexham, 1995.

Ellis, Osian, *The Story of the Harp in Wales,* University of Wales, 1991.

Joyner, Paul Ed, *Dolbadarn, Studies on a Theme*, Aberystwyth, 1990.

Kirk, David, *Snowdonia, A Historical Anthology*, Llanwrst, 1994.

Schama, Simon, *Landscape and Memory*, London, 1995.

Sir Watkin Williams Wynn & Wynnstay

Colman, George, *Random Records*, 1830.

Ford, Brinsley, 'Sir Watkin Williams Wynn, A Welsh Maecenas', *Apollo* Vol 99, 1974.

Girouard, Mark, *Life in the English Country House*, London, 1978.

Hinde, Thomas, *Capability Brown*, London, 1986.

Hughes, Peter, 'Paul Sandby and Sir Watkin Williams Wynn', *Burlington Magazine* CXIV, 1971.

Lord, Peter, *The Visual History of Wales – Imagining the Nation*, Cardiff.

Mowl, Timothy & Earnshaw, Brian, *Trumpet at a Distant Gate*, London, 1985.

Mowl, Timothy, *A Roman Palace on the Dee*, Cardiff, 1997 (exhibition catalogue).

Price, Cecil, *The English Theatre in Wales*, (Chapter XI Wynnstay) Cardiff, 1948.

Pritchard, T. W. *Remembering Ruabon*, Wrexham, 2000.

> *The Wynns at Wynnstay*, Caerwys, 1982.

'Wynnstay, Denbighshire', *Country Life*, March 1930, April 1972 (with P. Howell).

Transactions of the Denbighshire Historical Society, Vols 27, 28, 29, 30.

Roberts, Askew, *Wynnstay and the Wynns*, Oswestry, 1895.

GENERAL INDEX OF PEOPLE & PLACES

The number following the entry, in italics and in parenthesis, is the page number in the account book in which mention is made. Persons known by title e.g. 'the Secretary of State', 'the King' are not included. Other page numbers refer to the main text. Illustrations are denoted by bold type.

In consideration of the fact that the same people are encountered time after time, references are for the main or most important entries within the text.